Microsoft® Official Academic Course

Security Fundamentals,
Exam 98-367

WILEY

Credits

EDITOR	Bryan Gambrel
DIRECTOR OF SALES	Mitchell Beaton
DIRECTOR OF MARKETING	Chris Ruel
MICROSOFT SENIOR PRODUCT MANAGER	Merrick Van Dongen of Microsoft Learning
EDITORIAL PROGRAM ASSISTANT	Jennifer Lartz
CONTENT MANAGER	Micheline Frederick
PRODUCTION EDITOR	Amy Weintraub
CREATIVE DIRECTOR	Harry Nolan
COVER DESIGNER	Jim O'Shea
TECHNOLOGY AND MEDIA	Tom Kulesa/Wendy Ashenberg

Cover photo: Credit: © José Carlos Pires Pereira/iStockphoto

This book was set in Garamond by Aptara, Inc. and printed and bound by Bind Rite Robbinsville.
The cover was printed by Bind Rite Robbinsville.

Microsoft, ActiveX, Excel, InfoPath, Microsoft Press, MSDN, OneNote, Outlook, PivotChart, PivotTable, PowerPoint, SharePoint, SQL Server, Visio, Visual Basic, Visual C#, Visual Studio, Windows, Windows 7, Windows Mobile, Windows Server, and Windows Vista are either registered trademarks or trademarks of Microsoft Corporation in the United States and/or other countries. Other product and company names mentioned herein may be the trademarks of their respective owners.

The example companies, organizations, products, domain names, e-mail addresses, logos, people, places, and events depicted herein are fictitious. No association with any real company, organization, product, domain name, e-mail address, logo, person, place, or event is intended or should be inferred.

The book expresses the author's views and opinions. The information contained in this book is provided without any express, statutory, or implied warranties. Neither the authors, John Wiley & Sons, Inc., Microsoft Corporation, nor their resellers or distributors will be held liable for any damages caused or alleged to be caused either directly or indirectly by this book.

Founded in 1807, John Wiley & Sons, Inc. has been a valued source of knowledge and understanding for more than 200 years, helping people around the world meet their needs and fulfill their aspirations. Our company is built on a foundation of principles that include responsibility to the communities we serve and where we live and work. In 2008, we launched a Corporate Citizenship Initiative, a global effort to address the environmental, social, economic, and ethical challenges we face in our business. Among the issues we are addressing are carbon impact, paper specifications and procurement, ethical conduct within our business and among our vendors, and community and charitable support. For more information, please visit our website: www.wiley.com/go/citizenship.

ISBN 978-0-470-90184-7

Printed in the United States of America

10 9 8 7 6 5 4 3 2 1

Foreword from the Publisher

Wiley's publishing vision for the Microsoft Official Academic Course series is to provide students and instructors with the skills and knowledge they need to use Microsoft technology effectively in all aspects of their personal and professional lives. Quality instruction is required to help both educators and students get the most from Microsoft's software tools and to become more productive. Thus our mission is to make our instructional programs trusted educational companions for life.

To accomplish this mission, Wiley and Microsoft have partnered to develop the highest quality educational programs for Information Workers, IT Professionals, and Developers. Materials created by this partnership carry the brand name "Microsoft Official Academic Course," assuring instructors and students alike that the content of these textbooks is fully endorsed by Microsoft, and that they provide the highest quality information and instruction on Microsoft products. The Microsoft Official Academic Course textbooks are "Official" in still one more way—they are the officially sanctioned courseware for Microsoft IT Academy members.

The Microsoft Official Academic Course series focuses on *workforce development*. These programs are aimed at those students seeking to enter the workforce, change jobs, or embark on new careers as information workers, IT professionals, and developers. Microsoft Official Academic Course programs address their needs by emphasizing authentic workplace scenarios with an abundance of projects, exercises, cases, and assessments.

The Microsoft Official Academic Courses are mapped to Microsoft's extensive research and job-task analysis, the same research and analysis used to create the Microsoft Technology Associate (MTA) and Microsoft Certified Technology Specialist (MCTS) exams. The textbooks focus on real skills for real jobs. As students work through the projects and exercises in the textbooks, they enhance their level of knowledge and their ability to apply the latest Microsoft technology to everyday tasks. These students also gain resume-building credentials that can assist them in finding a job, keeping their current job, or furthering their education.

The concept of life-long learning is today an utmost necessity. Job roles, and even whole job categories, are changing so quickly that none of us can stay competitive and productive without continuously updating our skills and capabilities. The Microsoft Official Academic Course offerings, and their focus on Microsoft certification exam preparation, provide a means for people to acquire and effectively update their skills and knowledge. Wiley supports students in this endeavor through the development and distribution of these courses as Microsoft's official academic publisher.

Today educational publishing requires attention to providing quality print and robust electronic content. By integrating Microsoft Official Academic Course products, *WileyPLUS*, and Microsoft certifications, we are better able to deliver efficient learning solutions for students and teachers alike.

Bonnie Lieberman

General Manager and Senior Vice President

Preface

Welcome to the Microsoft Official Academic Course (MOAC) program for Security Fundamentals. MOAC represents the collaboration between Microsoft Learning and John Wiley & Sons, Inc. publishing company. Microsoft and Wiley teamed up to produce a series of textbooks that deliver compelling and innovative teaching solutions to instructors and superior learning experiences for students. Infused and informed by in-depth knowledge from the creators of Microsoft products, and crafted by a publisher known worldwide for the pedagogical quality of its products, these textbooks maximize skills transfer in minimum time. Students are challenged to reach their potential by using their new technical skills as highly productive members of the workforce.

Because this knowledge base comes directly from Microsoft, creator of the Microsoft Certified IT Professional (MCITP), Microsoft Certified Technology Specialist (MCTS), and Microsoft Technology Associate (MTA) exams (www.microsoft.com/learning/certification), you are sure to receive the topical coverage that is most relevant to students' personal and professional success. Microsoft's direct participation not only assures you that MOAC textbook content is accurate and current—it also means that students will receive the best instruction possible to enable their success on certification exams and in the workplace.

■ The Microsoft Official Academic Course Program

The *Microsoft Official Academic Course* series is a complete program for instructors and institutions to prepare and deliver great courses on Microsoft software technologies. With MOAC, we recognize that, because of the rapid pace of change in the technology and curriculum developed by Microsoft, there is an ongoing set of needs beyond classroom instruction tools for an instructor to be ready to teach the course. The MOAC program endeavors to provide solutions for all these needs in a systematic manner in order to ensure a successful and rewarding course experience for both instructor and student—technical and curriculum training for instructor readiness with new software releases; the software itself for student use at home for building hands-on skills, assessment, and validation of skill development; and a great set of tools for delivering instruction in the classroom and lab. All are important to the smooth delivery of an interesting course on Microsoft software, and all are provided with the MOAC program. We think about the model below as a gauge for ensuring that we completely support you in your goal of teaching a great course. As you evaluate your instructional materials options, you may wish to use the model for comparison purposes with other available products.

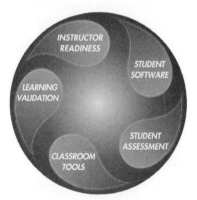

www.wiley.com/college/microsoft *or*
call the MOAC Toll-Free Number: 1+(888) 764-7001 (U.S. & Canada only)

▪ Pedagogical Features

The MOAC textbook for Security Fundamentals is designed to cover all the learning objectives for that MTA exam 98-367, which is referred to as its "objective domain." The Microsoft Technology Associate (MTA) exam objectives are highlighted throughout the textbook. Many pedagogical features have been developed specifically for the *Microsoft Official Academic Course* program.

Presenting the extensive procedural information and technical concepts woven throughout the textbook raises challenges for the student and instructor alike. The Illustrated Book Tour that follows provides a guide to the rich features contributing to the *Microsoft Official Academic Course* program's pedagogical plan. The following is a list of key features in each lesson designed to prepare students for success as they continue in their IT education, on the certification exams, and in the workplace:

- Each lesson begins with an **Objective Domain Matrix**. More than a standard list of learning objectives, the Domain Matrix correlates each software skill covered in the lesson to the specific exam objective domain.

- Concise and frequent **Step-by-Step** instructions teach students new features and provide an opportunity for hands-on practice. Numbered steps give detailed, step-by-step instructions to help students learn software skills.

- **Illustrations**—in particular, screen images—provide visual feedback as students work through the exercises. These images reinforce key concepts, provide visual clues about the steps, and allow students to check their progress.

- Lists of **Key Terms** at the beginning of each lesson introduce students to important technical vocabulary. When these terms are used later in the lesson, they appear in bold, italic type and are defined. The Glossary also contains all of the key terms and their definitions.

- Engaging point-of-use **Reader Aids**, located throughout the lessons, tell students why a topic is relevant (*The Bottom Line*) or provide students with helpful hints (*Take Note*). Reader Aids also provide additional relevant or background information that adds value to the lesson.

- **Certification Ready** features throughout the text signal students where a specific certification objective is covered. They provide students with a chance to check their understanding of that particular MTA objective and, if necessary, review the section of the lesson where it is covered. MOAC offers complete preparation for MTA certification.

- **End-of-Lesson Questions:** The Knowledge Assessment section provides a variety of multiple-choice, true-false, matching, and fill-in-the-blank questions.

- **End-of-Lesson Exercises:** Competency Assessment case scenarios, Proficiency Assessment case scenarios, and Workplace Ready exercises are projects that test students' ability to apply what they've learned in the lesson.

■ Lesson Features

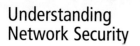

Understanding
Network Security

LESSON 4

OBJECTIVE DOMAIN MATRIX ———————————————— **Objective Domain Matrix**

Skills/Concepts	MTA Exam Objective	MTA Exam Objective Number
Using Dedicated Firewalls to Protect a Network	Understand dedicated firewalls.	3.1
Controlling Access with Network Access Protection (NAP)	Understand Network Access Protection (NAP).	3.2
Using Isolation to Protect a Network	Understand network isolation.	3.3
Protecting Data with Protocol Security	Understand protocol security.	3.4
Securing Wireless Networks	Understand wireless security.	1.4

KEY TERMS

application-level firewall
circuit-level firewall
DMZ (demilitarized zone)
DNS Security Extensions (DNSsec)
DNS poisoning
DNS spoofing
firewall
honey net
honeypot
host firewall
intrusion detection systems (IDS)

intrusion prevention systems (IPS)
MAC address
Network Access Protection (NAP)
network firewall
Open Systems Interconnect (OSI)
padded cell
personal firewall
Secure Content Management (SCM)
spoofing
stateful inspection
Unified Threat Management (UTM)

———————— **Key Terms**

Traditionally, when building an information security infrastructure, the first point of focus was the network. As soon as networks began interconnecting, it was obvious that the network offered the main vector of attack. In other words, it was the primary way to get to an organization's information from the outside.

At this point, the driving philosophy around network protection was reminiscent of the castles of old. According to this mindset, the best way to secure your network was to build strong walls, dig moats, and control access to the castle through the main gate. In network

87

———————— **X Ref Reader Aid**

———————— **The Bottom Line Reader Aid**

terms, this meant deploying multiple layers of firewalls, then controlling who could enter the network with firewall rules, access control, and demilitarized zones (DMZs). This practice is known as securing the perimeter, or defense in depth.

This model worked quite well until the next round of technological evolution in the late 1990s, when the concept of the virtual private network (VPN) was introduced. VPNs allowed companies to securely extend their network across untrusted networks like the Internet, but this also impacted the perimeter of the network. Next came wireless network technologies, literally moving the perimeter that required protection into the air and offering additional challenges to the layered security model.

The good news is that as network technologies have evolved and securing a networks' perimeter has become more challenging, the security technologies available for addressing these challenges have evolved as well. In this lesson, we will discuss such security solutions and how they can be used to address the challenges you will encounter.

■ Using Dedicated Firewalls to Protect a Network

THE BOTTOM LINE
Even today, firewalls remain the foundation of network security technology. There are a number of options, types, and technologies associated with selecting, implementing, and maintaining firewalls in your network. There are also a number of drivers to help you determine the proper solution for your organization.

CERTIFICATION READY
Where would most companies place their dedicated firewall?
3.1

One of the first things that comes to mind when people talk about information security is the firewall. Firewalls have long been the foundation of an organization's network security infrastructure. But what exactly is a firewall?

A *firewall* is a system that is designed to protect a computer or a computer network from network-based attacks. A firewall does this by filtering the data packets that are traversing the network. A typical perimeter firewall is implemented with two (or more) network connections (see Figure 4-1), namely:

• A connection to the network being protected; and
• A connection to an external network.

———————— **Certification Ready Alert**

Figure 4-1
A firewall implementation

Internet → Internet Traffic → Traffic Permitted After Filters Are Applied → Corporate Network

There are numerous variations on this model, but ultimately, all firewalls protect hosts on one network from hosts on another network.

Firewalls are used to divide and isolate networking areas for an organization. For example, one of the most common uses of a firewall would be to divide the network of your organization (internal network) from the external network (Internet). The internal network may also be referred to as clean, secure, and local while the external network may be referred to as dirty, unsecure, and remote. They all reference the same model, but occasionally, you may find you need to translate a particular term into terminology you are familiar with.

In addition to sniffers that are used to attack wired networks, there are now sniffers that have the ability to capture wireless data as well. Whenever you are connected to your business wireless, perhaps while at the local coffee shop or even while attending a meeting at a hotel, you are potentially at risk of having your data literally pulled out of the air and made available to an attacker. The use of encryption remains the best mechanism for combating this type of attack.

Another area of concern with sniffers is wireless keyboards. At its core, a wireless keyboard is a broadcast technology that sends keystrokes from the keyboard to a receiver connected to the computer. If you can get a receiver tuned to the same frequency close enough to the computer, you can capture every keystroke entered into the wireless keyboard—without needing to install a keylogger. Most wireless keyboards now support additional security, such as encrypted connections, but they are still broadcasting all information that the user types, so as long as people continue to enter the majority of their data via keyboard, this will be a significant potential source for attackers to exploit. In fact, many companies only permit their employees to use wired keyboards in order to mitigate this risk.

X REF
Sniffing is discussed in more detail in Lesson 4.

LOOKING AT GUESSED PASSWORDS

Although not as prevalent an issue as it was in years past, the possibility still exists that someone could sit down at your computer and guess your password. As we have seen in countless movies, an attacker may be familiar with the person whose system they are trying to compromise, or they may look around and see a postcard from a trip or pictures of an employee's kids with their names listed and ascertain a password from these items. Indeed, if a user does not follow corporate rules requiring a strong, not easily guessable password, but instead selects a password based on a spouse's, child's, or pet's name and birthday, an attacker could more easily guess the password and access the employee's data.

That being said, this type of attack is almost never seen these days. With the widespread availability of password cracking tools, the type of individual targeting required to guess someone's password is seldom worth the effort. It is generally much easier to leverage an attack using one of the other methods currently available. Typically, only co-workers or close friends will try to guess a user's password.

SKILL SUMMARY

IN THIS LESSON YOU LEARNED:

• The strength of a password can be determined by looking at the password's length, complexity, and randomness.
• A complex password uses characters from at least three of the following categories: uppercase, lowercase, numeric characters, and nonalphanumeric characters.
• Account lockout refers to the number of incorrect logon attempts permitted before a system will lock an account.
• The Minimum Password Age setting controls how many days users must wait before they can reset their password.
• The Maximum Password Age setting controls the maximum period of time that can elapse before users are forced to reset their password.
• A Group Policy Object (GPO) is a set of rules that allow an administrator granular control over the configuration of objects in Active Directory (AD), including user accounts, operating systems, applications, and other AD objects.
• Passwords have long been recognized as one of the weak links in many security programs.
• During a dictionary attack, the attacker tries an extensive list of potential passwords in conjunction with a user ID to try to guess the appropriate password.

56 | Lesson 2

Figure 2-18

Turning on BitLocker

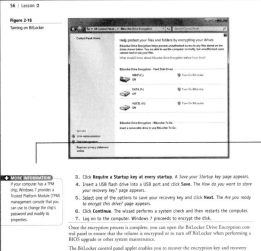

More Infomation Reader Aid

◆ **MORE INFORMATION**

If your computer has a TPM chip, Windows 7 provides a Trusted Platform Module (TPM) management console that you can use to change the chip's password and modify its properties.

3. Click **Require a Startup key at every startup.** A *Save your Startup key* page appears.

4. Insert a USB flash drive into a USB port and click **Save.** The *How do you want to store your recovery key?* page appears.

5. Select one of the options to save your recovery key and click **Next.** The *Are you ready to encrypt this drive?* page appears.

6. Click **Continue.** The wizard performs a system check and then restarts the computer.

7. Log on to the computer. Windows 7 proceeds to encrypt the disk.

Once the encryption process is complete, you can open the BitLocker Drive Encryption control panel to ensure that the volume is encrypted or to turn off BitLocker when performing a BIOS upgrade or other system maintenance.

The BitLocker control panel applet enables you to recover the encryption key and recovery password at will. You should carefully consider how to store this information, because it will allow access to the encrypted data. It is also possible to escrow this information into Active Directory.

USING DATA RECOVERY AGENTS AND BITLOCKER

If for some reason, a user loses the startup key and/or startup PIN needed to boot a system with BitLocker, that user can supply the recovery key created during the BitLocker configuration process and gain access to the system. However, if the user loses the recovery key, you can use a data recovery agent designated with Active Directory to recover the data on the drive.

A data recovery agent (DRA) is a user account that an administrator has authorized to recover BitLocker drives for an entire organization with a digital certificate on a smart card. In most cases, administrators of Active Directory Domain Services (AD DS) networks use DRAs to ensure access to their BitLocker-protected systems and to avoid having to maintain large numbers of individual keys and PINs.

Easy-to-Read Tables

32 | Lesson 2

EXAMINING GROUP SCOPES

Any group, whether it is a security group or a distribution group, is characterized by a scope that identifies the extent to which the group is applied in the domain tree or forest. The three group scopes are as follows:

• **Domain local:** Contains global and universal groups, even though it can also contain user accounts and other domain local groups. A domain local group is usually in the domain with the resource to which you want to assign permissions or rights.

• **Global:** Designed to contain user accounts, although they can also contain other global groups. Global groups are designed to be "global" for a domain. After you place user accounts into global groups, these groups are typically placed into domain local groups or universal groups.

• **Universal:** Designed to contain global groups from multiple domains, although they can also contain other universal groups and user accounts. Because global catalogs replicate universal group membership, you should limit membership to global groups. This way, if you change a member within a global group, the global catalog will not have to replicate the change.

See Table 2-1.

Table 2-1

Group scopes

SCOPE	MEMBERS CAN INCLUDE...	MEMBER PERMISSIONS CAN BE ASSIGNED...	GROUP SCOPE CAN BE CONVERTED TO...
Universal	Accounts from any domain within the forest in which this universal group resides Global groups from any domain within the forest in which this universal group resides Universal groups from any domain within the forest in which this universal group resides	In any domain or forest	Domain local Global (as long as no other universal groups exist as members)
Global	Accounts from the same domain as the parent global group Global groups from the same domain as the parent global group	In any domain	Universal (as long as the group is not a member of any other global groups)
Domain local	Accounts from any domain, global groups from any domain, universal groups from any domain, and domain local groups but only from the same domain as the parent domain local group	Only within the same domain as the parent domain local group	Universal (as long as no other domain local groups exist as members)

When assigning rights and permissions, you should always try to place your users into groups and assign the rights and permissions to these groups instead of to individual users. To effectively manage the use of global and domain local groups when assigning access to network resources, remember the mnemonic AGDLP (accounts, global, domain local, permissions):

• First, add the user account (A) into the global group (G) in the domain where the user exists.

• Next, add the global group (G) from the user domain into the domain local group (DL) in the resource domain.

---

24 | Lesson 2

RADIUS and extended it to meet their needs. From a features viewpoint, TACACS+ can be considered an extension of RADIUS.

Using Run As

Because administrators have full access to individual computers or entire networks, it is recommended that you use a standard nonadministrator user account to perform most tasks. Then, when you need to perform administrative tasks, you can use the Run as command or the built-in options that are included with the Windows operating system.

In previous versions of Windows, you had to use an administrator account to do certain things, such as changing system settings or installing software. If you were logged on as a limited user, the Run as command eliminated the need to log off and then log back on as an administrator.

In newer versions of Windows, including Windows 7 and Windows Server 2008 R2, the Run as command has been changed to Run as administrator. With User Account Control (UAC), you will rarely have to use the Run as administrator command, because Windows automatically prompts you for an administrator password when needed. UAC is discussed in detail in Lesson 5.

⊙ **RUN A PROGRAM AS AN ADMINISTRATOR**

GET READY. To run a program as an administrator, perform the following steps:

1. Right-click the program icon or file that you want to open, and then click **Run as administrator.** See Figure 2-2.

2. Select the administrator account that you want to use, type the password, and then click **Yes.**

You can also use the runas.exe command. For example, to run the widget.exe as an administrator, you would enter the following command:

runas /user:admin /widget.exe

Figure 2-2

Using the Run as administrator option

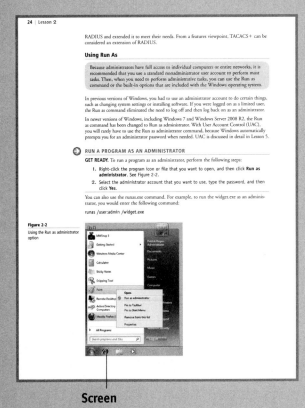

Screen Images

To use biometric devices (see Figure 2-1), you must have a biometric reader or scanning device, software that converts the scanned information into digital form and compares match points, and a database that stores the biometric data for comparison.

Figure 2-1
Finger scanner

Photos

To launch the biometric system, you will need to set up a station where an administrator enrolls each user; this includes scanning the biometric feature you want to use for authentication. When selecting a biometric method, you should consider its performance, difficulty, reliability, acceptance, and cost. You also need to look at the following characteristics:

- **False reject rate (false negative):** This is the percentage of authorized users who are incorrectly denied access.
- **False accept rate (false positive):** This is the percentage of unauthorized users who are incorrectly granted access.

Introducing RADIUS and TACACS+

When you buy a new computer and create a local user account and login, you are being authenticated with the username and password. For corporations, computers can be part of the domain, and authentication can be provided by the domain controllers. In other situations, you may need to provide centralized authentication, authorization, and accounting when users need to connect to a network service. Two commonly used protocols that provide these functions are Remote Authentication Dial In User Service (RADIUS) and Terminal Access Controller Access-Control System Plus (TACACS+).

A RADIUS or TACACS+ server resides on a remote system and responds to queries from clients such as VPN clients, wireless access points, routers, and switches. The server then authenticates username/password combinations (authentication), determines whether users are allowed to connect to the client (authorization), and logs the connection (accounting).

RADIUS is a mechanism that allows authentication of dial-in and other network connections, including modem dial-up, wireless access points, VPNs, and web servers. As an IETF standard, it has been implemented by most major operating system manufacturers, including Microsoft. For example, in Windows Server 2008, Network Policy Server (NPS) can be used as a RADIUS server to perform authentication, authorization, and accounting for RADIUS clients. It can be configured to use a Microsoft Windows NT Server 4.0 domain, an Active Directory Domain Services (AD DS) domain, or the local Security Accounts Manager (SAM) user accounts database to authenticate user credentials for connection attempts. NPS uses the dial-in properties of the user account and network policies to authorize a connection.

Another competing centralized AAA server is TACACS+, which was developed by Cisco. When designing TACACS+, Cisco incorporated much of the existing functionality of

---

Take Note
Reader Aid

been encrypted, you do not have to manually decrypt the encrypted file before you can use it. Rather, once you encrypt a file or folder, you work with the encrypted file or folder just as you would with any other file or folder.

EFS is keyed to a specific user account, using the public and private keys that are the basis of the Windows public key infrastructure (PKI). The user who creates a file is the only person who can read it. As the user works, EFS encrypts the files he or she creates using a key generated from the user's public key. Data encrypted with this key can be decrypted only by the user's personal encryption certificate, which is generated using his or her private key.

ENCRYPT A FOLDER OR FILE USING EFS

GET READY. To encrypt a folder or file, perform the following steps:

1. Right-click the folder or file you want to encrypt, then click **Properties**.
2. Click the **General** tab, and then click **Advanced**.
3. Select the **Encrypt contents to secure data** check box, click **OK**, and then click **OK** again. See Figure 2-16.

TAKE NOTE
You cannot encrypt a file with EFS while compressing a file with NTFS. You can only do one or the other.

Figure 2-16
Encrypting data with EFS

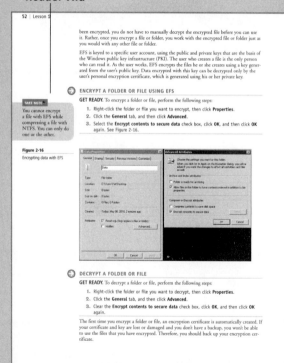

DECRYPT A FOLDER OR FILE

GET READY. To decrypt a folder or file, perform the following steps:

1. Right-click the folder or file you want to decrypt, then click **Properties**.
2. Click the **General** tab, and then click **Advanced**.
3. Clear the **Encrypt contents to secure data** check box, click **OK**, and then click **OK** again.

The first time you encrypt a folder or file, an encryption certificate is automatically created. If your certificate and key are lost or damaged and you don't have a backup, you won't be able to use the files that you have encrypted. Therefore, you should back up your encryption certificate.

---

2. Send the generated certificate request to the CA, usually using the vendor's website.
3. Receive a digital certificate from the CA and install it on the IIS server. Again, open **IIS Manager**, double-click the server within IIS Manager, and double-click **Server Certificates** in the **Features** view. Then select **Complete Certificate Request**.

If you have a web farm that consist of multiple web servers, you will need to install the digital certificate from the first server and export the digital certificate to a pfx format, and you will need to copy the public and private key to the other servers. Therefore, you will need to export the key from the first server and import to the other servers.

EXPORT A DIGITAL CERTIFICATE

GET READY. To export a digital certificate, perform the following steps:

1. Open **IIS Manager** and navigate to the level you want to manage.
2. In the **Features** view, double-click **Server Certificates**.
3. In the **Actions** pane, click **Export**.
4. In the **Export** dialog box, type a filename in the **Export to** box or click the **Browse** button to navigate to the name of a file in which to store the certificate for exporting.
5. Type a password in the **Password** box if you want to associate a password with the exported certificate. Retype the password in the **Confirm password** box.
6. Click **OK**.

IMPORT A DIGITAL CERTIFICATE

GET READY. To import a certificate, perform the following steps:

1. Open **IIS Manager** and navigate to the level you want to manage.
2. In the **Features** view, double-click **Server Certificates**.
3. In the **Actions** pane, click **Import**.
4. In the **Import Certificate** dialog box, type a filename in the **Certificate file** box or click the **Browse** button to navigate to the name of the file where the exported certificate is stored. Type a password in the **Password** box if the certificate was exported with a password.
5. Select **Allow this certificate to be exported** if you want to be able to export the certificate, or clear **Allow this certificate to be exported** if you want to prevent additional exports of this certificate.
6. Click **OK**.

EXAMINING A CERTIFICATE CHAIN

There are only so many root CA certificates that are assigned to commercial third-party organizations. Therefore, when you acquire a digital certificate from a third-party organization, you might need to use a certificate chain to obtain the root CA certificate. In addition, you may need to install an intermediate digital certificate that will link the assigned digital certificate to a trusted root CA certificate. The *certificate chain*, also known as the certification path, is a list of certificates used to authenticate an entity. It begins with the certificate of the entity and ends with the root CA certificate. See Figure 2-15.

Step-by-Step Exercises

Skill Summary

Knowledge Assessment

Case Scenarios

Workplace Ready

Conventions and Features
Used in This Book

This book uses particular fonts, symbols, and heading conventions to highlight important information and to call attention to special steps. For more information about the features in each lesson, refer to the Illustrated Book Tour section.

CONVENTION	MEANING
↓ THE BOTTOM LINE	This feature provides a brief summary of the material to be covered in the section that follows.
CLOSE	Words in all capital letters indicate instructions for opening, saving, or closing files or programs. They also point out items you should check or actions you should take.
CERTIFICATION READY	This feature signals a point in the text where a specific certification objective is covered. It provides you with a chance to check your understanding of that particular MTA objective and, if necessary, review the section of the lesson where the objective is covered.
TAKE NOTE*	Reader aids appear in shaded boxes found in your text. *Take Note* provides helpful hints related to particular tasks or topics.
DOWNLOAD	Download provides information on where to download useful software.
X REF	These notes provide pointers to information discussed elsewhere in the textbook or describe interesting features that are not directly addressed in the current topic or exercise.
Alt + Tab	A plus sign (+) between two key names means that you must press both keys at the same time. Keys that you are instructed to press in an exercise will appear in the font shown here.
Example	Key terms appear in bold, italic font.

Instructor Support Program

The *Microsoft Official Academic Course* programs are accompanied by a rich array of resources that incorporate the extensive textbook visuals to form a pedagogically cohesive package. These resources provide all the materials instructors need to deploy and deliver their courses. Resources available online for download include:

- The **MSDN Academic Alliance** is designed to provide the easiest and most inexpensive developer tools, products, and technologies available to faculty and students in labs, classrooms, and on student PCs. A free three-year membership is available to qualified MOAC adopters.

  Note: Microsoft Windows Server 2008, Microsoft Windows 7, and Microsoft Visual Studio can be downloaded from MSDN AA for use by students in this course.

- The **Instructor's Guide** contains solutions to all the textbook exercises and Syllabi for various term lengths. The Instructor's Guide also includes chapter summaries and lecture notes. The Instructor's Guide is available from the Book Companion site (http://www.wiley.com/college/microsoft).

- The **Test Bank** contains hundreds of questions in multiple-choice, true-false, short answer, and essay formats, and is available to download from the Instructor's Book Companion site (www.wiley.com/college/microsoft). A complete answer key is also provided.

- A complete set of **PowerPoint presentations and images** is available on the Instructor's Book Companion site (http://www.wiley.com/college/microsoft) to enhance classroom presentations. Approximately 50 PowerPoint slides are provided for each lesson. Tailored to the text's topical coverage and Skills Matrix, these presentations are designed to convey key concepts addressed in the text. All images from the text are on the Instructor's Book Companion site (http://www.wiley.com/college/microsoft). You can incorporate them into your PowerPoint presentations or use them to create your own overhead transparencies and handouts. By using these visuals in class discussions, you can help focus students' attention on key elements of technologies covered and help them understand how to use these technologies effectively in the workplace.

- When it comes to improving the classroom experience, there is no better source of ideas and inspiration than your fellow colleagues. The **Wiley Faculty Network** connects teachers with technology, facilitates the exchange of best practices, and helps enhance instructional efficiency and effectiveness. Faculty Network activities include technology training and tutorials, virtual seminars, peer-to-peer exchanges of experiences and ideas, personal consulting, and sharing of resources. For details, visit www.WhereFacultyConnect.com.

MSDN ACADEMIC ALLIANCE—FREE 3-YEAR MEMBERSHIP AVAILABLE TO QUALIFIED ADOPTERS!

The Microsoft Developer Network Academic Alliance (MSDN AA) is designed to provide the easiest and most inexpensive way for universities to make the latest Microsoft developer tools, products, and technologies available in labs, in classrooms, and on student PCs. MSDN AA is an annual membership program for departments teaching Science, Technology, Engineering, and Mathematics (STEM) courses. The membership provides a complete solution to keep academic labs, faculty, and students on the leading edge of technology.

Software available in the MSDN AA program is provided at no charge to adopting departments through the Wiley and Microsoft publishing partnership.

As a bonus to this free offer, faculty will be introduced to Microsoft's Faculty Connection and Academic Resource Center. It takes time and preparation to keep students engaged while giving them a fundamental understanding of theory, and the Microsoft Faculty Connection is designed to help STEM professors with this preparation by providing articles, curriculum, and tools that professors can use to engage and inspire today's technology students.

*Contact your Wiley representative for details.

For more information about the MSDN Academic Alliance program, go to:

http://msdn.microsoft.com/academic/

Note: Microsoft Windows Server 2008, Microsoft Windows 7, and Microsoft Visual Studio can be downloaded from MSDN AA for use by students in this course.

■ Important Web Addresses and Phone Numbers

To locate the Wiley Higher Education Representative in your area, go to http://www. wiley.com/college and click on the "*Who's My Rep?*" link at the top of the page, or call the MOAC Toll-Free Number: 1 + (888) 764-7001 (U.S. & Canada only).

To learn more about becoming a Microsoft Certified Technology Specialist and about exam availability, visit www.microsoft.com/learning/mcp/mcp.

▪ Additional Resources

Book Companion Web Site (www.wiley.com/college/microsoft)

The students' book companion site for the MOAC series includes any resources, exercise files, and Web links that will be used in conjunction with this course.

Wiley Desktop Editions

Wiley MOAC Desktop Editions are innovative, electronic versions of printed textbooks. Students buy the desktop version for up to 50% off the U.S. price of the printed text, and they get the added value of permanence and portability. Wiley Desktop Editions also provide students with numerous additional benefits that are not available with other e-text solutions.

Wiley Desktop Editions are NOT subscriptions; students download the Wiley Desktop Edition to their computer desktops. Students own the content they buy to keep for as long as they want. Once a Wiley Desktop Edition is downloaded to the computer desktop, students have instant access to all of the content without being online. Students can print the sections they prefer to read in hard copy. Students also have access to fully integrated resources within their Wiley Desktop Edition. From highlighting their e-text to taking and sharing notes, students can easily personalize their Wiley Desktop Edition as they are reading or following along in class.

▪ About the Microsoft Technology Associate (MTA) Certification

Preparing Tomorrow's Technology Workforce

Technology plays a role in virtually every business around the world. Possessing the fundamental knowledge of how technology works and understanding its impact on today's academic and workplace environment is increasingly important—particularly for students interested in exploring professions involving technology. That's why Microsoft created the Microsoft Technology Associate (MTA) certification—a new entry-level credential that validates fundamental technology knowledge among students seeking to build a career in technology.

The Microsoft Technology Associate (MTA) certification is the ideal and preferred path to Microsoft's world-renowned technology certification programs, such as Microsoft Certified Technology Specialist (MCTS) and Microsoft Certified IT Professional (MCITP). MTA is positioned to become the premier credential for individuals seeking to explore and pursue a career in technology, or augment related pursuits such as business or any other field where technology is pervasive.

MTA Candidate Profile

The MTA certification program is designed specifically for secondary and post-secondary students interested in exploring academic and career options in a technology field. It offers students a certification in basic IT and development. As the new recommended entry point for Microsoft technology certifications, MTA is designed especially for students new to IT and software development. It is available exclusively in educational settings and easily integrates into the curricula of existing computer classes.

MTA Empowers Educators and Motivates Students

MTA provides a new standard for measuring and validating fundamental technology knowledge right in the classroom while keeping your budget and teaching resources intact. MTA helps institutions stand out as innovative providers of high-demand industry credentials and is easily deployed with a simple, convenient, and affordable suite of entry-level technology certification exams. MTA enables students to explore career paths in technology without requiring a big investment of time and resources, while providing a career foundation and the confidence to succeed in advanced studies and future vocational endeavors.

In addition to giving students an entry-level Microsoft certification, MTA is designed to be a stepping stone to other, more advanced Microsoft technology certifications, like the Microsoft Certified Technology Specialist (MCTS) certification.

Delivering MTA Exams: The MTA Campus License

Implementing a new certification program in your classroom has never been so easy with the MTA Campus License. Through the one-time purchase of the 12-month, 1,000-exam MTA Campus License, there's no more need for ad hoc budget requests and recurrent purchases of exam vouchers. Now you can budget for one low cost for the entire year, and then administer MTA exams to your students and other faculty across your entire campus where and when you want.

The MTA Campus License provides a convenient and affordable suite of entry-level technology certifications designed to empower educators and motivate students as they build a foundation for their careers.

The MTA Campus License is administered by Certiport, Microsoft's exclusive MTA exam provider.

To learn more about becoming a Microsoft Technology Associate and exam availability, visit www.microsoft.com/learning/mta.

■ Activate Your FREE MTA Practice Test!

Your purchase of this book entitles you to a free MTA practice test from GMetrix (a $30 value). Please go to www.gmetrix.com/mtatests and use the following validation code to redeem your free test: **MTA98-367-792A4C4E9036**

The **GMetrix Skills Management System** provides everything you need to practice for the Microsoft Technology Associate (MTA) Certification.

Overview of Test features:

- Practice tests map to the Microsoft Technology Associate (MTA) exam objectives
- GMetrix MTA practice tests simulate the actual MTA testing environment
- 50+ questions per test covering all objectives
- Progress at own pace, save test to resume later, return to skipped questions
- Detailed, printable score report highlighting areas requiring further review

To get the most from your MTA preparation, take advantage of your free GMetrix MTA Practice Test today!

For technical support issues on installation or code activation, please email support@gmetrix.com.

Acknowledgments

■ MOAC MTA Technology Fundamentals Reviewers

We'd like to thank the many reviewers who pored over the manuscript and provided invaluable feedback in the service of quality instructional materials:

Yuke Wang, University of Texas at Dallas

Palaniappan Vairavan, Bellevue College

Harold "Buz" Lamson, ITT Technical Institute

Colin Archibald, Valencia Community College

Catherine Bradfield, DeVry University Online

Robert Nelson, Blinn College

Kalpana Viswanathan, Bellevue College

Bob Becker, Vatterott College

Carol Torkko, Bellevue College

Bharat Kandel, Missouri Tech

Linda Cohen, Forsyth Technical Community College

Candice Lambert, Metro Technology Centers

Susan Mahon, Collin College

Mark Aruda, Hillsborough Community College

Claude Russo, Brevard Community College

David Koppy, Baker College

Sharon Moran, Hillsborough Community College

Keith Hoell, Briarcliffe College and Queens College—CUNY

Mark Hufnagel, Lee County School District

Rachelle Hall, Glendale Community College

Scott Elliott, Christie Digital Systems, Inc.

Gralan Gilliam, Kaplan

Steve Strom, Butler Community College

John Crowley, Bucks County Community College

Margaret Leary, Northern Virginia Community College

Sue Miner, Lehigh Carbon Community College

Gary Rollinson, Cabrillo College

Al Kelly, University of Advancing Technology

Katherine James, Seneca College

www.wiley.com/college/microsoft *or*
call the MOAC Toll-Free Number: 1+(888) 764-7001 (U.S. & Canada only)

Brief Contents

Contents

www.wiley.com/college/microsoft or
call the MOAC Toll-Free Number: 1+(888) 764-7001 (U.S. & Canada only)

Understanding Security Layers

OBJECTIVE DOMAIN MATRIX

SKILLS/CONCEPTS	MTA EXAM OBJECTIVE	MTA EXAM OBJECTIVE NUMBER
Introducing Security	Understand core security principles.	1.1
Looking at Physical Security as the First Line of Defense	Understand physical security.	1.2

KEY TERMS

access control

attack surface

availability

confidentiality

defense in depth

flash drive

integrity

keylogger

mobile device

principle of least privilege

removable device

residual risk

risk

risk acceptance

risk assessment

risk avoidance

risk management

risk mitigation

risk transfer

social engineering

threat

When you think about security, you can start by thinking about your stuff. We all have stuff. We have stuff that we really care about, stuff that would be difficult to replace, and stuff that has great sentimental value. We have stuff we don't want other people to find out about. We even have stuff that we could probably live without. Now think about where you keep your stuff. It could be in your house, car, school, or office; in a locker, backpack, or suitcase; or in a number of other places. Think about all of the bad things that could happen to your stuff. You could be robbed, or you could experience a disaster such as a fire, earthquake, or flood. In any case, you want to protect your possessions—no matter where the threat comes from.

At a high level, security is about protecting stuff. In the case of your personal stuff, it's about making sure you lock the door when you leave the house; remembering to take your purse with you when you leave a restaurant; or even making sure you hide all the presents you bought for the holidays in the back of your car before you head back into the mall.

Many of the security topics we discuss in this lesson boil down to the same common sense you use every day to protect your stuff. In the business environment, however, the stuff we're protecting is assets, information, systems, and networks, and we can protect these valuables with a variety of tools and techniques that we discuss at length in this book.

In this lesson, we start with the basics. We'll look at some of the underlying principles of a security program to set the foundation for your understanding of the more advanced topics covered later in the book. We'll also discuss the concept of physical security, which is critical not only for securing physical assets, but for securing information assets as well. By the time we're done, you'll have a good idea how to protect stuff for a living.

■ Introducing Security

↓
THE BOTTOM LINE

Before you can start securing your environment, you need to have a fundamental understanding of the standard concepts of security. It's easy to start buying firewalls, but until you understand what you're trying to protect, why it needs to be protected, and what you're protecting it from, you're just throwing your money away.

CERTIFICATION READY
Can you list and describe what CIA stands for as it relates to security?
1.1

When you are working in the information security field, one of the first acronyms you will encounter is CIA—but don't confuse this with the government agency with the same acronym. Rather, in this context, CIA represents the core goals of an information security program:

• Confidentiality

• Integrity

• Availability

Understanding Confidentiality

Confidentiality is a concept we deal with frequently in real life. For instance, we expect our doctors to keep our medical records confidential, and we trust our friends to keep our secrets confidential. In the business world, we define confidentiality as the characteristic of a resource ensuring access is restricted to only permitted users, applications, or computer systems. But what does this mean in reality? In short, confidentiality deals with keeping information, networks, and systems secure from unauthorized access.

Confidentiality is particularly critical in today's environment. Lately, in a few high-profile instances, several large companies have leaked people's personal information. These breaches in confidentiality made the news largely because the leaked information could be used to perpetrate identity theft against the people whose information was disseminated.

There are several technologies that support confidentiality in an enterprise security implementation. These include:

• Strong encryption

• Strong authentication

• Stringent access controls

Lesson 2 contains more details on strong encryption, strong authentication, and stringent access controls.

Another key component to consider when discussing confidentiality is how to determine what information is considered confidential. Some common classifications of data are "Public," "Internal Use Only," "Confidential," and "Strictly Confidential." You will also see the classification "Privileged" used frequently in the legal profession. Similarly, the military often categorizes information as "Unclassified," "Restricted," "Confidential," "Secret," or "Top Secret." These classifications are then used to determine what measures are appropriate to protect the information. If your information is not classified, you are left with two options— you can either protect all your information as if it were confidential (an expensive and daunting task), or you can treat all your information as if it were "Public" or "Internal Use Only" and not take stringent protection measures.

Understanding Integrity

In the information security context, *integrity* is defined as the consistency, accuracy, and validity of data or information. One of the goals of a successful information security program is to ensure that data is protected against any unauthorized or accidental changes. Therefore, a security program should include processes and procedures to manage intentional changes, as well as the ability to detect changes. Some of the many processes that can be used to effectively ensure the integrity of information include authentication, authorization, and accounting. For example, you could use rights and permissions to control who can access certain information or resources. You can also use a hashing function (a mathematical function) that can be calculated on data or a message before and after a designated period of time to show whether information has been modified during the specified time. You could also use an auditing or accounting system that records when changes have been made.

Understanding Availability

Availability is the third core security principle, and it describes a resource being accessible to a user, application, or computer system when required. In other words, availability means that when a user needs to get to information, he or she has the ability to do so.

Typically, threats to availability come in two types: accidental and deliberate. Accidental threats include natural disasters like storms, floods, fire, power outages, earthquakes, and so forth. This category also includes outages due to equipment failure, software problems, and other unplanned system, network, or user issues. The second category—deliberate threats—is related to outages that result from the exploitation of a system vulnerability. Some examples of this type of threat include denial of service attacks or network worms that impact vulnerable systems and their availability. In some cases, one of the first actions you will need to take following an outage is determining which category the outage fits into. Companies handle accidental outages very differently than deliberate ones.

Defining Threats and Risk Management

Risk management is the process of identifying, assessing, and prioritizing threats and risks. A *risk* is generally defined as the probability that an event will occur. In reality, businesses are only concerned about risks that would negatively impact the computing environment. For instance, there is a risk that you might win the lottery on Friday—but that's not a risk your company is going to actively address, because it would be something positive. Rather, your company would be more concerned with the specific type of risk known as a *threat*, which is defined as an action or occurrence that could result in the breach, outage, or corruption of a system by exploiting known or unknown vulnerabilities. Typically, when people refer to risk management, they are focusing on this type of negative risk.

The goal of any risk management plan is to remove risks when possible and to minimize the consequences of risks that cannot be eliminated. The first step in creating a risk management plan is to conduct a *risk assessment*. Risk assessments are used to identify the risks that might impact your particular environment.

TAKE NOTE *

In a mature risk assessment environment, it is common to record your risks in a risk register, which provides a formal mechanism for documenting the risks, impacts, controls, and other information required by the risk management program.

Once you have completed your assessment and identified your risks, you need to evaluate each risk for two factors. First, you need to determine the likelihood that a risk will occur in your environment. For example, a tornado is much more likely in Oklahoma than in Vermont. A meteor strike is probably not very likely anywhere, although it's one example commonly used to represent the complete loss of a facility when discussing risk. After you have determined the likelihood of a specific risk, you then need to determine the impact of that risk on your environment. For instance, a virus on a user's workstation generally has a relatively low impact on the company (although a high impact on the user.) A virus on your financial system has a much higher overall impact, although hopefully a lower likelihood.

Once you have evaluated your risks, it's time to prioritize them. One of the best mechanisms to assist with prioritization is to create a risk matrix, which can be used to determine an overall risk ranking. A risk matrix should include the following elements:

- The risk
- The likelihood that the risk will actually occur
- The impact of the risk
- A total risk score
- The relevant business owner (individual, team or department) for the risk
- The core security principles affected by the risk—confidentiality, integrity, and/or availability
- The appropriate strategy or strategies to deal with the risk

Some additional fields that may prove useful in your risk register are as follows:

- A deliverable date for the risk to be addressed
- Documentation about the residual risk (i.e., the risk that remains after measures have been taken to reduce the likelihood or minimize the effect of an event)
- The status of the strategy or strategies being used to address the risk; this can include indicators like "Planning," "Awaiting Approval," "Implementation," and "Complete"

One easy way to calculate a total risk score is to assign numeric values to your likelihood and impact. For example, you can rank likelihood and impact on a scale from 1 to 5, where 1 equals low likelihood or low probability and 5 equals high likelihood or high impact. You can then multiply the likelihood and impact together to generate a total risk score. By sorting from high to low, you have an easy method to initially prioritize your risks. You should then review the specific risks to determine the final order in which you want to address them. At this point, you may find that external factors, like cost or available resources, affect your priorities.

After you have prioritized your risks, you are ready to choose from among the four generally accepted responses to these risks. They include:

- Avoidance
- Acceptance
- Mitigation
- Transfer

Risk avoidance is the process of eliminating a risk by choosing not to engage in an action or activity. As an example of risk avoidance, consider a person who understands that there is a risk that the value of a stock might drop, so he or she avoids the risk by not purchasing the stock. One problem with risk avoidance is that there is frequently a reward associated with a risk—so if you avoid the risk, you also avoid the reward. For instance, if the stock in the example were to triple in price, the risk-averse investor would lose out on the reward because he or she wanted to avoid the risk.

Risk acceptance is the act of identifying and then making an informed decision to accept the likelihood and impact of a specific risk. To reuse the stock example, risk acceptance is the process in which a buyer thoroughly researches a company whose stock he or she is interested in, and after considering this information, makes the decision to accept the risk that the stock price might drop.

Risk mitigation consists of taking steps to reduce the likelihood or impact of a risk. A common example of risk mitigation is the use of redundant hard drives in a server. There is a risk of hard drive failure in any system. By using redundant drive architecture, you can mitigate the risk of a drive failure by having the redundant drive. In other words, although the risk still exists, it has been reduced by your actions.

Risk transfer is the act of taking steps to move responsibility for a risk to a third party through insurance or outsourcing. For example, there is a risk that you may have an accident while driving your car. You transfer this risk by purchasing insurance so that in the event of an accident, your insurance company is responsible for paying the majority of the associated costs.

TAKE NOTE *

There are many different ways to identify, assess, and prioritize risks. There is no one right way. Use the techniques that best fit your environment and requirements.

As mentioned earlier, one other important concept in risk management is that of **residual risk**. Residual risk is the risk that remains after measures have been taken to reduce the likelihood or minimize the effect of a particular event. To continue with the car insurance example, your residual risk in the event of an accident would be the deductible you have to pay before your insurance company assumes responsibility for the remainder of the damage.

Now, as part of our discussion of risk, we also need to look at two final concepts that will help you understand the foundations of security principles and risk management: the principle of least privilege and the idea of an attack surface.

Understanding the Principle of Least Privilege

The **principle of least privilege** is a security discipline that requires that a particular user, system, or application be given no more privilege than necessary to perform its function or job. This sounds like a very commonsense approach to assigning permissions, and when seen on paper, it is. However, when you start to apply this principle in a complex production environment, it becomes significantly more challenging.

The principle of least privilege has been a staple in the security arena for a number of years, and many organizations have struggled to implement it successfully. However, with today's increased focus on security from both a business and a regulatory perspective, organizations are working harder than ever before to build their models around this principle. The regulatory requirements of Sarbanes-Oxley, HIPAA, HITECH, and various state regulations, coupled with organizations' increased focus on the security practices of their business partners, vendors, and consultants, are driving companies to invest in tools, processes, and other resources to ensure this principle is followed.

But why is a principle that sounds so simple on paper so difficult to implement in reality? The challenge is largely related to the complexity of the typical work environment. It is easy to visualize application of the principle of least privilege for a single employee. On a physical basis, the employee needs access to the building he or she works in, any common areas, and his or her office. Logically, the employee also needs to be able to log in to his or her computer, have access to some centralized applications, and have access to a file server, a printer, and an internal web site. Now, imagine that single user multiplied by a thousand—and imagine that these thousand employees work in six different office locations. Some employees need access to all six locations, whereas others only need access to their own location. Still others need access to specific subsets of the six locations; for example, they might need access to the two offices in their region, or they might require access to the data center so they can provide IT support.

In this situation, instead of a single set of access requirements, you now have multiple departments with varying application requirements. You also have different user types, varying from "regular" users to power users to administrators; therefore, you need to determine not only what type of user each employee is, but also which internal applications he or she can access.

Add to this mix new hires, employees who are transferred or promoted, and employees who leave the company, and you can start to see how making sure each employee has the minimum amount of access required to do his or her job can be a time-intensive activity.

But wait—we're not done. In addition to physical and user permissions, you also need to be aware that in many IT environments, certain applications require access to data and/or other applications. Thus, to follow the principle of least privilege, you must ensure that these applications have the minimum necessary access in order to function properly. This can be extremely difficult when working in a Microsoft Active Directory environment, due to the detailed permissions included in Active Directory. Determining which permissions an application requires to function properly with Active Directory can be challenging in the extreme.

To further complicate matters, in industries where there is heavy regulation, like the financial or medical fields, or when regulations like Sarbanes-Oxley are in effect, there are additional requirements stating that you must audit regularly to ensure you have successfully implemented and validated privileges across the enterprise.

A detailed discussion of how to implement and maintain the principle of least privilege is beyond the scope of this book, but there are some high-level tools and strategies you should be aware of, including the following:

- **Groups:** Groups allow you to logically group users and applications so that permissions are not applied on a user-by-user or application-by-application basis.

- **Multiple user accounts for administrators:** Administrators are one of the biggest challenges when implementing the principle of least privilege. Administrators are typically also users, and it is seldom a good idea for administrators to perform their daily user tasks as an administrator. To address this issue, many companies issue their administrators two accounts—one for their role as a user of the company's applications and systems and the other for their role as an administrator.

- **Account standardization:** The best way to simplify a complex environment is to standardize a limited number of account types. Each different account type permitted in your environment adds an order of magnitude to your permissions management strategy. By standardizing a limited set of account types, you make your job much easier.

- **Third-party applications:** A variety of third-party tools have been designed to make managing permissions easier. These range from account life-cycle management applications to auditing applications to application firewalls.

- **Processes and procedures:** One of the easiest ways to manage permissions in your environment is to have a solid framework of processes and procedures for managing accounts. With this framework to rely on, you don't have to address each account as a unique circumstance. Rather, you can rely on the defined process to determine how all accounts are created, classified, permissioned, and maintained.

TAKE NOTE*

Perfect implementation of the principle of least privilege is very rare. A best effort is typically what is expected and what is achievable.

Understanding Attack Surface

One final concept to tackle when evaluating the security of your environment is that of an *attack surface*. With respect to systems, networks, and applications, this is another idea that has been around for quite some time. An attack surface consists of the set of methods and avenues an attacker can use to enter a system and potentially cause damage. The larger the attack surface of a particular environment, the greater the risk of a successful attack.

To calculate the attack surface of an environment, it's frequently easiest to divide the evaluation into three components:

- Application
- Network
- Employee

When evaluating the *application attack surface*, you need to look at things like:

- The amount of code in an application
- The number of data inputs to an application
- The number of running services
- Which ports the application is listening on

Similarly, when evaluating the *network attack surface*, you should consider the following:

- Overall network design
- Placement of critical systems
- Placement and rule sets on firewalls
- Other security-related network devices, such as IDS, VPN, and so on

Finally, when evaluating the *employee attack surface*, you should consider the following factors:

- The risk of social engineering
- The potential for human errors
- The risk of malicious behavior

Once you have evaluated these three types of attack surfaces, you will have a solid understanding of the total attack surface presented by your environment, as well as how an attacker might try to compromise your environment.

Understanding Social Engineering

As previously mentioned, one of the key factors to consider when evaluating the employee attack surface is the risk of a social engineering attack. **Social engineering** is a method used to gain access to data, systems, or networks, primarily through misrepresentation. This technique typically relies on the trusting nature of the person being attacked.

In a typical social engineering attack, the attacker will try to appear as harmless or respectful as possible. These attacks can be perpetrated in person, through email, or via phone. Attackers will try techniques ranging from pretending to be a help desk or support department staffer, claiming to be a new employee, or in some cases, even offering credentials that identify them as an employee of the company.

Generally, these attackers will ask a number of questions in an attempt to identify possible avenues to exploit during an attack. If they do not receive sufficient information from one employee, they may reach out to several others until they have sufficient information for the next phase of an attack.

To avoid social engineering attacks, remember the following techniques:

- **Be suspicious:** Phone calls, emails, or visitors who ask questions about the company, its employees, or other internal information should be treated with extreme suspicion, and if appropriate, reported to security personnel.
- **Verify identity:** If you receive inquiries that you are unsure of, verify the identity of the requestor. If a caller is asking questions that seem odd, try to get his or her number so you can call back. Then, verify that the phone number you have been given is from a legitimate source. Similarly, if someone approaches you with a business card as identification, ask to see a picture ID. Business cards are easy to print, and they are even easier to take from the "Win a Free Lunch" bowl at a local restaurant.
- **Be cautious:** Do not provide sensitive information unless you are certain not only of the person's identity, but also his or her right to have the information.
- **Don't use email:** Email is inherently insecure and prone to a variety of address spoofing techniques. Therefore, don't reveal personal or financial information via email. Never

respond to email requests for sensitive information—and be especially cautious of providing this information after following web links embedded in email. A common trick is to embed a survey link in an email, possibly offering a prize or prize drawing, and then asking questions about the computing environment like "How many firewalls do you have deployed?" or "What firewall vendor do you use?" Employees are so accustomed to seeing these types of survey requests in their inboxes that they seldom think twice about responding to them.

Linking Cost with Security

There are some points that you should keep in mind when developing a security plan. First, security costs money. Typically, the more money you spend, the more secure your information or resources will be (up to a point). So, when looking at risk and threats, you need to consider how valuable certain confidential data or resources are to your organization and also how much money you are willing to spend to protect those data or resources.

In addition to considering cost, you should also strive to make the security measures as seamless as possible to authorized users who are accessing the confidential information or resource. If security becomes a heavy burden, users will often look for methods to circumvent the measures you have established. Of course, training goes a long way in protecting your confidential information and resources because it shows users what warning signs to watch for.

■ Looking at Physical Security as the First Line of Defense

THE BOTTOM LINE

There are a number of factors to consider when designing, implementing, or reviewing physical security measures taken to protect assets, systems, networks, and information. These include understanding site security and computer security; securing removable devices and drives; access control; mobile device security; disabling the Log On Locally capability; and identifying and removing keyloggers.

CERTIFICATION READY
Why is physical security so important to a server even when you need usernames and passwords to access that server?
1.2

Most businesses exercise some level of control over who is able to access their physical environment. When securing computer-related assets and data, there is a tendency to only look at the virtual world, paying little attention to the issue of physical security. However, if you work for a large company in a location with a data center, you may see badge readers and/or keypads to access the building and any secure areas, along with guards and perhaps even logbooks to control and track the people who enter in the building. Office keys and desk drawer keys provide yet another layer of security. In smaller offices, similar measures may be in place, albeit on a smaller scale.

TAKE NOTE*
If someone can get physical access to a server where confidential data is stored, with the right tools and enough time, that person can bypass any security the server uses to protect the data.

This multilayered approach to physical security is known as defense in depth or a layered security approach. See Figure 1-1. Securing a physical site is more than just putting a lock on the front door and making sure you use that lock. Rather, it is a complex challenge for any security professional.

TAKE NOTE*
Security does not end with physical security. You also need to look at protecting confidential information with technology based on authentication, authorization, and accounting—including use of rights, permissions, and encryption.

Understanding Site Security

Site security is a specialized area of the security discipline. This section is meant to introduce you to some of the more common concepts and technologies you may encounter when working in the site security field.

UNDERSTANDING ACCESS CONTROL

Before we jump into site security details, you must first understand what is meant by the term "access control." **Access control** is a key concept when thinking about physical security. It is also a little confusing, because you will frequently hear the phrase used when discussing information security. In the context of physical security, access control is the process of restricting access to a resource to only permitted users, applications, or computer systems.

If you think about it, you can probably come up with several everyday examples of access control. For instance, when you close a door and lock it, you are practicing access control. When you use a baby gate to keep a toddler from falling down a staircase, you are practicing access control. Similarly, when you put a fence around your yard to keep your dog out of the neighbor's flowers, you are practicing access control.

The difference between the access control you practice in your everyday life and the access control you will encounter in the business world is the nature of what you are protecting and the technologies you have available to secure it. We will cover these topics in more detail through the rest of this lesson.

Figure 1-1

Layered site security model

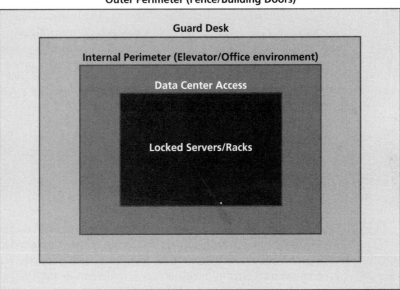

As previously mentioned, site security involves securing the physical premises. One fundamental concept used when designing a security environment is that of defense in depth. **Defense in depth** means using multiple layers of security to defend your assets. That way, even if an attacker breaches one layer of your defense, you have additional layers to keep that person out of the critical areas of your environment.

A simple example of defense in depth that you may have encountered in the "real world" is a hotel room that contains a locked suitcase. To get into the locked hotel room, you must get the key to work. After you accomplish this task, there is a deadbolt that must be bypassed. And once you are past the deadbolt, there is still the lock on the suitcase that must be breached.

Beyond the idea of defense in depth, there are several other goals to keep in mind when designing a physical security plan:

- **Authentication:** Site security must address the need to identify and authenticate the people who are permitted access to an area.
- **Access control:** Once a person's identity has been proven and authenticated, site security must determine what areas that person has access to.
- **Auditing:** Site security must also provide the ability to audit activities within the facility. This can be done by reviewing camera footage, badge reader logs, visitor registration logs, or other mechanisms.

For the purposes of this lesson, we will break the physical premises into three logical areas:

- **The external perimeter**, which makes up the outermost portion of the location. This typically includes the driveways, parking lots, and any green space the location may support. This does not include things like public roads.
- **The internal perimeter**, which consists of any buildings on the premises. If the location supports multiple tenants, your internal perimeter is restricted to only the buildings you occupy.
- **Secure areas**, which are locations within the building that have additional access restrictions and/or security measures in place. These might include data centers, network rooms, wiring closets, or departments like Research and Development or Human Resources.

UNDERSTANDING EXTERNAL PERIMETER SECURITY

The external security perimeter is the first line of defense surrounding your office. However, security measures in this area probably vary the most of any area we will discuss. For instance, if you are trying to protect a top-secret government installation, your external perimeter security will likely consist of multiple fences, roving guard patrols, land mines, and all sorts of other measures you won't see in the corporate world. On the other hand, if your office is in a multitenant office park, the external perimeter security may consist only of streetlights. Most companies fall somewhere in between. Common security measures you may encounter with respect to an organization's external perimeter include the following:

TAKE NOTE

Test your camera's playback capabilities regularly. Because cameras are almost always used to review events after the fact, you need to be sure your system is successfully recording the data.

- Security cameras
- Parking lot lights
- Perimeter fence
- Gate with guard
- Gate with access badge reader
- Guard patrols

One challenge associated with security cameras is that these cameras are only as good as the people monitoring them. Because monitoring cameras is a resource-intensive, expensive undertaking, in most office environments, there isn't anyone actively watching these cameras. Instead, cameras are used after an incident occurs to determine what happened or who is responsible.

UNDERSTANDING THE INTERNAL PERIMETER

The internal security perimeter starts with the building walls and exterior doors and includes any internal security measures, with the exception of secure areas within the building. Some of the features you may use to secure an internal perimeter include the following:

- Locks (on exterior doors, internal doors, office doors, desks, filing cabinets, etc.)
- Keypads
- Security cameras
- Badge readers (on doors and elevators)
- Guard desks

- Guard patrols
- Smoke detectors
- Turnstiles
- Mantraps

The key security measures implemented in the internal perimeter are those that are used to divide the internal space into discrete segments. This is a physical implementation of the principle of least privilege. For example, if an organization's office includes finance, human resources, and sales departments, it would not be unusual to restrict access to the finance department to only those people who work in finance. You generally don't need human resources staffers wandering around your finance area. These sorts of segregations may be based on floors, areas, or even series of offices, depending on the physical layout.

DEFINING SECURE AREAS

Secure areas within an office would include places like a data center, the research and development department, a lab, a telephone closet, a network room, or any other area that requires additional security controls not only to restrict external attackers, but also to limit internal employee access. Secure area security technologies include the following:

- Badge readers
- Keypads
- Biometric technologies (e.g., fingerprint scanners, retinal scanners, voice recognition systems, etc.)
- Security doors
- X-ray scanners
- Metal detectors
- Cameras
- Intrusion detection systems (light beam, infrared, microwave, and/or ultrasonic)

UNDERSTANDING SITE SECURITY PROCESSES

Although technology forms a significant component of an organization's physical security, the processes you put in place to support this technology are just as critical. In fact, you should have such processes at all levels of your site.

In the external perimeter, you might have a process to manage entry to the parking lot through a gate, or there may be a process for how often the guards patrol the parking lot. Included in those processes should be how to document findings, track entry and exits, and respond to incidents. For example, your guard tour process should include instructions on how to handle an unlocked car or a suspicious person, or, with the heightened awareness of possible terrorist attacks, how to handle an abandoned package.

In the internal perimeter, you might have processes that include guest sign-in procedures, equipment removal procedures, guard rotations, or when the front door is to be left unlocked. You should probably also have processes to handle deliveries, how/when to escort visitors in the facility, and even what types of equipment may be brought into the building. For example, many companies prohibit bringing personal equipment into the office due to the risk that an employee could use his or her personal laptop to steal valuable company information.

Once you reach the secure area layer, you will generally have procedures for controlling who is permitted to enter the data center and how they will access the data center. In addition, you will have multiple mechanisms to ensure that only authorized people are granted access including locked doors, biometric devices, cameras, and security guards.

TAKE NOTE★

Smaller offices that are not occupied at night may take advantage of remote monitoring and intrusion detection systems in their internal perimeter. Larger locations typically have some activities occurring on nights and weekends, which makes use of these technologies more challenging.

TAKE NOTE★

Cameras are available on virtually every cell phone on the market today. If you need to ensure that cameras are not used in your facility, plan on taking phones at the door or disabling their camera function.

Understanding Computer Security

Computer security consists of the processes, procedures, policies, and technologies used to protect computer systems. For the purposes of this lesson, computer security will refer specifically to physically securing computers; other facets of computer security are discussed throughout the rest of the book.

In addition to the many physical security measures already described, there are some additional tools that can be used to secure actual computers. Before we start discussing these tools, however, we first need to differentiate among three main types of computers:

- **Servers:** These are computers used to run centralized applications and deliver the applications across a network. This can be an internal network (such as for a business) or perhaps even the Internet (for public access). The computer that hosts your favorite website is an excellent example of a server. Servers are typically configured with redundant capabilities, ranging from redundant hard drives to fully clustered servers.
- **Desktop computers:** These computers are usually found in office environments, schools, and homes. Such computers are meant to be used in a single location and to run applications like word processing, spreadsheets, games, and other local programs. They can also be used to interact with centralized applications or to browse websites.
- **Mobile computers:** This category includes laptop, notebook, tablet, and netbook computers. You could even include smartphones. These machines are used for the same types of functions as desktop computers, but they are meant to be used in multiple locations (for example, home and office). Due to their smaller size, mobile computers were once less powerful than desktop computers, but thanks to advances in microprocessor and storage technologies, this gap is rapidly narrowing.

Each type of computer—server, desktop, and mobile—requires different physical security considerations. For example, when securing a server, the first thing you must consider is where the server will be located. Servers are typically much more expensive than desktop or mobile computers and used to run critical applications, so the types of security typically used with servers are largely location based. Servers should be secured in data centers or computer rooms, where you can take advantage of locked doors, cameras, and various other security features described earlier in the lesson.

If you do not have the ability to place a server in a data center or computer room, you should utilize one of the following technologies:

- **Computer security cable:** A cable that is attached to the computer and to a piece of furniture or the wall.
- **Computer security cabinet/rack:** A storage container that is secured with a locking door.

Desktop computers are typically secured with the same types of computer security cables you can use with servers. Desktop computers are frequently used in secure office environments or in people's homes, and they are not particularly expensive relative to other technologies. Accordingly, most companies do not take extraordinary measures to protect the desktop computers in their offices.

Mobile computers, unlike servers and desktops, are highly portable, so there is a unique set of technologies and best practices for protecting these machines from theft or damage. Some of these methods are described in the following section.

UNDERSTANDING MOBILE DEVICE SECURITY

Mobile devices are one of the largest challenges facing many security professionals today. Mobile devices such as laptops, PDAs (personal digital assistants), and smartphones are used to process information, send and receive mail, store enormous amounts of data, surf the Internet, and interact remotely with internal networks and systems. When you consider that you can place a 32 GB MicroSD memory card (see Figure 1-2) in a smartphone that a senior vice president can then use to store all of a company's research and development information, the potential impact to the company should someone steal that phone is staggering. As a result, the industry offers a number of technologies for physically securing mobile devices, including the following:

Docking station security only works if you enable it and make sure the docking station is secured to an immovable object. It's frequently just as easy to steal a laptop and its docking station as it is to steal just the laptop.

- **Docking stations:** Virtually all laptop docking stations are equipped with security features. This may involve a key, a padlock, or both, depending on the vendor and model.
- **Laptop security cables:** Used in conjunction with the USS (Universal Security Slot), these cables attach to a laptop and can be wrapped around a secure object like a piece of furniture.
- **Laptop safes:** These are steel safes specifically designed to hold a laptop and be secured to a wall or piece of furniture.
- **Theft recovery software:** These applications enable the tracking of a stolen computer so it can be recovered.
- **Laptop alarms:** These are motion-sensitive alarms that sound in the event that a laptop is moved. Some are also designed in conjunction with a security cable system so that they sound whenever the cable is cut.

PDAs and smartphones are typically more difficult to secure than laptops; because they are a new technology that just recently exploded in popularity, only limited security tools are available. For now, you can configure passwords to protect these devices, enable encryption, and remotely wipe phones that are managed by an organization. Some smartphones and PDAs also include GPS components that allow you to track their location.

Of course, there are some best practices (and yes, these are based on common sense) that can be followed when securing both laptops and PDAs or smartphones, including the following:

- **Keep your equipment with you:** Mobile devices should be kept with you whenever possible. This means you should keep your mobile devices on your person or in your hand luggage when traveling. Similarly, keep your mobile devices in your sight when going through airport checkpoints.
- **Use your trunk:** If you are traveling by car and are unable to take your mobile device with you, lock it in the trunk when you park. Do not leave a mobile device in view in an unattended vehicle, even for a short period of time, and never leave it in a vehicle overnight.
- **Use the safe:** If you are staying in a hotel, lock your mobile device in a safe if one is available.

USING REMOVABLE DEVICES AND DRIVES

In addition to mobile devices, another technology that presents unique challenges to security professionals is removable devices and drives. You can see some examples of common removable devices in Figure 1-2.

Figure 1-2

Removable devices

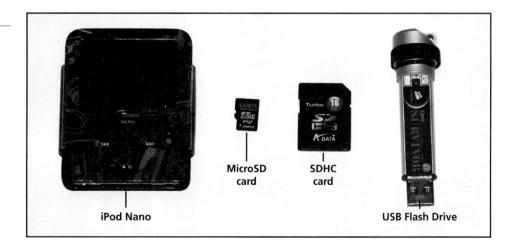

A *removable device* or drive is a storage device that is designed to be taken out of a computer without turning the computer off. These devices range from the MicroSD memory card, which is the size of your fingernail and can store up to 32 GB of information, to an external hard drive, which can store up to 2 terabytes of data. Floppy disks, CDs, and DVDs are also considered removable drives because they can be used to store critical data.

Removable devices typically connect to a computer through a drive, through external communications ports like USB or Firewire, or, in the case of memory cards, through built-in or USB-based readers. These devices are used for a variety of purposes, including backing up critical data, providing supplemental storage, transferring data between computers, and sometimes even running applications. This form of storage is also used in music players like iPods and Zunes, as well as in personal media players like the Archos and Creative's Zen devices.

There are three basic types of security issues associated with removable storage:

- Loss
- Theft
- Espionage

The loss of a storage device is one of the most common security issues you will encounter. USB drives are especially problematic in this regard. Typically the size of a pack of gum or smaller, these drives are frequently left in conference rooms, in hotel rooms, or in seat pockets on airplanes. Your challenge is how to secure the gigabytes of data that are lost along with these drives. Currently, these devices can be protected with both authentication and encryption. Also, with Windows 7 and Windows Server 2008 R2, Microsoft released BitLocker To Go, which can be used to protect data on mobile storage devices. In addition, some companies may offer their own protection mechanism, such as IronKey. Of course, you need to impress on your users the value of these types of storage. Many users do not give a second thought to throwing a confidential presentation on a *flash drive* (a small drive based on flash memory) for a meeting. As part of your awareness efforts, you must educate these users about the value of data, as well as how easy it is to misplace portable storage devices.

Theft is a problem with any portable piece of equipment. Many of the theft-prevention measures discussed with respect to mobile devices apply to removable storage devices as well. For example, keep drives with you whenever possible. When you cannot keep them with you, secure them in a hotel safe, locked desk drawer, or other secure location. Do not leave portable storage out where it can be easily removed from your area. Remember, even though removable devices themselves are relatively inexpensive, the data on them can be irreplaceable, or worse, confidential.

The final area in which these types of devices present a security issue is in conjunction with espionage. Many storage devices come in very small forms, which make them particularly well suited to espionage. For example, you can purchase flash drives disguised as pens, watches, or even as part of a pocketknife. To further compound the problem, everyday technological devices like music players and cell phones often have multiple gigabytes of storage. Even if you manage to ban unauthorized external drives and music players from the work setting, removing employee cell phones is virtually impossible. So, how can you protect your environment from this type of security threat?

The key to this threat is not to try to defend the environment from portable devices, but instead to protect the data from any unauthorized access. This is where the principle of least privilege is critical—if you ensure that employees can only access the data, systems, and networks they need to do their jobs, then you make the task of keeping critical data off portable drives much easier.

UNDERSTANDING KEYLOGGERS

A *keylogger* is a physical or logical device used to capture keystrokes. An attacker will either place a device between the keyboard and the computer or install a software program to record each keystroke taken, and then he or she can use software to replay the data and capture critical information like user IDs and passwords, credit card numbers, Social Security numbers, or

TAKE NOTE*

Some workplaces address the issues associated with removable storage by using hardware or software configurations that prohibit their use. Although this can be an effective strategy, it is also expensive and resource intensive. Accordingly, there are only a limited number of businesses in which this strategy can be effectively implemented.

X REF

Encryption is frequently used to secure the data on removable drives. This method is discussed in detail in Lesson 2.

even confidential emails or other data. There are also wireless keyboard sniffers that can intercept the broadcast keystrokes sent between a wireless keyboard and a computer.

To protect against a physical keylogger, your best tool is visual inspection. Take a look at the connection between the keyboard and the computer. If there is an extra device in between the two, someone is trying to capture your keystrokes. This is especially important when working with shared or public computers, where attackers will utilize keyloggers to cast a wide net and grab whatever critical data someone might enter.

The best defense against a software keylogger is the use of up-to-date antimalware software. Many software keyloggers are identified as malware by these applications. You can also leverage User Account Control and host-based firewalls to prevent a software keylogger from being installed.

To defend against a wireless keyboard sniffer, your best bet is to ensure your wireless keyboard supports encrypted connections. Most current wireless keyboards will either operate in an encrypted mode by default or at least permit you to configure encryption during installation.

X REF

Lesson 5 contains a more in-depth discussion of antimalware and workstation firewall technologies.

SKILL SUMMARY

IN THIS LESSON YOU LEARNED:

- Before you can start securing your environment, you need to have a fundamental understanding of the standard concepts of security.
- CIA, short for confidentiality, integrity, and availability, represents the core goals of an information security program.
- Confidentiality deals with keeping information, networks, and systems secure from unauthorized access.
- One of the goals of a successful information security program is to ensure integrity, or that information is protected against any unauthorized or accidental changes.
- Availability is defined as the characteristic of a resource being accessible to a user, application, or computer system when required.
- Threat and risk management is the process of identifying, assessing, and prioritizing threats and risks.
- A risk is generally defined as the probability that an event will occur.
- Once you have prioritized your risks, there are four generally accepted responses to these risks: avoidance, acceptance, mitigation, and transfer.
- The principle of least privilege is a security discipline that requires that a user, system, or application be given no more privilege than necessary to perform its function or job.
- An attack surface consists of the set of methods and avenues an attacker can use to enter a system and potentially cause damage. The larger the attack surface of an environment, the greater the risk of a successful attack.
- The key to thwarting a social engineering attack is employee awareness. If your employees know what to look out for, an attacker will find little success.
- Physical security uses a defense in depth or layered security approach that controls who can physically access an organization's resources.
- Physical premises can be divided into three logical areas: the external perimeter, the internal perimeter, and secure areas.
- Computer security consists of the processes, procedures, policies, and technologies used to protect computer systems.
- Mobile devices and mobile storage devices are among the biggest challenges facing many security professionals today because of their size and portability.
- A keylogger is a physical or logical device used to capture keystrokes.

Knowledge Assessment

Multiple Choice

Circle the letter or letters that correspond to the best answer or answers.

1. Which of the following are valid risk responses? (Choose all that apply.)
   a. Mitigation
   b. Transfer
   c. Investment
   d. Avoidance

2. Which of the following are considered removable devices or drives? (Choose all that apply.)
   a. iPod
   b. Netbook
   c. USB flash drive
   d. Floppy drive

3. Which of the following would be considered appropriate security measures for a building's external security perimeter? (Choose all that apply.)
   a. Motion detector
   b. Parking lot lights
   c. Turnstile
   d. Security guards

4. You are traveling on business and are headed out to dinner with a client. You cannot take your laptop with you to the restaurant. What should you do with the device? (Choose the best answer.)
   a. Lock the laptop in your car trunk.
   b. Store the laptop out of sight in a dresser drawer.
   c. Secure the laptop to a piece of furniture with a laptop security cable.
   d. Check the laptop at the front desk.

5. The process of eliminating a risk by choosing not to engage in an action or activity describes which of the following?
   a. Mitigation
   b. Residual risk
   c. Avoidance
   d. Acceptance

6. You have just been promoted to Chief Security Officer for your auto parts manufacturing business, and you are trying to identify technologies that will help ensure the confidentiality of your proprietary manufacturing techniques. Which of the following are technologies you could use to help with this endeavor? (Choose all that apply.)
   a. Strong encryption
   b. Security guards
   c. Laptop safes
   d. Strong authentication

7. The acronym CIA stands for which of the following?
   a. Confidentiality, identity, access control
   b. Confidentiality, integrity, access control
   c. Confidentiality, integrity, availability
   d. Control, identity, access control

8. You have been placed in charge of the corporate security department, and your boss has asked you to help her understand what is meant by core security principles. Which of these explanations should you give to your boss?
   a. Core security principles refer to the internal security perimeter when setting up a layered physical security environment.
   b. Core security principles refer to the principles of confidentiality, availability, and integrity.
   c. Core security principles refer to leveraging security best practices.
   d. Core security principles refer to the four methods of addressing risk.

9. As the Chief Security Officer for a small medical records processing company, you have just finished setting up the physical security for your new office. In particular, you have made sure that the parking lot is illuminated, that you have guards both at the door and performing periodic patrols, and that you have badge readers throughout the building at key locations. You also have put biometric access technology on the data center door. In addition, you have cameras in the parking lot, at building entrances, and at the data center entrances. This type of implementation is known as: (Choose the best answer.)
   a. Access control
   b. Core security principles
   c. Security best practices
   d. Defense in depth

10. What do you call the process of disabling unneeded services and ports to make a system more secure?
    a. Reducing the surface attack area
    b. Mitigating a Trojan horse
    c. Security avoidance
    d. Defense in depth

Fill in the Blank

1. _____ is the characteristic of a resource that ensures that access is restricted to only permitted users, applications, or computer systems.

2. If you are deploying technologies to restrict access to a resource, you are practicing the security principle known as _____.

3. Deploying multiple layers of security technology is called _____.

4. An action or occurrence that could result in the breach, outage, or corruption of a system by exploiting known or unknown vulnerabilities is a(n) _____.

5. You have just taken a new job as the Risk Manager for a medium-sized pharmaceutical company, and your first assignment is to perform a formal risk assessment. You will most likely record the results of your risk assessment in a(n) _____.

6. A secretary at your office just got off the phone with someone who said he was calling from the corporate IT department. The caller had a number of questions about the secretary's computer setup, and he asked for her user ID and password. In this situation, the secretary was most likely a victim of _____.

7. The consistency, accuracy, and validity of data or information is called _____.

8. You are traveling for work and decide to use a computer in the hotel business center to check your email and pay several bills. When you sit down at the computer, you notice there is an extra connector between the keyboard and the computer. You have most likely encountered a(n) _____.

9. You are the Risk Manager for a regional bank, and you have just deployed a new badge reader system to address an access control risk. Although your solution has mitigated the risk, there is still a small remaining risk associated with access control. This risk is known as the _____.

10. The larger the _____ of a particular environment, the greater the risk of a successful attack.

■ Competency Assessment

Scenario 1-1: Designing a Physical Security Solution

You are the Security Manager for a medium-sized bank. You have been asked to design a security solution to keep intruders out of the bank after hours. The three areas of the bank you need to secure are the parking lot, the building perimeter, and the vault. List what technologies you would use in each of these areas.

Scenario 1-2: Securing a Mobile Device

You are the IT Manager for a 5,000-employee legal services company. You are in the process of rolling out new mobile devices to your sales department. What processes and technologies will you use to keep these systems physically secure?

■ Proficiency Assessment

Scenario 1-3: Looking at Confidentiality, Integrity, and Availability

Within your organization, you have a server called Server1 that is running Windows Server 2008 R2. On Server1, you create and share a folder called Data on the C drive. Within the Data folder, you create a folder for each user within your organization. You then place each person's electronic paycheck in his or her folder. Later, you find out that John was able to go in and change some of the electronic paychecks and delete others. Explain which of the CIA components was not followed in this scenario.

Scenario 1-4: Examining Social Engineering

You work for the Contoso Corporation. Your manager wants you to put together a training class about end-user security. To begin, use the Internet to research three cases or instances in which individuals used social engineering to break into a system, and list how they attempted to get access.

✳ Workplace Ready

Understanding the Basics

Understanding security concepts is only the first step in learning about security. As a network administrator or security officer, you will be amazed by how much considering these basics will help you plan, implement, and update your organization's overall security program.

Authentication, Authorization, and Accounting

OBJECTIVE DOMAIN MATRIX

SKILLS/CONCEPTS	MTA EXAM OBJECTIVE	MTA EXAM OBJECTIVE NUMBER
Starting Security with Authentication	Understand user authentication.	2.1
Comparing Rights and Permissions	Understand permissions.	2.2
Using Auditing to Complete the Security Picture	Understand audit policies.	2.4
Using Encryption to Protect Data	Understand encryption.	2.5

KEY TERMS

access control list (ACL)

accounting

Active Directory

administrative share

asymmetric encryption

auditing

authentication

authorization

biometrics

BitLocker To Go

brute force attack

built-in groups

certificate chain

certificate revocation list (CRL)

computer account

decryption

dictionary attack

digital certificate

digital signature

domain controller

domain user

effective permissions

encryption

explicit permission

group

hash function

inherited permission

IP Security (IPsec)

Kerberos

key

local user account

member server

multifactor authentication

nonrepudiation

NTFS	Secure Sockets Layer (SSL)
NTFS permission	Security Account Manager (SAM)
NTLM	security token
organizational units (OU)	share permissions
owner	shared folder
password	single sign-on (SSO)
permission	smart card
personal identification number (PIN)	symmetric encryption
public key infrastructure (PKI)	syslog
registry	user account
right	virtual private network (VPN)

The CIO for your company approaches you to discuss security. During the conversation, he asks you what measures the company has in place to ensure that users can access only what they need and nothing else. You respond by explaining that you have built the organization's security model using the three As: authentication, authorization, and accounting. Unfortunately, he wants to know more about this model. How would you respond?

■ Starting Security with Authentication

↓ THE BOTTOM LINE

In the world of information security, AAA (authentication, authorization, and accounting) is a leading model for access control. Here, *authentication* is the process of identifying an individual, usually based on a username and password. After a user is authenticated, he or she can access network resources based on his or her authorization. *Authorization* is the process of giving individuals access to system objects based on their identity. Finally, *accounting*, also known as *auditing*, is the process of keeping track of a user's activity while accessing network resources, including the amount of time spent in the network, the services accessed while there, and the amount of data transferred during each session.

Nonrepudiation prevents one party from denying the actions it has carried out. If you have established proper authentication, authorization, and accounting, appropriate mechanisms of nonrepudiation should be in place, and no user should be able to deny the actions he or she has carried out while in your organization's system.

CERTIFICATION READY
Can you list the different methods for authentication?
2.1

Before users can access a computer or a network resource, they will most likely log in to prove they are who they say they are and to see whether they have the required rights and permissions to access the network resources.

Logging in is the process through which you are recognized by a computer system or network so that you can begin a session. A user can authenticate via one or more of the following methods:

- **By using what he or she knows:** For instance, by supplying a password or personal identification number (PIN)
- **By using what he or she owns or possesses:** For example, by providing a passport, smart card, or ID card
- **By proving what he or she is:** For instance, by supplying biometric factors based on fingerprints, retinal scans, voice input, etc.

When two or more authentication methods are used to authenticate someone, a ***multifactor authentication*** system is said to be in place. Of course, a system that uses two authentication methods (such as smart cards and passwords) can be referred to as a two-factor authentication system.

Authenticating with What You Know

> For both individual computers and entire networks, the most common method of authentication is the password. A ***password*** is a secret series of characters that enables a user to access a particular file, computer, or program.

USING PASSWORDS

When seeking access to a file, computer, or network, hackers will first attempt to crack passwords by trying obvious possibilities, including the names and birthdays of a user's spouse or children, key words used by the user, or the user's hobbies. If these efforts don't work, most hackers will next attempt ***brute force attacks***, which consist of trying as many possible combinations of characters as time and money permit. A subset of the brute force attack is the ***dictionary attack***, which attempts all words in one or more dictionaries. Lists of common passwords are also typically tested.

To make a password more secure, you need to choose a word that nobody can guess. Therefore, whatever you choose should be long enough and should be considered a strong or complex password. For more information about creating strong passwords, visit the following websites:

http://www.microsoft.com/protect/fraud/passwords/create.aspx

https://www.microsoft.com/protect/fraud/passwords/checker.aspx?WT.mc_id=Site_Link

Because today's computers are much more powerful than the computers of years past (which are often used to crack passwords), some people recommend passwords that are at least 14 characters long. However, remembering long passwords can be cumbersome for some people, and these individuals may write their passwords on a piece of paper near their desk. In these situations, you should start looking for other forms of authentication, such as smart cards or biometrics.

Users should also change their passwords regularly; that way, if a user's password is revealed to someone else, it won't be long until that password is no longer valid. In addition, changing passwords routinely also shortens the amount of time that an individual has to guess your password, because he or she will have to start the entire cracking process all over again once your password is changed.

Microsoft includes password policy settings within group policies so that you can easily enforce standards such as minimum number of characters, minimum level of password complexity, how often users must change their passwords, how often users can reuse passwords, and so on.

Although passwords are the easiest security method to implement and the most popular authentication method, use of passwords also has significant disadvantages, including the likelihood of passwords being stolen, spoofed, and/or forgotten. For example, a hacker might call a company's IT department for support and pretend to be a legitimate user, eventually convincing the department to reset that user's password to whatever he or she requests.

Given such scenarios, it's essential that you establish a secure process to reset all user passwords. For instance, you could establish a self-service process in which a user's identity is verified by asking questions and comparing the answers to responses that have been stored previously, such as the person's birthday, the name of his or her favorite movie, the name of his or her pet, and so on. However, these can be relatively easily guessed by an attacker, determined though low-effort research, or discovered through social engineering.

Accordingly, when resetting passwords, you must have a method to positively identify the user who is asking for the password change. Also, you should not send new passwords via email because if a user's existing password is compromised, the hacker will likely be able to access the user's email account and obtain the new password as well. To avoid these problems, you could meet face-to-face with the person who is requesting a password change and ask for identification. Unfortunately, with large networks and networks that include multiple sites, this may not be plausible. You could also call back and leave the password on the person's voicemail where he or she will need to provide a PIN to access it, or you could send the password to the user's manager or administrative assistant. In either case, you should have the user reset the password immediately after he or she logs on.

USING A PERSONAL IDENTIFICATION NUMBER (PIN)

A *personal identification number (PIN)* is a secret numeric password shared between a user and a system that can be used to authenticate the user to the system. Because they only consist of digits and are relatively short (usually four digits), PINs are used for relatively low-security scenarios, such as gaining access to a system, or in combination with another method of authentication.

Authenticating with What You Own or Possess

A second category of authentication is based on what you own or possess. The most common examples of this type of authentication involve use of digital certificates, smart cards, and security tokens.

A *digital certificate* is an electronic document that contains an identity, such as a user or organization name, along with a corresponding public key. Because a digital certificate is used to prove a person's identity, it can also be used for authentication. You can think of a digital certificate as similar to a driver's license or passport that contains a user's photograph and thumbprint so that there is no doubt who that user is.

A *smart card* is a pocket-sized card with embedded integrated circuits consisting of nonvolatile memory storage components and perhaps dedicated security logic. Nonvolatile memory is memory that does not forget its content when power is discontinued. This kind of memory may contain digital certificates to prove the identity of the person who is carrying the card, and it may also contain permissions and access information. Because smart cards can be stolen, some do not have any markings on them; this makes it difficult for a thief to identify what the card can be used to access. In addition, many organizations require users to supply passwords or PINs in combination with their smart cards.

A *security token* (or sometimes a hardware token, hard token, authentication token, USB token, cryptographic token, or key fob) is a physical device that an authorized computer services user is given to ease authentication. Hardware tokens are typically small enough to be carried in a pocket and are often designed to attach to a user's keychain. Some of these security tokens include a USB connector, RFID functions, or Bluetooth wireless interface to enable transfer of a generated key number sequence to a client system. Some security tokens may also include additional technology, such as a static password or digital certificate built into the security token, much like a smart card. Other security tokens may automatically generate a second code that users must input in order to be authenticated.

Authenticating with What You Are

Biometrics is an authentication method that identifies and recognizes people based on physical traits, such as fingerprints, face recognition, iris recognition, retinal scans, and voice recognition. Many mobile computers include a finger scanner, and it is relatively easy to install biometric devices on doors and cabinets to ensure that only authorized people enter secure areas.

To use biometric devices (see Figure 2-1), you must have a biometric reader or scanning device, software that converts the scanned information into digital form and compares match points, and a database that stores the biometric data for comparison.

Figure 2-1

Finger scanner

To launch the biometric system, you will need to set up a station where an administrator enrolls each user; this includes scanning the biometric feature you want to use for authentication. When selecting a biometric method, you should consider its performance, difficulty, reliability, acceptance, and cost. You also need to look at the following characteristics:

- **False reject rate (false negative):** This is the percentage of authorized users who are incorrectly denied access.
- **False accept rate (false positive):** This is the percentage of unauthorized users who are incorrectly granted access.

Introducing RADIUS and TACACS+

When you buy a new computer and create a local user account and login, you are being authenticated with the username and password. For corporations, computers can be part of the domain, and authentication can be provided by the domain controllers. In other situations, you may need to provide centralized authentication, authorization, and accounting when users need to connect to a network service. Two commonly used protocols that provide these functions are Remote Authentication Dial In User Service (RADIUS) and Terminal Access Controller Access-Control System Plus (TACACS+).

A RADIUS or TACACS+ server resides on a remote system and responds to queries from clients such as VPN clients, wireless access points, routers, and switches. The server then authenticates username/password combinations (authentication), determines whether users are allowed to connect to the client (authorization), and logs the connection (accounting).

RADIUS is a mechanism that allows authentication of dial-in and other network connections, including modem dial-up, wireless access points, VPNs, and web servers. As an IETF standard, it has been implemented by most major operating system manufacturers, including Microsoft. For example, in Windows Server 2008, Network Policy Server (NPS) can be used as a RADIUS server to perform authentication, authorization, and accounting for RADIUS clients. It can be configured to use a Microsoft Windows NT Server 4.0 domain, an Active Directory Domain Services (AD DS) domain, or the local Security Accounts Manager (SAM) user accounts database to authenticate user credentials for connection attempts. NPS uses the dial-in properties of the user account and network policies to authorize a connection.

Another competing centralized AAA server is TACACS+, which was developed by Cisco. When designing TACACS+, Cisco incorporated much of the existing functionality of

RADIUS and extended it to meet their needs. From a features viewpoint, TACACS+ can be considered an extension of RADIUS.

Using Run As

Because administrators have full access to individual computers or entire networks, it is recommended that you use a standard nonadministrator user account to perform most tasks. Then, when you need to perform administrative tasks, you can use the Run as command or the built-in options that are included with the Windows operating system.

In previous versions of Windows, you had to use an administrator account to do certain things, such as changing system settings or installing software. If you were logged on as a limited user, the Run as command eliminated the need to log off and then log back on as an administrator.

In newer versions of Windows, including Windows 7 and Windows Server 2008 R2, the Run as command has been changed to Run as administrator. With User Account Control (UAC), you will rarely have to use the Run as administrator command, because Windows automatically prompts you for an administrator password when needed. UAC is discussed in detail in Lesson 5.

 RUN A PROGRAM AS AN ADMINISTRATOR

GET READY. To run a program as an administrator, perform the following steps:

1. Right-click the program icon or file that you want to open, and then click **Run as administrator**. See Figure 2-2.
2. Select the administrator account that you want to use, type the password, and then click **Yes**.

You can also use the runas.exe command. For example, to run the widget.exe as an administrator, you would enter the following command:

```
runas /user:admin /widget.exe
```

Figure 2-2

Using the Run as administrator option

Introducing Directory Services with Active Directory

THE BOTTOM LINE

A directory service stores, organizes, and provides access to information in a directory. It is used for locating, managing, and administering common items and network resources, such as volumes, folders, files, printers, users, groups, devices, telephone numbers, and other objects. One popular directory service used by many organizations is Microsoft's Active Directory.

Active Directory is a technology created by Microsoft that provides a variety of network services, including the following:

- Lightweight Directory Access Protocol (LDAP)
- Kerberos-based and single sign-on (SSO) authentication
- DNS-based naming and other network information
- A central location for network administration and delegation of authority

The Lightweight Directory Access Protocol, or LDAP, is an application protocol for querying and modifying data using directory services running over TCP/IP. Within the directory, the set of objects is organized in a logical hierarchical manner so that you can easily find and manage those objects. The structure can reflect geographical or organizational boundaries, although it tends to use DNS names for structuring the topmost levels of the hierarchy. Deeper inside the directory, there might be entries representing people, organizational units, printers, documents, groups of people, or anything else that represents a given tree entry (or multiple entries). LDAP uses TCP port 389.

Kerberos is the default computer network authentication protocol, which allows hosts to prove their identity over a nonsecure network in a secure manner. It can also provide mutual authentication so that both the user and server verify each other's identity. To ensure security, Kerberos protocol messages are protected against eavesdropping and replay attacks.

Single sign-on (SSO) allows you to log on once and access multiple related but independent software systems without having to log in again. As you log on with Windows using Active Directory, you are assigned a token, which can then be used to sign on to other systems automatically.

Finally, Active Directory allows you to organize all of your network resources—including users, groups, printers, computers, and other objects—so that you can assign passwords, permissions, rights, and so on to the identity that needs it. You can also assign who is permitted to manage a group of objects.

Looking at Domain Controllers

A *domain controller* is a Windows server that stores a replica of the account and security information of a domain and defines the domain boundaries. To make a computer running Windows Server 2008 a domain controller, you will first have to install Active Directory Domain Services. You will then have to execute the dcpromo (short for dc promotion) command to make the server a domain controller from the Search programs and files box, or from the command prompt.

After a computer has been promoted to a domain controller, there are several MMC snap-in consoles to manage Active Directory, including:

- **Active Directory Users and Computers:** Used to manage users, groups, computers, and organizational units.

- **Active Directory Domains and Trusts:** Use to administer domain trusts, domain and forest functional levels, and user principal name (UPN) suffixes.
- **Active Directory Sites and Services:** Used to administer the replication of directory data among all sites in an Active Directory Domain Services (AD DS) forest.
- **Active Directory Administrative Center:** Used to administer and publish information in the directory, including managing users, groups, computers, domains, domain controllers, and organizational units. Active Directory Administrative Center is new in Windows Server 2008 R2.
- **Group Policy Management Console (GPMC):** Provides a single administrative tool for managing Group Policy across the enterprise. GPMC is automatically installed in Windows Server 2008 and newer domain controllers and needs to be downloaded and installed on Windows Server 2003 domain controllers.

Although these tools are typically installed on domain controllers, they can also be installed on client PCs so that you can manage Active Directory without logging on to a domain controller.

Active Directory uses multimaster replication, which means that there is no master domain controller, commonly referred to as a primary domain controller in Windows NT domains. However, there are certain functions that can only be handled by one domain controller at a time.

One role is the PDC Emulator, which provides backwards compatibility for NT4 clients, which is uncommon. However, it also acts as the primary authority for password changes and acts as the master time server within the domain.

A server that is not running as a domain controller is known as a *member server*. To demote a domain controller to a member server, you would rerun the dcpromo program.

Introducing NTLM

Although Kerberos is the default authentication protocol for today's domain computers, **NTLM** is the default authentication protocol for Windows NT, stand-alone computers that are not part of a domain, and situations in which you are authenticating to a server using an IP address. NTLM also acts as a fall-back authentication protocol if Kerberos authentication cannot be completed, such as when it is blocked by a firewall.

NTLM uses a challenge-response mechanism for authentication in which clients are able to prove their identities without sending a password to the server. After a random eight-byte challenge message is sent to the client from the server, the client uses the user's password as a key to generate a response back to the server using an MD4/MD5 hashing algorithm (one-way mathematical calculation) and DES encryption (a commonly used encryption algorithm that encrypted and decrypted data with the same key).

Introducing Kerberos

With Kerberos, security and authentication are based on secret key technology, and every host on the network has its own secret key. The Key Distribution Center maintains a database of these secret keys.

When a user logs in to a network resource using Kerberos, the client transmits the username to the authentication server, along with the identity of the service the user wants to connect to (e.g., a file server). The authentication server constructs a ticket, which randomly generates a key, encrypted with the file server's secret key, and sends it to the client as part of its credentials, which includes the session key encrypted with the client's key. If the user types the right password, then the client can decrypt the session key, present the ticket to the file server, and give the user the shared secret session key to communicate between them. Tickets are time stamped and typically have an expiration time of only a few hours.

For all of this to work and to ensure security, the domain controllers and clients must have the same time. Windows operating systems include the Time Service tool (W32Time service). Kerberos authentication will work if the time interval between the relevant computers is within the maximum enabled time skew. The default is five minutes. You can also turn off the Time Service tool and install a third-party time service. Of course, if you have problems authenticating, you should make sure that the time is correct for the domain controllers and the client having the problem.

Using Organizational Units

As mentioned earlier, an organization could have thousands of users and thousands of computers. With Windows NT, the domain could only handle so many objects before some performance issues arose. With later versions of Windows, however, the size of the domain was dramatically increased. Whereas with Windows NT you may have required several domains to define your organization, you can now have just one domain to represent a large organization. However, if you have thousands of such objects, you still need a way to organize and manage them.

To help organize objects within a domain and minimize the number of domains, you can use *organizational units*, or OUs, which can be used to hold users, groups, computers, and other organizational units. See Figure 2-3. An organizational unit can only contain objects that are located in a domain. Although there is no restriction as to how many nested OUs (an OU inside of another OU) you can have, you should design a shallow hierarchy for better performance.

Figure 2-3

Active Directory organizational unit

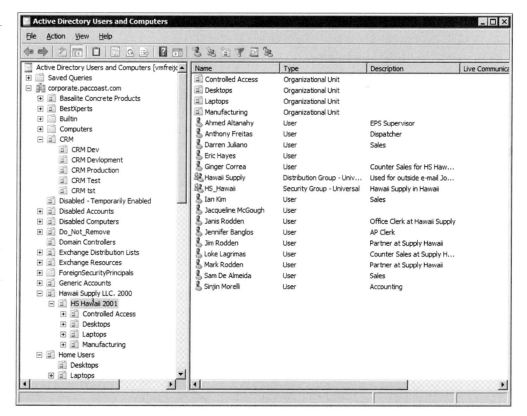

When you first install Active Directory, there are several organizational units already created. They include computers, users, domain controllers, and built-in OUs. Unlike OUs that you create, these OUs do not allow you to delegate permissions or assign group policies. (Group policies will be explained later in the text.) Containers are objects that can store or hold other objects. They include the forest, tree, domain, and organizational unit. To help you manage your objects, you can delegate authority to a container, particularly the domain or organizational unit.

For example, let's say that you have your domain divided by physical location. You can then assign a site administrator authoritative control to the OU that represents a particular physical location, and the user will only have administrative control to the objects within that OU. You can also structure your OUs by function or areas of management. For instance, you could create a Sales OU to hold all of your sales users. You could also create a Printers OU to hold all of the printer objects and then assign a printer administrator to that OU.

Similar to NTFS and the registry, you can assign permissions to users and groups over an Active Directory object. However, you would normally delegate control to the user or group. You can assign basic administrative tasks to regular users or groups and leave domain-wide and forest-wide administration to members of the Domain Admins and Enterprise Admins groups. By delegating administration, you allow groups within your organization to take more control of their local network resources. You also help secure your network from accidental or malicious damage by limiting the membership of administrator groups.

You can delegate administrative control to any level of a domain tree by creating organizational units within a domain, then delegating administrative control for specific organizational units to particular users or groups.

 DELEGATE CONTROL

GET READY. To delegate control of an organizational unit, perform the following steps:

1. Open **Active Directory Users and Computers.**
2. In the console tree, right-click the organizational unit for which you want to delegate control.
3. Click **Delegate control** to start the Delegation of Control Wizard, and then follow the instructions.

Looking at Objects

> An object is a distinct, named set of attributes or characteristics that represent a network resource. Common objects used within Active Directory are computers, users, groups, and printers. Attributes have values that define the specific object. For example, a user could have the first name John, the last name Smith, and the login name jsmith, all of which identify the user.

When working with objects, administrators typically use the names of those objects, such as usernames. However, all Active Directory objects are also assigned a 128-bit unique number called a security identifier (SID), sometimes referred to as a globally unique identifier (GUID), to uniquely identify them. Therefore, if a user changes his or her username, you can change that name on the network, but he or she will still be able to access all of the same objects and have all of the same rights as before because those objects and rights are assigned to the GUID.

GUIDs also provide some security if a user is deleted. You cannot create a new user account with the same username and expect to have access to all of the objects and all of the rights that the previous user had. Rather, if you decide to let someone in your organization go and you later replace that person, you should instead disable the first person's account, hire the new person, rename the user account, change the password, and re-enable the account. That way, the new person will be able to access all of the same resources and have all of the same rights that the previous user had.

The schema of Active Directory defines the format of each object and the attributes or fields within each object. The default schema contains definitions of commonly used objects like user accounts, computers, printers, and groups. For example, the schema defines that the user account has fields for first name, last name, and telephone numbers.

To allow Active Directory to be flexible so that it can support other applications, you can extend a schema to include additional attributes. For example, you could add badge number or employee identification fields to the user object. When you install some applications, such as Microsoft Exchange, they will extend the schema, usually by adding additional attributes or fields so that it can support the application.

EXAMINING USERS

A *user account* enables a user to log on to a computer and domain. As a result, it can be used to prove the identity of a user, which can then be used to determine what a user can access and what kind of access the user will have (authorization). User accounts can also be used for auditing. For instance, if there is a security problem in which something was inappropriately accessed or deleted, user account data can be used to show who accessed or deleted the object.

On today's Windows networks, there are two types of user accounts:

- Local user account
- Domain user account

A user account allows users to log on and gain access to the computer where the account was created. The *local user account* is stored in the *Security Account Manager (SAM)* database on the local computer. The only Windows computer that does not have a SAM database is the domain controller. The administrator local user account is the only account that is created and enabled by default in Windows. Although this account cannot be deleted, it can be renamed.

The only other account created by default is the guest account. It was designed for the occasional user who needs access to network resources on a low-security network. The guest local user account is disabled by default and not recommended for general use.

A *domain user* account is stored on the domain controller and allows you to gain access to resources within the domain, assuming you have been granted permissions to access those objects. The administrator domain user account is the only account that is created and enabled by default in Windows when you first create a domain. Again, although this account cannot be deleted, it can be renamed.

When you create a domain user account, you must supply a first name, last name, and a user login name. The user login name must be unique with the domain. See Figure 2-4. After the user account is created, you can then open the user account properties and configure a person's username, logon hours, telephone numbers and addresses, which computers the user can log on to, what groups the person is a member of, and so on. You can also specify whether a

Figure 2-4

User account in Active Directory

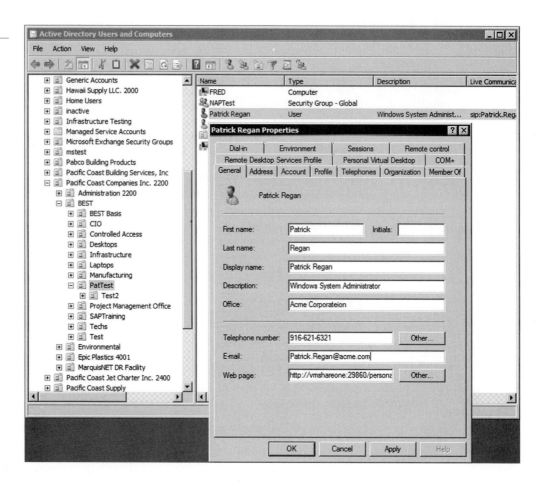

password expires, whether a password can be changed, and whether an account is disabled. Finally, on the Profile tab, you can define the user's home directory, logon script, and profile path. See Figure 2-5.

Figure 2-5

Profile tab

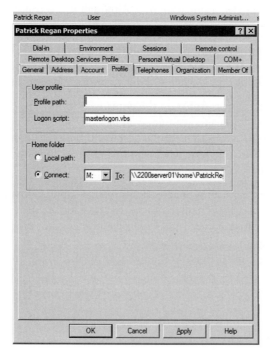

LOOKING AT COMPUTERS

Like user accounts, Windows *computer accounts* provide a means for authenticating and auditing a computer's access to a Windows network, as well as its access to domain resources. Each Windows computer to which you want to grant resource access must have a unique computer account. These accounts can also be used for auditing purposes, because they specify what systems were used to access particular resources. See Figure 2-6.

Figure 2-6

Computer account

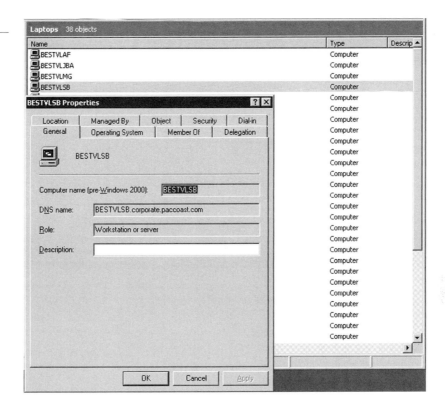

Using Groups

A *group* is a collection or list of user accounts or computer accounts. Different from a container, a group does not store users or computers; rather, it just lists them. Using groups can simplify administration, especially when assigning rights and permissions.

A group is used to group users and computers together so that when you assign rights and permissions, you assign them to the group rather than to each user individually. Users and computers can be members of multiple groups, and in some instances, one group can be designated as part of another group.

EXAMINING GROUP TYPES

In Windows Active Directory, there are two types of groups: security and distribution. A security group is used to assign rights and permissions and to gain access to network resources. It can also be used as a distribution group. A distribution group is employed only for nonsecurity functions, such as distributing email, and it cannot be used to assign rights and permissions.

EXAMINING GROUP SCOPES

Any group, whether it is a security group or a distribution group, is characterized by a scope that identifies the extent to which the group is applied in the domain tree or forest. The three group scopes are as follows:

- **Domain local:** Contains global and universal groups, even though it can also contain user accounts and other domain local groups. A domain local group is usually in the domain with the resource to which you want to assign permissions or rights.
- **Global:** Designed to contain user accounts, although they can also contain other global groups. Global groups are designed to be "global" for a domain. After you place user accounts into global groups, these groups are typically placed into domain local groups or universal groups.
- **Universal:** Designed to contain global groups from multiple domains, although they can also contain other universal groups and user accounts. Because global catalogs replicate universal group membership, you should limit membership to global groups. This way, if you change a member within a global group, the global catalog will not have to replicate the change.

See Table 2-1.

Table 2-1

Group scopes

Scope	Members Can Include...	Member Permissions Can Be Assigned...	Group Scope Can Be Converted to...
Universal	Accounts from any domain within the forest in which this universal group resides. Global groups from any domain within the forest in which this universal group resides. Universal groups from any domain within the forest in which this universal group resides	In any domain or forest	Domain local. Global (as long as no other universal groups exist as members)
Global	Accounts from the same domain as the parent global group. Global groups from the same domain as the parent global group	In any domain	Universal (as long as the group is not a member of any other global groups)
Domain local	Accounts from any domain, global groups from any domain, universal groups from any domain, and domain local groups but only from the same domain as the parent domain local group	Only within the same domain as the parent domain local group	Universal (as long as no other domain local groups exist as members)

When assigning rights and permissions, you should always try to place your users into groups and assign the rights and permissions to these groups instead of to individual users. To effectively manage the use of global and domain local groups when assigning access to network resources, remember the mnemonic AGDLP (accounts, global, domain local, permissions):

- First, add the user account (A) into the global group (G) in the domain where the user exists.
- Next, add the global group (G) from the user domain into the domain local group (DL) in the resource domain.

- Finally, assign permissions (P) on the resource to the domain local group (DL) in its domain.

If you are using universal groups, the mnemonic is expanded to AGUDLP:

- First, add the user account (A) into the global group (G) in the domain where the user exists.
- Then add the global group (G) from the user domain into the universal group (U).
- Next, add the universal group (U) to the domain local group (DL).
- Finally, assign permissions (P) on the resource to the domain local group (DL) in its domain.

USING BUILT-IN GROUPS

Similar to administrator and guest accounts, Windows has default groups called ***built-in groups***. These default groups have been granted the essential rights and permissions to get you started. Some of Windows' built-in groups are as follows:

- **Domain Admins:** Members of this group can perform administrative tasks on any computer within the domain. By default, the Administrator account is a member.
- **Domain Users:** Windows automatically adds each new domain user account to the Domain Users group.
- **Account Operators:** Members of this group can create, delete, and modify user accounts and groups.
- **Backup Operators:** Members of this group can back up and restore all domain controllers using Windows Backup.
- **Authenticated Users:** This group includes all users with a valid user account on the computer or in Active Directory. Use the Authenticated Users group instead of the Everyone group to prevent anonymous access to a resource.
- **Everyone:** This group includes all users who access a computer with a valid user account.

For more information on the available groups, visit the following website:

http://technet.microsoft.com/en-us/library/cc756898(WS.10).aspx

Looking at Web Server Authentication

When a person accesses a web server, such as those running on Microsoft's Internet Information Server (IIS), several methods of authentication can be used.

When authenticating to web servers, IIS provides a variety of authentication schemes:

- **Anonymous (enabled by default):** Anonymous authentication gives users access to a website without prompting them for a username or password. Instead, IIS uses a special Windows user account called IUSR_*machinename* for access. By default, IIS controls the password for this account.
- **Basic:** Basic authentication prompts the user for a username and password. However, even though the username and password are sent as Base64 encoding, it is basically sent in plain text since Base64 encoding is used as a format and not an encryption. If you need to encrypt usernames and passwords while using basic authentication, you can use digital certificates so that this information is encrypted with https.

- **Digest:** Digest authentication is a challenge/response mechanism that sends a digest or hash using the password as the key instead of sending the password over the network.
- **Integrated Windows authentication:** Integrated Windows authentication (formerly known as NTLM authentication and Windows NT Challenge/Response authentication) can use either NTLM or Kerberos V5 authentication.
- **Client Certificate Mapping:** Client Certificate Mapping uses a digital certificate that contains information about an entity and the entity's public key for authentication purposes.

■ Comparing Rights and Permissions

 THE BOTTOM LINE
What a user can do on a system or to a resource is determined by two things: rights and permissions.

CERTIFICATION READY
Can you describe how the permissions are stored for an object?
2.2

A *right* authorizes a user to perform certain actions on a computer, such as logging on to a system interactively or backing up files and directories on a system. User rights are assigned through local policies or Active Directory group policies. See Figure 2-7.

Figure 2-7

Group policy user rights assignment

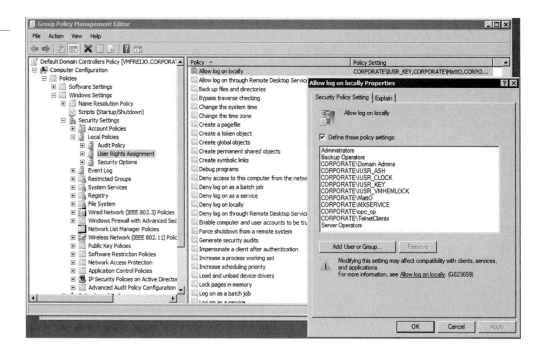

A *permission* defines the type of access that is granted to an object (an object can be identified with a security identifier) or object attribute. The most common objects assigned permissions are NTFS files and folders, printers, and Active Directory objects. Information about which users can access an object and what they can do is stored in the *access control list (ACL)*, which lists all users and groups that have access to an object. NTFS and printer permissions are discussed in the next lesson.

■ Looking at NTFS

THE BOTTOM LINE

A file system is a method of storing and organizing computer files and the data they contain. It also maintains the physical location of the files so that you can easily find and access the files in the future. Windows Server 2008 supports FAT16, FAT32, and NTFS file systems on hard drives.

After you partition a disk, you then need to format the disk. You can format the disk as FAT16, FAT32, or NTFS. Of these, *NTFS* is the preferred file system for today's operating systems.

FAT16, sometimes referred to generically as File Allocation Table (FAT), is a simple file system that uses minimal memory and has been used with DOS. Originally it supported the 8.3 naming scheme, which allowed up to an eight-character filename and three-character filename extension. Later, it was revised to support longer filenames. Unfortunately, FAT volumes can only support up to 2 GB.

FAT32 was released with the second major release of Windows 95. Although this file system can support larger drives, today's Windows supports volumes up to 32 GB. It also supports long filenames.

Today, NTFS is the preferred file system because it supports both volumes up to 16 exabytes and long filenames. In addition, NTFS is more fault tolerant than previous file systems used in Windows because it is a journaling file system. A journaling file system makes sure that a transaction is written to disk properly before being recognized. Finally, NTFS offers better security through permissions and encryption.

Using NTFS Permissions

NTFS permissions allow you to control which users and groups can gain access to files and folders on an NTFS volume. The advantage with NTFS permissions is that they affect both local users and network users.

Usually, when assigning NTFS permissions, you would assign the following standard permissions:

- **Full Control:** Permission to read, write, modify, and execute the files in a folder; change attributes and permissions; and take ownership of the folder or files within
- **Modify:** Permission to read, write, modify, and execute the files in the folder, as well as to change the attributes of the folder or files within
- **Read and Execute:** Permission to display a folder's contents; to display the data, attributes, owner, and permissions for files within the folder; and to run files within the folder
- **List Folder Contents:** Permission to display a folder's contents; and display the data, attributes, owner, and permissions for files within the folder
- **Read:** Permission to display a file's data, attributes, owner, and permissions
- **Write:** Permission to write to a file, append to the file, and read or change the file's attributes

To manage NTFS permissions, you can right-click a drive, folder, or file and select Properties, then select the Security tab. As shown in Figure 2-8, you should see the group and users who have been given NTFS permissions and their respective standard NTFS permissions. To change the permissions, you would click the Edit button.

Figure 2-8

NTFS permissions

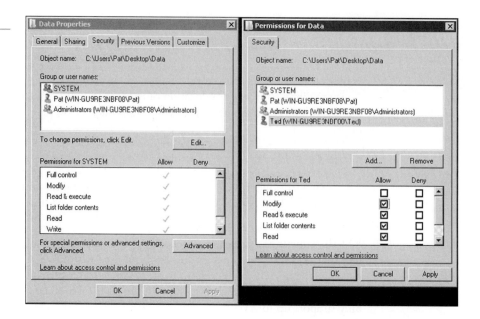

Groups or users who are granted Full Control permission on a folder can delete any files in that folder regardless of the permissions protecting the file. In addition, List Folder Contents is inherited by folders but not files, and it should only appear when you view folder permissions. In Windows Server 2008, the Everyone group does not include the Anonymous Logon group by default, so permissions applied to the Everyone group do not affect the Anonymous Logon group.

To simplify administration, it is recommended that you grant permissions using groups. By assigning NTFS permissions to a group, you are granting permissions to one or more people, reducing the number of entries in each access list and reducing the amount of effort to configure situations in which multiple people need access to certain files or folders.

Looking at Effective NTFS Permissions

The folder/file structure on an NTFS drive can be very complicated and include many folders and many nested folders. In addition, because it is recommended that you assign permissions to groups and at different levels on an NTFS volume, figuring out the effective permissions of a particular folder or file for a particular user can be tricky.

There are two types of permissions used in NTFS:

- *Explicit permissions:* Permissions granted directly to a file or folder
- *Inherited permissions:* Permissions granted to a folder (parent object or container) that flows into child objects (subfolders or files) inside that folder

When permissions are assigned to a folder, by default, they apply to both the folder and any subfolders and files of that folder. To stop permissions from being inherited in this way, you can select the "Replace all existing inheritable permissions on all descendants with inheritable permissions from this object" in the Advanced Security Settings dialog box. The dialog box will then ask whether you are sure you want to do this. You can also clear the "Allow inheritable permissions from parent to propagate to this object" check box. When the check box is clear, Windows will respond with a Security dialog box. When you click on the Copy button, the explicit permission will be copied from the parent folder to the subfolder or file. You can then change the subfolder's or file's explicit permissions. If you click the Remove button, it will remove the inherited permission altogether.

By default, all objects within a folder inherit the permissions from that folder when they are created. However, explicit permissions take precedence over inherited permissions. So, if you grant different permissions at a lower level, the lower-level permissions will take precedence.

For example, say you have a folder called Data. Within the Data folder, you have Folder 1, and within Folder 1, you have Folder 2. If you grant Allow Full Control to a user account, the Allow Full Control permission will flow down to all the subfolders and files within the Data folder.

Object	NTFS Permissions
Data	Grant Allow Full Control (Explicit)
Folder 1	Allow Full Control (Inherited)
Folder 2	Allow Full Control (Inherited)
File 1	Allow Full Control (Inherited)

Thus, if you grant Allow Full Control on the Data folder to a user account, the Allow Full Control permission will normally flow down to Folder 1. However, if you grant Allow Read permission to Folder 1 to the same user account, the Allow Read permission will overwrite the inherited permission and also flow downward to Folder 2 and File 1.

Object	NTFS Permissions
Data	Grant Allow Full Control (Explicit)
Folder 1	Allow Read (Explicit)
Folder 2	Allow Read (Inherited)
File 1	Allow Read (Inherited)

If a user has access to a file, that user will still be able to gain access to the file even if he or she does not have access to the folder containing the file. Of course, because the user doesn't have access to the folder, the user cannot navigate or browse through the folder to get to the file. Therefore, the user would have to use the universal naming convention (UNC) or local path to open the file.

When you view permissions for an object, they will be one of the following:

- **Checked:** Here, permissions have been explicitly assigned.
- **Cleared (unchecked):** Here, no permissions are assigned.
- **Shared:** Here, permissions are granted through inheritance from a parent folder.

Besides granting Allow permissions, you can also grant the Deny permission. The Deny permission always overrides the other permissions that have been granted, including situations in which a user or group has been given Full Control. For example, if a group has been granted Read and Write permissions yet one member of the group has been denied the Write permission, that user's effective rights would only include the Read permission.

When you combine applying Deny versus Allow permissions and explicit versus inherited permissions, the hierarchy of precedence is as follows:

1. Explicit Deny
2. Explicit Allow
3. Inherited Deny
4. Inherited Allow

Because users can be members of several groups, it is possible for them to have several sets of explicit permissions to a folder or file. When this occurs, the permissions are combined to form the *effective permissions*, which are the actual permissions when logging in and accessing a file or folder. They consist of explicit permissions plus any inherited permissions.

When you calculate effective permissions, you must first calculate the explicit and inherited permissions for an individual or group and then combine them. When combining user and group permissions for NTFS security, the effective permission is the cumulative permission. The only exception is that Deny permissions always apply.

For example, say you have a folder called Data. Within the Data folder, you have Folder 1, and within Folder 1, you have Folder 2. Imagine also that User 1 is a member of Group 1 and Group 2. If you assign Allow Write permission to the Data folder to User 1, the Allow Read permission to Folder 1 to Group 1, and the Allow Modify permission to Folder 2 to Group 2, then the user's effective permissions would be as follows:

Object	User 1 NTFS Permissions	Group 1 Permissions	Group 2 Permissions	Effective Permissions
Data	Allow Write permission (Explicit)			Allow Write permission
Folder 1	Allow Write permission (Inherited)	Allow Read permission (Explicit)		Allow Read and Write permission
Folder 2	Allow Write permission (Inherited)	Allow Read permission (Inherited)	Allow Modify permission* (Explicit)	Allow Modify permission*
File 1	Allow Write permission (Inherited)	Allow Read permission (Inherited)	Allow Modify permission* (Inherited)	Allow Modify permission*

*The Modify permission includes the Read and Write permissions.

Now, say you have a folder called Data. Within the Data folder, you have Folder 1 and within Folder 1, you have Folder 2. User 1 is a member of Group 1 and Group 2. You assign the Allow Write permission to the Data folder to User 1, the Allow Read permission to Folder 1 to Group 1, and the Deny Modify permission to Folder 2 to Group 2. Here, the user's effective permission would be shown as follows:

Object	User 1 NTFS Permissions	Group 1 Permissions	Group 2 Permissions	Effective Permissions
Data	Allow Write permission (Explicit)			Allow Write permission
Folder 1	Allow Write permission (Inherited)	Allow Read permission (Explicit)		Allow Read and Write permission
Folder 2	Allow Write permission (Inherited)	Allow Read permission (Inherited)	Deny Modify permission (Explicit)	Deny Modify permission
File 1	Allow Write permission (Inherited)	Allow Read permission (Inherited)	Deny Modify permission (Inherited)	Deny Modify permission

VIEW NTFS EFFECTIVE PERMISSIONS

GET READY. To view the NTFS effective permissions granted to a user for a file or folder, perform the following steps:

1. Right-click the file or folder and select **Properties**.
2. Select the **Security** tab.
3. Click the **Advanced** button.
4. Click the **Effective Permissions** tab.
5. Click the **Select** button and type in the name of the user or group you want to view. Click the **OK** button. See Figure 2-9.

Figure 2-9

NTFS effective permissions

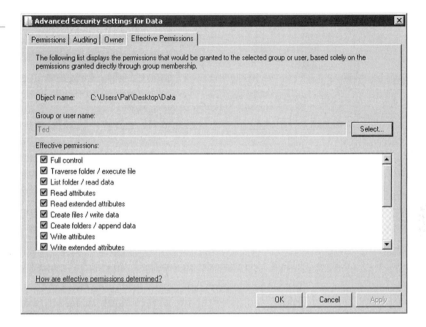

Copying and Moving Files

When you move or copy files from one location to another, you need to understand what happens to the NTFS permissions associated with these files.

When copying and moving files, you will encounter one of three scenarios:

- If you copy a file or folder, the new file or folder will automatically acquire the same permissions as the drive or folder it is being copied to.
- If a file or folder is moved within the same volume, that file or folder will retain the same permissions that were already assigned to it.
- If a file or folder is moved from one volume to another volume, that file or folder will automatically acquire the permissions of the drive or folder it is being copied to.

Using Folder and File Owners

The **owner** of an object controls what permissions are set on the object and to whom permissions are granted. If for some reason, you have been denied access to a file or folder and you need to reset the permissions, you can take ownership of the file or folder and then modify the permissions. All administrators automatically have the Take Ownership permission for all NTFS objects.

TAKE OWNERSHIP OF A FILE OR FOLDER

GET READY. To take ownership of a file or folder, perform the following steps:

1. Open **Windows Explorer** and locate the file or folder you want to take ownership of.
2. Right-click the file or folder, click **Properties**, and then click the **Security** tab.
3. Click **Advanced**, and then click the **Owner** tab. See Figure 2-10.

Figure 2-10

Owner tab

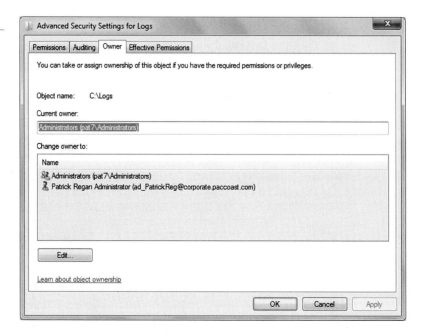

4. Click **Edit**, and then do one of the following:
   - To change the owner to a user or group that is not listed, click **Other users and groups** and, in **Enter the object name to select (examples)**, type the name of the user or group. Then click **OK**.
   - To change the owner to a user or group that is listed, click the name of the new owner in the **Change owner to** box.
5. To change the owner of all subcontainers and objects within the tree, select the **Replace owner on subcontainers and objects** check box.

■ Sharing Drives and Folders

THE BOTTOM LINE

Most users are not going to log on to a server directly to access their data files. Instead, a drive or folder will be shared (known as a ***shared folder***), and they will access the data files over the network. To help protect against unauthorized access to such folders, you will use share permissions along with NTFS permissions (assuming the shared folder is on an NTFS volume). Then, when users need to access a network share, they will use the Universal Naming Convention UNC, which is \\servername\sharename.

 SHARE A FOLDER

GET READY. To share a folder, perform the following steps:

1. In Windows Server 2003, right-click the drive or folder you want to share and select **Sharing and security**. In Windows Server 2008, right-click the drive or folder, select **Properties**, select the **Sharing** tab, and then click the **Advanced Sharing** button.

2. Select **Share this folder.**

3. Type the name of the shared folder.

4. If necessary, you can specify the maximum number of people that can access the shared folder at the same time.

5. Click the **Permissions** button.

6. By default, **Everyone** is given **Allow Read share permission.** Unless you actually want everyone to have access to the folder, you can remove **Everyone**, assign additional permissions, or add additional people.

7. After the desired users and groups have been added with the proper permissions, click the **OK** button to close the **Permissions** dialog box. See Figure 2-11.

8. Click **OK** to close the **Properties** dialog box.

Figure 2-11

Sharing a folder

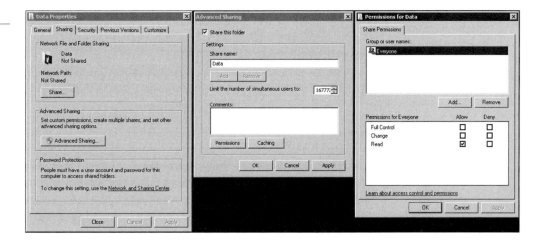

The *share permissions* that are available are as follows:

- **Full control:** Users with this permission have Read and Change permissions, as well as the additional capabilities to change file and folder permissions and take ownership of files and folders.

- **Change:** Users with this permission have Read permissions and the additional capabilities to create files and subfolders, modify files, change attributes on files and subfolders, and delete files and subfolders.

- **Read:** Users with this permission can view file and subfolder names, access the subfolders of the share, read file data and attributes, and run program files.

It should be noted that share permissions always apply when accessed remotely using a UNC, even if it is on the FAT, FAT32, or NTFS volume.

As with NTFS, you can also allow or deny each share permission. To simplify managing share and NTFS permissions, Microsoft recommends giving Everyone Full Control, then controlling access using NTFS permissions. In addition, because a user can be member of several groups, it is possible for the user to have several sets of permissions to a shared drive or folder. The effective share permissions are the combination of the user permissions and the permissions for all groups that the user is a member of.

When a person logs directly on to the server console and accesses the files and folders without using the UNC, only the NTFS permissions—and not the share permissions—apply. In contrast, when a person accesses a shared folder using the UNC, you must combine the NTFS and shared permissions to see what a user can do. To determine the overall access, first calculate the effective NTFS permissions, then determine the effective shared permissions. Finally, apply the more restrictive permissions between the NTFS and shared permissions.

Looking at Special and Administrative Shares

In Windows, there are several special shared folders that are automatically created for administrative and system use. Different from regular shares, these shares do not show when a user browses the computer resources using Network Neighborhood, My Network Place, or similar software. In most cases, special shared folders should not be deleted or modified. For Windows Servers, only members of the Administrators, Backup Operators, and Server Operators group can connect to these shares.

An *administrative share* is a shared folder typically used for administrative purposes. To make a shared folder or drive into a hidden share, the share name must have a $ at the end of it. Because the share folder or drive cannot be seen during browsing, you would have to use a UNC name that includes the share name (including the $). By default, all volumes with drive letters automatically have administrative shares (C$, D$, E$, and so on). Other administrative shares can be created as needed for individual folders.

Besides the administrative shares for each drive, you will also have the following special shares:

- **ADMIN$:** A resource used by the system during remote administration of a computer. The path of this resource is always the path to the Windows 7 system root (the directory in which Windows 7 is installed—for example, C:\Windows).
- **IPC$:** A resource sharing the named pipes that are essential for communication between programs. It is used during remote administration of a computer and when viewing a computer's shared resources.
- **PRINT$:** A resource used during remote administration of printers.

■ Introducing the Registry

THE BOTTOM LINE

The *registry* is a central, secure database in which Windows stores all hardware configuration information, software configuration information, and system security policies. Components that use the registry include the Windows kernel, device drivers, setup programs, hardware profiles, and user profiles.

Most of the time, you will not need to access the registry because programs and applications typically make all necessary changes automatically. For example, when you change your desktop background or change the default color for Windows, you access the Display settings within the Control Panel and your changes are automatically saved to the registry.

If you do need to access the registry and make changes to it, you should closely follow instructions from a reputable source, because an incorrect change to your computer's registry could render your computer inoperable. However, there may be a time when you need to make a change in the registry because there is no interface or program to make the change. To view and manually change the registry, you will use the Registry Editor (Regedit.exe), which can be executed from the command prompt, Start Search box, or Run box. See Figure 2-12.

Figure 2-12

Registry Editor

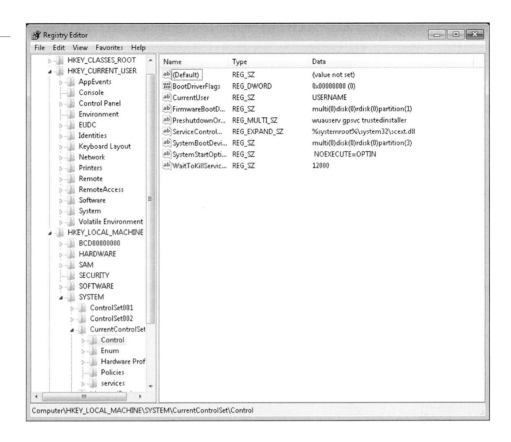

The registry is split into a several logical sections, often referred to as hives, which are generally named by their Windows API definitions. The hives begin with HKEY and are often abbreviated to a three- or four-letter short name starting with "HK." For example, HKCU is HKEY_CURRENT_USER, and HKLM is HKEY_LOCAL_MACHINE. Windows 7 has five Root Keys/HKEYs:

- **HKEY_CLASSES_ROOT:** Stores information about registered applications, such as file association data that tells which default program opens files with a certain extension.
- **HKEY_CURRENT_USER:** Stores settings that are specific to the currently logged-in user. When a user logs off, the HKEY_CURRENT_USER is saved to HKEY_USERS.
- **HKEY_LOCAL_MACHINE:** Stores settings that are specific to the local computer.
- **HKEY_USERS:** Contains subkeys corresponding to the HKEY_CURRENT_USER keys for each user profile actively loaded on the machine.
- **HKEY_CURRENT_CONFIG:** Contains information gathered at run time. Information stored in this key is not permanently stored on disk, but rather regenerated at boot time.

Registry keys are similar to folders that contain values or subkeys. The keys within the registry follow a syntax similar to a Windows folder or file path that uses backslashes to separate each level. For example:

HKEY_LOCAL_MACHINE\Software\Microsoft\Windows

refers to the subkey "Windows" of the subkey "Microsoft" of the subkey "Software" of the HKEY_LOCAL_MACHINE key.

Registry values include a name and a value. There are multiple types of values. Some of the most common key types are shown in Table 2-2.

Table 2-2

Common registry key types

NAME	DATA TYPE	DESCRIPTION
Binary value	REG_BINARY	Raw binary data. Most hardware component information is stored as binary data and displayed in Registry Editor in hexadecimal format.
DWORD value	REG_DWORD	Data represented by a number that is four bytes long (a 32-bit integer). Many parameters for device drivers and services are this type and are displayed in Registry Editor in binary, hexadecimal, or decimal format.
Expandable string value	REG_EXPAND_SZ	A variable-length data string. This data type includes variables that are resolved when a program or service uses the data.
Multi-string value	REG_MULTI_SZ	A multiple string. Values that contain lists or multiple values in a form that people can read are generally this type. Entries are separated by spaces, commas, or other marks.
String value	REG_SZ	A fixed-length text string.
QWORD value	REG_QWORD	Data represented by a number that is a 64-bit integer. This data is displayed in Registry Editor as a binary value and was introduced in Windows 2000.

Reg files (also known as registration entries) are text files for storing portions of a registry. These files have a .reg filename extension. If you double-click a reg file, it will add the registry entries into the registry. You can export any registry subkey by right-clicking the subkey and choosing Export. You can back up the entire registry to a reg file by right-clicking Computer at the top of Regedit and selecting export, or you can back up the system state with Windows Backup.

 ACCESS REGISTRY PERMISSIONS

GET READY. The registry uses permissions that are stored in Access Control Lists (ACLs). To access the registry permissions, perform the following steps:

1. Open **Registry Editor**.
2. Click the key to which you want to assign permissions.
3. On the **Edit** menu, click **Permissions**.

You will then add the prospective user and assign either Allow or Deny Full Control or Read permission.

■ Using Encryption to Protect Data

THE BOTTOM LINE

Encryption is the process of converting data into a format that cannot be read by another user. Once a user has encrypted a file, that file automatically remains encrypted when it is stored on disk. *Decryption* is the process of converting data from an encrypted format back to its original format.

CERTIFICATION READY
Can you list and contrast the three primary methods of encryption?
2.5

With commonly used encryption, the encryption algorithm needs to provide a high level of security yet still be available to the public. Because the algorithm is made available to the public, the security resides in the key, not in the algorithm itself.

One of the simplest cipher algorithms is the substitution cipher, which changes one character or symbol into another. For example, if you have

clear text

and you substitute each "e" with a "y," each "c" with the letter "j," and each letter "t" with a "y," you would get the following cipher text:

jlyar yexy

Another simple technique is based on the transposition cipher, which involves transposing or scrambling letters in a certain manner. For example, if you have

clear text

and you switch every two letters, you get:

lcae rettx

A *key*, which can be thought of as a password, is applied mathematically to plain text to provide cipher or encrypted text. Different keys produce different encrypted output. With computers, encryption is often based on bits, not characters. For example, if you have the Unicode letters "cl," it could be expressed in the following binary format:

01100011 01101100

If you mathematically add the binary form of 'z'(01111010), which is the key, you get:

01100011	01101100
+01111010	+01111010
11011101	1110 0110

which would appear as strange Unicode characters: ýæ.

Like a password, the longer a key is (usually expressed in bits), the more secure it is. For a hacker to figure out a key, he or she would also have to use a brute force attack, which means the hacker would have to try every combination of bits until he or she figured out the correct key. Although a key could be broken given enough time and processing power, long keys are chosen so that key cracking will take months, maybe even years, to accomplish. Of course, as with passwords, some encryption algorithms change their key frequently. Therefore, a key length of 80 bits is generally considered the minimum for strong security with symmetric encryption algorithms. 128-bit keys are commonly used and are also considered very strong.

Examining Types of Encryption

Encryption algorithms can be divided into three classes: symmetric, asymmetric and hash function.

LOOKING AT SYMMETRIC ENCRYPTION

Symmetric encryption uses a single key to encrypt and decrypt data. Therefore, it is also referred to as secret-key, single-key, shared-key, and private-key encryption. To use symmetric key algorithms, you need to initially exchange the secret key between both sender and receiver.

Symmetric-key ciphers can be divided into block ciphers and stream ciphers. A block cipher takes a block of plain text and a key, and then outputs a block of cipher text of the same size. Two popular block ciphers include the Data Encryption Standard (DES) and the Advanced Encryption Standard (AES), which have been designated cryptography standards by the U.S. government.

The National Bureau of Standards selected the Data Encryption Standard as an official Federal Information Processing Standard (FIPS) for the United States in 1976. It is based on a symmetric-key algorithm that uses a 56-bit key.

Because DES is based on a relatively small 56-bit key size, it was subject to brute force attacks. Therefore, instead of designing a completely new block cipher algorithm, Triple DES (3DES), which uses three independent keys, was developed. DES and the more secure 3DES are still popular and used across a wide range of applications, ranging from ATM encryption, to email privacy, to secure remote access.

Although DES and 3DES remain popular, a more secure encryption method called Advanced Encryption Standard (AES) was announced in 2001 and is currently growing in popularity. This standard comprises three block ciphers—AES-128, AES-192, and AES-256—used on 128-bit blocks with key sizes of 128, 192, and 256 bits, respectively. The AES ciphers have been analyzed extensively and are now used worldwide, including with Wi-Fi Protected Access 2 (WPA2) wireless encryption.

In contrast with block ciphers, stream ciphers create an arbitrarily long stream of key material, which is combined bit-by-bit or character-by-character with the plain text. RC4 is one widely used stream cipher, employed in both Secure Sockets Layer (SSL) and Wired Equivalent Privacy (WEP). Although RC4 is simple and known for its speed, it can be vulnerable if the key stream is not discarded, nonrandom or related keys are used, or a single key stream is used twice.

LOOKING AT ASYMMETRIC ENCRYPTION

Asymmetric encryption, also known as public key cryptography, uses two mathematically related keys for encryption. One key is used to encrypt the data, while the second is used to decrypt it. Unlike symmetric key algorithms, this method does not require a secure initial exchange of one or more secret keys to both sender and receiver. Instead, you can make the public key known to anyone and use the other key to encrypt or decrypt the data. The public key could be sent to someone or could be published within a digital certificate via a Certificate Authority (CA). Secure Sockets Layer (SSL)/Transport Layer Security (TLS) and Pretty Good Privacy (PGP) all use asymmetric keys. Two popular asymmetric encryption protocols are Diffie-Hellman and RSA.

For example, say you want a partner to send you data. To begin the asymmetric encryption process, you send your partner the public key. Your partner will then encrypt the data with the key and send you the encrypted message. You will next use the private key to decrypt the message. If the public key falls into someone else's hands, that person still could not decrypt the message because you need the private key to decrypt a message that has been encrypted with the public key.

LOOKING AT HASH FUNCTION

The last type of encryption is the hash function. Different from the symmetric and asymmetric algorithms, a *hash function* is meant as a one-way encryption. That means that after something has been encrypted with this method, it cannot be decrypted. For example, a hash function can be used to encrypt a password that is stored on disk and for digital signatures. Anytime a password is entered, the same hash calculation is performed on the entered password and compared to the hash value of the password stored on disk. If the two match, the user must have typed in the password. This avoids storing passwords in a readable format where a hacker might be able to gain access to them.

Introducing Public Key Infrastructure

Public key infrastructure (PKI) is a system consisting of hardware, software, policies, and procedures that create, manage, distribute, use, store, and revoke digital certificates. Within the PKI, the certificate authority (CA) binds a public key with respective user identities and issues digital certificates containing the public key.

For the PKI system to work, the CA must be trusted. Typically within an organization, you may install a CA on Windows server, specifically on a domain controller, and it would be trusted within your organization. If you require a CA that is trusted outside your organization, you would have to use a trusted third-party CA, such as VeriSign or Entrust. Established commercial CAs charge to issue certificates that will automatically be trusted by most web browsers. See Figure 2-13.

Figure 2-13

Trusted CAs in Internet Explorer

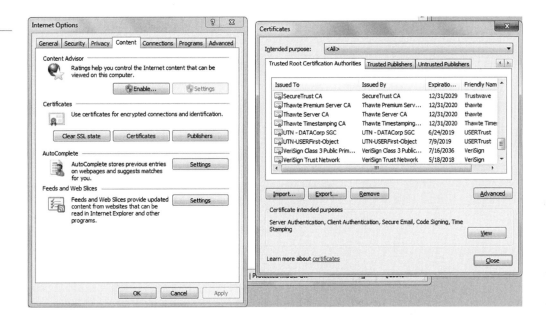

The registration authority (RA), which may or may not be the same server as the CA, is used to distribute keys, accept registrations for the CA, and validate identities. The RA does not distribute digital certificates; instead, the CA does.

Besides having an expiration date, a digital certificate can be revoked if it was compromised or if the situation has changed for the system to which the certificate was assigned. A *certificate revocation list (CRL)* is a list of certificates (or more specifically, a list of serial numbers for certificates) that have been revoked or are no longer valid and therefore should not be relied on.

As previously mentioned, Windows servers can host a certificate authority. The Enterprise Root CA is at the top level of the certificate authority hierarchy. Once Enterprise Root CA is configured, it registers automatically within Active Directory, and all computers within the domain trust it. This authority will support auto enrollment and auto-renewal of digital certificates.

If you need to support outside clients and customers, you would most likely build a stand-alone CA. Unlike the Enterprise Root CA, a stand-alone CA does not use Active Directory. Because stand-alone CAs do not support auto enrollment, all requests for certificates are pending until an administrator approves them.

USING DIGITAL CERTIFICATES

A *digital certificate* is an electronic document that contains a person's or organization's name, a serial number, an expiration date, a copy of the certificate holder's public key (used for encrypting messages and creating digital signatures), and the digital signature of the CA that assigned the certificate so that recipients can verify that the certificate is real.

The most common digital certificate is the X.509 version 3. The X.509 version 3 standard specifies the format for the public key certificate, certificate revocation lists, attribute certificates, and a certificate path validation algorithm. See Figure 2-14.

Figure 2-14

X.509 digital certificate

Digital certificates can be imported and exported via electronic files. Four common formats are as follows:

- **Personal Information Exchange (PKCS #12):** The Personal Information Exchange format (PFX, also called PKCS #12) supports secure storage of certificates, private keys, and all certificates in a certification path. The PKCS #12 format is the only file format that can be used to export a certificate and its private key. It will usually have a .p12 filename extension.

- **Cryptographic Message Syntax Standard (PKCS #7):** The PKCS #7 format supports storage of certificates and all certificates in a certification path. It will usually have a .p7b or .p7c filename extension.

- **DER-encoded binary X.509:** The Distinguished Encoding Rules (DER) format supports storage of a single certificate. This format does not support storage of the private key or certification path. It will usually have a .cer, .crt, or .der filename extension.

- **Base64-encoded X.509:** The Base64 format supports storage of a single certificate. This format does not support storage of the private key or certification path.

 ACQUIRE A DIGITAL CERTIFICATE

GET READY. To acquire a digital certificate using IIS 7/7.5, perform the following steps:

1. Request an Internet server certificate from the IIS server. To do so, click the server within **IIS Manager**, then double-click **Server Certificates** in the **Features** view. Next click **Create Certificate Request** from the **Actions** pane.

2. Send the generated certificate request to the CA, usually using the vendor's website.

3. Receive a digital certificate from the CA and install it on the IIS server. Again, open **IIS Manager**, double-click the server within IIS Manager, and double-click **Server Certificates** in the **Features** view. Then select **Complete Certificate Request**.

If you have a web farm that consist of multiple web servers, you will need to install the digital certificate from the first server and export the digital certificate to a pfx format, and you will need to copy the public and private key to the other servers. Therefore, you will need to export the key from the first server and import to the other servers.

 EXPORT A DIGITAL CERTIFICATE

GET READY. To export a digital certificate, perform the following steps:

1. Open **IIS Manager** and navigate to the level you want to manage.

2. In the **Features** view, double-click **Server Certificates**.

3. In the **Actions** pane, click **Export**.

4. In the **Export** dialog box, type a filename in the **Export to** box or click the **Browse** button to navigate to the name of a file in which to store the certificate for exporting.

5. Type a password in the **Password** box if you want to associate a password with the exported certificate. Retype the password in the **Confirm password** box.

6. Click **OK**.

 IMPORT A DIGITAL CERTIFICATE

GET READY. To import a certificate, perform the following steps:

1. Open **IIS Manager** and navigate to the level you want to manage.

2. In the **Features** view, double-click **Server Certificates**.

3. In the **Actions** pane, click **Import**.

4. In the **Import Certificate** dialog box, type a filename in the **Certificate file** box or click the **Browse** button to navigate to the name of the file where the exported certificate is stored. Type a password in the **Password** box if the certificate was exported with a password.

5. Select **Allow this certificate to be exported** if you want to be able to export the certificate, or clear **Allow this certificate to be exported** if you want to prevent additional exports of this certificate.

6. Click **OK**.

EXAMINING A CERTIFICATE CHAIN

There are only so many root CA certificates that are assigned to commercial third-party organizations. Therefore, when you acquire a digital certificate from a third-party organization, you might need to use a certificate chain to obtain the root CA certificate. In addition, you may need to install an intermittent digital certificate that will link the assigned digital certificate to a trusted root CA certificate. The *certificate chain*, also known as the certification path, is a list of certificates used to authenticate an entity. It begins with the certificate of the entity and ends with the root CA certificate. See Figure 2-15.

Figure 2-15

Certificate chain

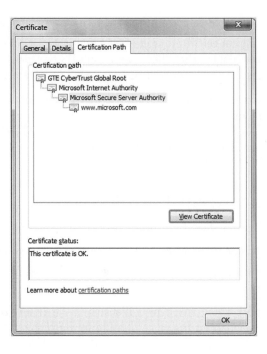

USING A DIGITAL SIGNATURE

A *digital signature* is a mathematical scheme that is used to demonstrate the authenticity of a digital message or document. It is also used to prove that the message or document has not been modified. With a digital signature, the sender uses the receiver's public key to create a hash of the message, which is stored in the message digest. The message is then sent to the receiver. The receiver will next use his or her private key to decrypt the hash value, perform the same hash function on the message, and compare the two hash values. If the message has not been changed, the hash values will match.

To prove that a message comes from a particular person, you can perform the hashing function with your private key and attach the hash value to the document to be sent. When the document is sent and received by the receiving party, the same hash function is completed. You then use the sender's public key to decrypt the hash value included in the document. If the two hash values match, the user who sent the document must have known the sender's private key, proving who sent the document. It will also prove that the document has not been changed.

USING SECURE SOCKETS LAYER (SSL) AND TRANSPORT LAYER SECURITY (TLS)

There are times when you need to transmit private data over the Internet, such as credit card numbers, Social Security numbers, and so on. In these instances, you should use SSL over http (https) to encrypt the data before sending it. By convention, URLs that require an SSL connection start with https: instead of http:.

SSL is short for *Secure Sockets Layer*. It is a cryptographic system that uses two keys to encrypt data, a public key known to everyone and a private or secret key known only to the recipient of the message. The public key is published in a digital certificate, which also confirms the identity of the web server.

When you connect to a site that is secured using SSL, a gold lock appears in the address bar, along with the name of the organization to which the CA issued the certificate. Clicking the lock icon displays more information about the site, including the identity of the CA that issued the certificate. For even more information, you can click the View Certificate link to open the Certificate dialog box.

Occasionally, Internet Explorer may find problems with a website's digital certificate—for instance, the certificate may be expired, may be corrupted, may have been revoked, or may not match the name of the website. When this happens, IE will block access to the site and display a warning stating that there is a problem with the certificate. You then have a chance to close the browser window or ignore the warning and continue on to the site. Of course, if you chose to ignore the warning, make sure you trust the website and you believe that you are communicating with the correct server.

Transport Layer Security (TLS) is an extension of SSL that was supported by the Internet Engineering Task Force (IETF) so that it could be an open, community-supported standard that could then be expanded with other Internet standards. Although TLS is often referred to as SSL 3.0, it does not interoperate with SSL. Also, even though TLS is usually the default for most browsers, it has a downgrade feature that allows SSL 3.0 to run as needed.

Encrypting Email

Because email is sent over the Internet, you may be concerned with the possibility that your data packets will be captured and read. Therefore, you may want to encrypt emails that contain confidential information.

There are multiple protocols that can be used to encrypt emails. Two prominent protocols include:

- Secure Multipurpose Internet Mail Extension (S/MIME)
- Pretty Good Privacy (PGP)

Secure Multipurpose Internet Mail Extension (S/MIME) is the secure version of MIME, used to embed objects within email messages. It is the most widely supported standard used to secure email communications, and it uses the PKCS #7 standard. S/MIME is included with popular web browsers and has also been endorsed by other messaging products vendors.

Pretty Good Privacy (PGP) is a freeware email encryption system that uses symmetrical and asymmetrical encryption. Here, when email is sent, the document is encrypted with the public key and also a session key. The session key is a one-use random number used to create the cipher text. The session key is encrypted into the public key and sent with the cipher text. When the message is received, the private key is used to extract the session key. The session key and the private key are then used to decrypt the cipher text.

Encrypting Files with EFS

If someone steals a hard drive that is protected by NTFS permissions, that person could take the hard drive, put it in a system of which he or she is an administrator, and access all files and folders on the hard drive. Therefore, to truly protect a drive that could be stolen or accessed illegally, you can encrypt the files and folders on that drive.

Windows 7 offers two file encrypting technologies, Encrypting File System (EFS) and BitLocker Drive Encryption. EFS protects individual files or folders, whereas BitLocker protects entire drives.

Encrypting File System (EFS) can encrypt files on an NTFS volume so that they cannot be used unless the user has access to the keys required to decrypt the information. After a file has been encrypted, you do not have to manually decrypt the encrypted file before you can use it. Rather, once you encrypt a file or folder, you work with the encrypted file or folder just as you would with any other file or folder.

EFS is keyed to a specific user account, using the public and private keys that are the basis of the Windows public key infrastructure (PKI). The user who creates a file is the only person who can read it. As the user works, EFS encrypts the files he or she creates using a key generated from the user's public key. Data encrypted with this key can be decrypted only by the user's personal encryption certificate, which is generated using his or her private key.

ENCRYPT A FOLDER OR FILE USING EFS

GET READY. To encrypt a folder or file, perform the following steps:

1. Right-click the folder or file you want to encrypt, then click **Properties**.
2. Click the **General** tab, and then click **Advanced**.
3. Select the **Encrypt contents to secure data** check box, click **OK**, and then click **OK** again. See Figure 2-16.

Figure 2-16

Encrypting data with EFS

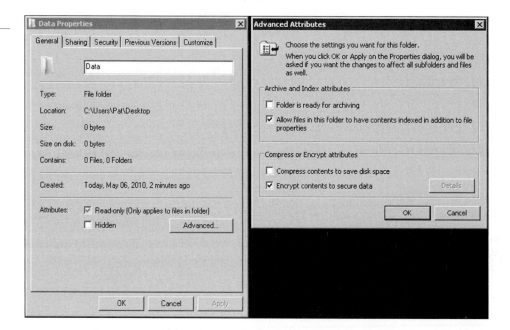

DECRYPT A FOLDER OR FILE

GET READY. To decrypt a folder or file, perform the following steps:

1. Right-click the folder or file you want to decrypt, then click **Properties**.
2. Click the **General** tab, and then click **Advanced**.
3. Clear the **Encrypt contents to secure data** check box, click **OK**, and then click **OK** again.

The first time you encrypt a folder or file, an encryption certificate is automatically created. If your certificate and key are lost or damaged and you don't have a backup, you won't be able to use the files that you have encrypted. Therefore, you should back up your encryption certificate.

BACK UP EFS CERTIFICATE

GET READY. To back up your EFS certificate, perform the following steps:

1. Execute **certmgr.msc**. If you are prompted for an administrator password or confirmation, type the password or provide confirmation.
2. In the left pane, double-click **Personal**.
3. Click **Certificates**.
4. In the main pane, click the certificate that lists **Encrypting File System** under **Intended Purposes**. If there is more than one EFS certificate, you should back up all of them.
5. Click the **Action** menu, Select **All Tasks**, and then click **Export**.
6. In the **Certificate Export** wizard, click **Next**, click **Yes, export the private key**, and then click **Next**.
7. Click **Personal Information Exchange**, and then click **Next**.
8. Type the password you want to use, confirm it, and then click **Next**. The export process will create a file to store the certificate.
9. Type a name for the file and the location (include the whole path) or instead click **Browse**, navigate to a location, type a filename, and then click **Save**.
10. Click **Next**, and then click **Finish**.

You should then place the certificate in a safe place.

If for some reason, a person leaves your organization and you cannot read his or her encrypted files, you can also set up recovery agents who can recover encrypted files for a domain.

 ADD USERS AS RECOVERY AGENTS

GET READY. To add new users as recovery agents, these users must first have recovery certificates issued by the enterprise CA structure.

1. Open the **Active Directory Users and Computers** console.
2. Right-click the domain and select **Properties**.
3. Select the **Group Policy** tab.
4. Select the **Default Domain Policy** and click **Edit**.
5. Expand **Computer Configuration\Windows Settings\Security Settings\Public Key Policies\Encrypted Data Recovery Agents**.
6. Right-click **Encrypted Data Recovery Agents** and select **Add**.
7. Click **Next** to the **Add Recovery Agent Wizard**.
8. Click **Browse Directory**. Locate the user and click **OK**.
9. Click **Next**.
10. Click **Finish**.
11. Close the **Group Policy Editor**.

If you copy a file or folder, the new file or folder will automatically acquire the encryption attribute of the original drive or folder. If the file or folder is moved within the same volume, it will retain the original assigned encryption attribute. Thus, if it is encrypted, it will remain encrypted at the new location. When the file or folder is moved from one volume to another, it is copied to the new location and then deleted from the old location. Therefore, the moved folder and files are new to the volume and acquire the new encryption attribute.

Encrypting Disks in Windows

> Unlike EFS, BitLocker allows you to encrypt entire disks. Therefore, if a drive or laptop is stolen, the data is still encrypted, even if the thief installs it on another system of which he or she is an administrator.

TAKE NOTE *

BitLocker is a feature of Windows 7 Enterprise and Windows 7 Ultimate. It is not supported on other editions of Windows 7.

BitLocker Drive Encryption is the feature in the Windows 7 Ultimate and Enterprise editions that makes use of a computer's Trusted Platform Module (TPM). A TPM is a microchip built into a computer that is used to store cryptographic information, such as encryption keys. Information stored on the TPM can be more secure from external software attacks and physical theft. For instance, BitLocker Drive Encryption can use a TPM to validate the integrity of a computer's boot manager and boot files at startup, as well as to guarantee that a computer's hard disk has not been tampered with while the operating system was offline. BitLocker Drive Encryption also stores measurements of core operating system files in the TPM.

The system requirements of BitLocker are as follows:

- Because BitLocker stores its own encryption and decryption key in a hardware device that is separate from your hard disk, you must have one of the following:
  - A computer with Trusted Platform Module (TPM). If your computer was manufactured with TPM version 1.2 or higher, BitLocker will store its key in the TPM.
  - A removable USB memory device, such as a USB flash drive. If your computer doesn't have TPM version 1.2 or higher, BitLocker will store its key on the flash drive.
- Your computer must also have at least two partitions: a system partition (which contains the files needed to start your computer and must be at least 200 MB) and an operating system partition (which contains Windows). The operating system partition will be encrypted, and the system partition will remain unencrypted so your computer can start. If your computer doesn't have two partitions, BitLocker will create them for you. Both partitions must be formatted with the NTFS file system.
- In addition, your computer must have a BIOS that is compatible with TPM and supports USB devices during computer startup. If this is not the case, you will need to update the BIOS before using BitLocker.

BitLocker has five operational modes, which define the steps involved in the system boot process. These modes, in descending order from most to least secure, are as follows:

- **TPM + startup PIN + startup key:** The system stores the BitLocker volume encryption key on the TPM chip, but an administrator must supply a personal identification number (PIN) and insert a USB flash drive containing a startup key before the system can unlock the BitLocker volume and complete the system boot sequence.
- **TPM + startup key:** The system stores the BitLocker volume encryption key on the TPM chip, but an administrator must insert a USB flash drive containing a startup key before the system can unlock the BitLocker volume and complete the system boot sequence.
- **TPM + startup PIN:** The system stores the BitLocker volume encryption key on the TPM chip, but an administrator must supply a PIN before the system can unlock the BitLocker volume and complete the system boot sequence.
- **Startup key only:** The BitLocker configuration process stores a startup key on a USB flash drive, which the administrator must insert each time the system boots. This mode does not require the server to have a TPM chip, but it must have a system BIOS that supports access to the USB flash drive before the operating system loads.
- **TPM only:** The system stores the BitLocker volume encryption key on the TPM chip, and it accesses this key automatically when the chip has determined that the boot environment is unmodified. This unlocks the protected volume and the computer continues

to boot. Therefore, no administrative interaction is required during the system boot sequence.

When you enable BitLocker using the BitLocker Drive Encryption control panel, you can select the TPM + startup key, TPM + startup PIN, or TPM only options. To use the TPM + startup PIN + startup key option, you must first configure the *Require additional authentication at startup* Group Policy setting, found in the Computer Configuration\Policies\ Administrative Templates\Windows Components\BitLocker Drive Encryption\Operating System Drives container.

ENABLING BITLOCKER

BitLocker is not enabled by default. If you don't know if your laptop comes with TPM, you should first verify that you have TPM. You will then turn on BitLocker for the volume that you wish to encrypt.

 DETERMINE WHETHER YOU HAVE TPM

GET READY. To find out whether your computer has Trusted Platform Module (TPM) security hardware, perform the following steps:

1. Open the **Control Panel**, click **System and Security**, and click **BitLocker Drive Encryption**.
2. In the left pane, click **TPM Administration**. If you are prompted for an administrator password or confirmation, type the password or provide confirmation.

The TPM Management on Local Computer snap-in tells you whether your computer has the TPM security hardware. See Figure 2-17. If your computer doesn't have it, you'll need a removable USB memory device to turn on BitLocker and store the BitLocker startup key that you'll need whenever you start your computer.

Figure 2-17

TMP management console

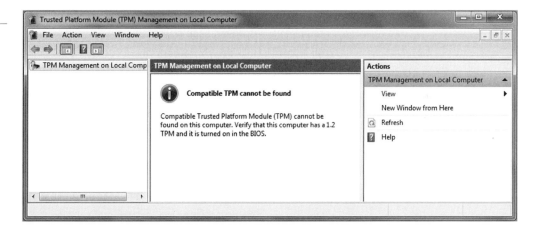

 TURN ON BITLOCKER

GET READY. Log on to Windows 7 using an account with administrative privileges. Then, perform the following steps:

1. Click **Start**, then click **Control Panel > System and Security > BitLocker Drive Encryption**. The BitLocker Drive Encryption control panel appears.
2. Click **Turn on BitLocker** for your hard disk drives. The *Set BitLocker startup preferences* page appears. See Figure 2-18.

Figure 2-18

Turning on BitLocker

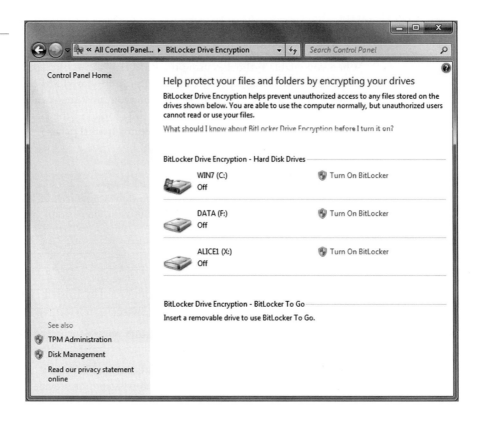

MORE INFORMATION

If your computer has a TPM chip, Windows 7 provides a Trusted Platform Module (TPM) management console that you can use to change the chip's password and modify its properties.

3. Click **Require a Startup key at every startup**. A *Save your Startup key* page appears.

4. Insert a USB flash drive into a USB port and click **Save**. The *How do you want to store your recovery key?* page appears.

5. Select one of the options to save your recovery key and click **Next**. The *Are you ready to encrypt this drive?* page appears.

6. Click **Continue**. The wizard performs a system check and then restarts the computer.

7. Log on to the computer. Windows 7 proceeds to encrypt the disk.

Once the encryption process is complete, you can open the BitLocker Drive Encryption control panel to ensure that the volume is encrypted or to turn off BitLocker when performing a BIOS upgrade or other system maintenance.

The BitLocker control panel applet enables you to recover the encryption key and recovery password at will. You should carefully consider how to store this information, because it will allow access to the encrypted data. It is also possible to escrow this information into Active Directory.

USING DATA RECOVERY AGENTS AND BITLOCKER

If for some reason, a user loses the startup key and/or startup PIN needed to boot a system with BitLocker, that user can supply the recovery key created during the BitLocker configuration process and gain access to the system. However, if the user loses the recovery key, you can use a data recovery agent designated with Active Directory to recover the data on the drive.

A data recovery agent (DRA) is a user account that an administrator has authorized to recover BitLocker drives for an entire organization with a digital certificate on a smart card. In most cases, administrators of Active Directory Domain Services (AD DS) networks use DRAs to ensure access to their BitLocker-protected systems and to avoid having to maintain large numbers of individual keys and PINs.

To create a DRA, you must first add the user account you want to designate to the Computer Configuration\Policies\Windows Settings\Security Settings\Public Key Policies\BitLocker Drive Encryption container in a GPO or to the system's Local Security Policy. Then, you must configure the Provide The Unique Identifiers For Your Organization policy setting in the Computer Configuration\Policies\Administrative Templates\Windows Components\ BitLocker Drive Encryption container with unique identification fields for your BitLocker drives.

Finally, you must enable DRA recovery for each type of BitLocker resource you want to recover by configuring the following policies:

- Choose How BitLocker-Protected Operating System Drives Can Be Recovered
- Choose How BitLocker-Protected Fixed Drives Can Be Recovered
- Choose How BitLocker-Protected Removable Drives Can Be Recovered

These policies enable you to specify how BitLocker systems should store their recovery information, and they also enable you to store that information in the AD DS database.

USING BITLOCKER TO GO

BitLocker To Go is a new feature in Windows 7 that enables users to encrypt removable USB devices, such as flash drives and external hard disks. Although BitLocker has always supported the encryption of removable drives, BitLocker To Go allows you to use the encrypted device on other computers without having to perform an involved recovery process. Because the system is not using the removable drive as a boot device, a TPM chip is not required.

To use BitLocker To Go, simply insert the removable drive and open the BitLocker Drive Encryption control panel. The device appears in the interface, with a *Turn on BitLocker* link just like that of the computer's hard disk drive.

■ Introducing IPsec

THE BOTTOM LINE

IP Security, more commonly known as *IPsec*, is a suite of protocols that provides a mechanism for data integrity, authentication, and privacy for the Internet Protocol. It is used to protect data that is sent between hosts on a network by creating secure electronic tunnels between two machines or devices. IPsec can be used for remote access, VPN server connections, LAN connections, or WAN connections.

IPsec ensures that data cannot be viewed or modified by unauthorized users while it is being sent to its destination. Before data is sent between two hosts, the source computer encrypts the information by encapsulating each data packet in a new packet that contains the information necessary to set up, maintain, and tear down the tunnel when it is no longer needed. The data is then decrypted at the destination computer.

There are a couple of modes and a couple of protocols available in IPsec depending on whether they are implemented by the end hosts (such as the server) or implemented on the routers and the desired level of security. In particular, IPsec can be used in one of two modes:

- **Transport mode:** Used to secure end-to-end communications, such as between a client and a server.
- **Tunnel mode:** Used for server-to-server or server-to-gateway configurations. The tunnel is the path a packet takes from the source computer to the destination computer. This way, any IP packets sent between the two hosts or between the two subnets, depending on the configuration, are secured.

In addition, the two IPsec protocols are as follows:

- **Encapsulating Security Payload (ESP):** Provides confidentiality, authentication, integrity, and antireplay for the IP payload only, not the entire packet. ESP operates directly on top of IP.
- **Authentication Header (AH):** Provides authentication, integrity, and antireplay for the entire packet (both the IP header and the data payload carried in the packet). It does not provide confidentiality, which means that it does not encrypt the payload. The data is readable but protected from modification. Some fields that are allowed to change in transit are excluded because they need to be modified as they are relayed from router to router. AH operates directly on top of IP.

ESP and AH can be combined to provide authentication, integrity, and antireplay for the entire packet (both the IP header and the data payload carried in the packet), as well as confidentiality for the payload.

Although AH and ESP provide the means to protect data from tampering, preventing eavesdropping and verifying the origin of the data, it is the Internet Key Exchange (IKE) that defines the method for the secure exchange of the initial encryption keys between the two endpoints. IKE allows nodes to agree on authentication methods, encryption methods, what keys to use, and the lifespan of the keys.

The information negotiated by IKE is stored in a Security Association (SA). An SA is like a contract laying out the rules of the VPN connection for the duration of the SA. Each SA is assigned a 32-bit number that, when used in conjunction with the destination IP address, uniquely identifies the SA. This number is called the Security Parameters Index (SPI).

IPsec can be used with Windows in various ways. To enable IPsec communications for a Windows Server 2008 computer, you would create group policies and assign them to individual computers or groups of computers. You could also use the Windows Firewall with advanced security.

Encrypting with VPN Technology

Today, it is common for organizations to use remote access server (RAS), which enables users to connect remotely via various protocols and connection types. By connecting to RAS over the Internet, users can connect to their organization's network so that they can access data files, read email, and access other applications just as if they were sitting at work. However, because the Internet is considered an insecure medium, you must use data encryption when setting up these types of connections.

A *virtual private network (VPN)* links two computers through a wide-area network such as the Internet. To keep the connection secure, the data sent between the two computers is encapsulated and encrypted. In one scenario, a client connects to the RAS server to access internal resources from offsite. Another scenario is to connect one RAS server on one site or organization to another RAS server on another site or organization so that the site or organizations can communicate with each other.

The four types of tunneling protocols used with a VPN server/RAS server running on Windows Server 2008 R2 are as follows:

- **Point-to-Point Tunneling Protocol (PPTP):** A VPN protocol based on the legacy Point-to-Point protocol used with modems. Unfortunately, PPTP is easy to set up but uses weak encryption technology.
- **Layer 2 Tunneling Protocol (L2TP):** Used with IPsec to provide security. This the industry standard when setting up secure tunnels.

- **Secure Sockets Tunneling Protocol (SSTP):** Introduced with Windows Server 2008, which users the HTTPS protocol over TCP port 443 to pass traffic through firewalls and web proxies that might block PPTP and L2TP/IPsec.
- **Internet Key Exchange version 2 (IKEv2):** Uses IPsec for encryption while supporting VPN Reconnect (also called Mobility), which enables VPN connections to be maintained when a VPN client moves between wireless cells or switches and to automatically reestablish broken VPN connectivity. Different from L2TP with IPsec, IKEv2 client computers do not need to provide authentication through a machine certificate or a pre-shared key.

When using VPNs, Windows 7 and Windows Server 2008 support the following forms of authentication:

- **Password Authentication Protocol (PAP):** Uses plain text (unencrypted passwords). PAP is the least secure form of authentication and is not recommended.
- **Challenge Handshake Authentication Protocol (CHAP):** A challenge-response authentication method that uses the industry standard md5 hashing scheme to encrypt the response. CHAP was an industry standard for years and is still quite popular.
- **Microsoft CHAP version 2 (MS-CHAPv2):** Provides two-way authentication (mutual authentication). MS-CHAPv2 provides stronger security than CHAP.
- **Extensible Authentication Protocol Microsoft CHAP version 2 (EAP-MS-CHAPv2):** EAP is a universal authentication framework that allows third-party vendors to develop custom authentication schemes including retinal scans, voice recognition, fingerprint identifications, smart cards, Kerberos, and digital certificates. It also provides a mutual authentication method that supports password-based user or computer authentication.

 CREATE A VPN TUNNEL

GET READY. To create a VPN tunnel on a computer running Windows 7 so that you can connect to a Remote Access Server, perform the following steps:

1. From **Control Panel**, select **Network and Internet** to access the **Network and Sharing Center**.
2. From the **Network and Sharing Center**, choose **Set up a new connection wizard**.
3. In the **Set Up a Connection or Network** page, choose **Connect to a workplace**.
4. In the **Connect to a Workplace** page, answer the question: **Do you want to use a connection that you already have?** Choose whether you want to create a new connection or use an existing connection.
5. On the next page, choose **Use my Internet connection (VPN)**.
6. On the next screen, either choose your VPN connection or specify the Internet address for the VPN server and a destination name. You can also specify the following options: **Use a Smart card for authentication, Allow other people to use this connection,** and **Don't connect now, just set up so I can connect later.**

Often, you may need additional configurations of your VPN connection, such as those specifying the type of protocol, which authentication protocol to use, and the type of encryption.

After the VPN connection is created and configured, to connect using the VPN, simply open the Network and Sharing Center and click Manage Network Connections. Then right-click your VPN connection and click the Connect button. See Figure 2-19.

Figure 2-19

VPN connection

Figure 2-19

VPN connection

By default, when you connect to a VPN using the previous configuration, all web browsing and network traffic goes through the default gateway on the Remote Network unless you are communicating with local home computers. Having this option enabled helps protect the corporate network because all traffic will also go through firewalls and proxy servers, which helps prevent a network from being infected or compromised.

If you wish to route your browsing through your home Internet connection rather than through the corporate network, you can disable the "Use Default Gateway on Remote Network" option. When you disable this option, you are using what is known as split tunneling.

 ENABLE SPLIT TUNNELING

GET READY. To enable split tunneling, perform the following steps:

1. Right-click a VPN connection and click **Properties**.
2. Click the **Networking** tab.
3. Double-click **Internet Protocol Version 4 (TCP/IPv4)**.
4. Click the **Advanced** button.
5. Deselect the **Use default gateway on remote network** option.

It can be a lot of work to configure multiple clients to connect to a remote access server. In fact, this task is often too complicated for computer novices, and it may be prone to errors. To help simplify administration of the VPN client into an easy-to-install executable, you could use the Connection Manager Administration Kit (CMAK). To install CMAK on Windows Server 2008, you must install it as a feature.

■ Using Auditing to Complete the Security Picture

↓ THE BOTTOM LINE

As mentioned earlier, security can be divided into three areas. Authentication is used to prove the identity of a user, whereas authorization gives access to an authenticated user. To complete the security picture, however, you need to enable auditing so that you can have a record of which users have logged in and what resources those users accessed or tried to access.

CERTIFICATION READY
Can you explain why
auditing is so important
to security?
2.4

It is important that you protect your information and service resources from people who should not have access to them, while at the same time making those resources available to authorized users. Therefore, along with authentication and authorization, you should also enable auditing so that you can have a record of the following details:

- Who has successfully logged in
- Who has attempted to log in but failed
- Who has changed accounts in Active Directory
- Who has accessed or changed certain files
- Who has used a certain printer
- Who has restarted a system
- Who has made some system changes

Auditing is not enabled by default in Windows. To enable auditing, you must specify what types of system events to audit using group policies or the local security policy (Security Settings\Local Policies\Audit Policy). See Figure 2-20. Table 2-3 shows the basic audit events that are available in Windows Server 2003 and 2008. Windows Server 2008 also has additional options for more granular control. After you enable logging, you then open the Event Viewer security logs to view the logged security events. By default, these logs can only be seen and managed by the Administrators group.

Figure 2-20

Enabling auditing using group policies

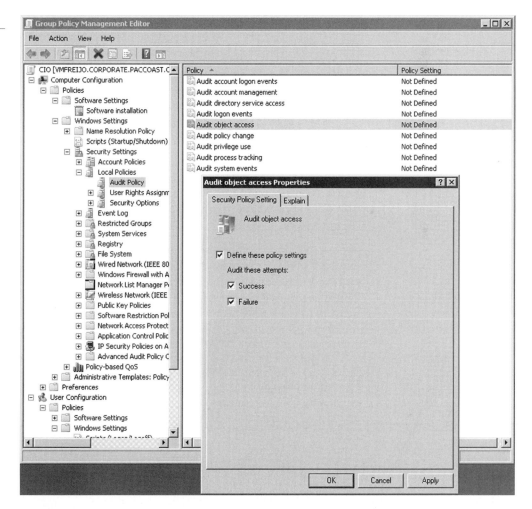

Table 2-3

Audit events

EVENT	EXPLANATION
Account Logon	Determines whether the OS audits each time the computer validates an account's credentials, such as account login.
Account Management	Determines whether to audit each event of account management on a computer, including changing passwords and creating or deleting user accounts.
Directory Service Access	Determines whether the OS audits user attempts to access Active Directory objects.
Logon	Determines whether the OS audits each instance of a user attempting to log on or log off of his or her computer.
Object Access	Determines whether the OS audits user attempts to access non-Active Directory objects, including NTFS files, folders, and printers.
Policy Change	Determines whether the OS audits each instance in which users attempt to change user rights assignments, auditing policy, account policy, or trust policy.
Privilege Use	Determines whether to audit each instance in which a user exercises a user right.
Process Tracking	Determines whether the OS audits process-related events, such as process creation, process termination, handle duplication, and indirect object access. This is usually used for troubleshooting.
System	Determines whether the OS audits changes to the system time, system start up or shut down, attempts to load extensible authentication components, losses of auditing events due to auditing system failure, and security logs exceeding a configurable warning threshold level.

Auditing NTFS files, folders, and printers is a two-step process. You must first enable Object Access using group policies. Then you must specify which files, folders, or printers you want to audit. After enabling logging, you can open the Event Viewer security logs to view the security events.

Because Windows is only part of what makes up a network, you also need to look at other areas to audit. For example, for Microsoft's web server IIS, you can enable logging of who visits each site. For Microsoft's Internet Security and Acceleration (ISA) and Microsoft's Threat Management Gateway (TMG) servers, you can choose to log who accesses your network through a VPN or what is accessed through the firewall. Also, if you have Cisco routers and firewalls, you should enable auditing so that if someone reconfigures the router and firewall, you have a record of it.

If you need to audit non-Microsoft products, you may need to use Syslog. *Syslog* is a standard for logging program messages that can be accessed by devices that would not otherwise have a method for communications. Cisco firewalls and routers, computers running Linux and UNIX, and many printers can use Syslog. It can be employed for computer system management and security auditing, as well as for generalized information, analysis, and debugging messages.

After you decide what you are going to audit, you need to decide where you are going to keep the logs. You need to choose a server or device that has enough storage to hold the logs for the time required by your organization. You should also limit access to this storage area only to essential people. You should also consider backing up these logs and keeping the backups as long as required by your organization.

Lastly, if your organization is large enough or you have high security standards, you should consider having different people as administrators and different people as auditors. By having isolation of duties, the auditors can make sure that the administrators are doing what they are supposed to be doing and more importantly to make sure they are not doing what they are not supposed to be doing.

Finally, you should make sure that you have a change management system and a ticket system. A change management system will record what changes are made. It gives the IT department a method to review changes before they are implemented so that if these changes cause problems with a system, they can be evaluated. In addition, if a problem does occur, this system provides a single list of all of the changes made to your environment.

In comparison, a ticket system gives you a record of all problems and requests by users. By having a ticket system, you can determine what your most common problems are and identify trends.

 AUDIT FILES AND FOLDERS

GET READY. Assuming that object auditing has been enabled, to audit files and folders, perform the following steps:

1. Open **Windows Explorer.**
2. Right-click the file or folder that you want to audit, click **Properties**, and then click the **Security** tab.
3. Click **Edit**, and then click **Advanced.**
4. In the **Advanced Security Settings for <object>** dialog box, click the **Auditing** tab.
5. Do one of the following:
   - To set up auditing for a new user or group, click **Add.** In **Enter the object name to select**, type the name of the user or group that you want, and then click **OK.**
   - To remove auditing for an existing group or user, click the group name or username, click **Remove**, click **OK**, and then skip the rest of this procedure.
   - To view or change auditing for an existing group or user, click the name of the group or user, then click **Edit.**
6. In the **Apply onto** box, click the location where you want auditing to take place.
7. In the **Access** box, indicate what actions you want to audit by selecting the appropriate check boxes:
   - To audit successful events, select the **Successful** check box.
   - To stop auditing successful events, clear the **Successful** check box.
   - To audit unsuccessful events, select the **Failed** check box.
   - To stop auditing unsuccessful events, clear the **Failed** check box.
   - To stop auditing all events, click **Clear All.**
8. If you want to prevent subsequent files and subfolders of the original object from inheriting these audit entries, select the **Apply these auditing entries to objects and/or containers within this container only** check box.
9. Click **OK** to close the Advanced Security Settings dialog box.
10. Click **OK** to close the Properties dialog box.

SKILL SUMMARY

IN THIS LESSON YOU LEARNED:

- AAA (authentication, authorization, and accounting) is a model for access control.
- Authentication is the process of identifying an individual.
- After a user is authenticated, he or she can access network resources based on his or her authorization. Authorization is the process of giving individuals access to system objects based on their identity.
- Accounting, also known as auditing, is the process of keeping track of a user's activity when accessing network resources, including the amount of time spent in the network, the services accessed while in the network, and the amount of data transferred during the session.
- Nonrepudiation prevents one party from denying the actions it has carried out.
- Users can authenticate using what they know, what they own or possess, and/or what they are.
- When you use two or more methods to authenticate a user, you are implementing a multifactor authentication system.
- The most common method of authentication with computers and networks is the password.
- A password is a secret series of characters that enables a user to access a file, computer, or program.
- To hack a password, users will try obvious passwords, brute force attacks, and dictionary attacks.
- For increased security, you need to choose a password that nobody can guess. Therefore, your password should be long enough, and it should be considered strong or complex.
- A personal identification number (PIN) is a secret numeric password shared between a user and a system that can be used to authenticate the user to the system.
- A digital certificate is an electronic document that contains an identity, such as a user or organization, and a corresponding public key.
- A smart card is a pocket-sized card with embedded integrated circuits that consist of nonvolatile memory storage components and perhaps dedicated security logic.
- A smart card can contain digital certificates to prove the identity of the person carrying the card, and it may also contain permissions and access information.
- Biometrics is an authentication method that identifies and recognizes people based on physical traits, such as fingerprints, face recognition, iris recognition, retinal scans, and voice recognition.
- Because administrators have full access to computers and networks, you should use a standard nonadministrator account to perform most tasks.
- Active Directory is a technology created by Microsoft that provides a variety of network services, including LDAP, Kerberos-based and single sign-on authentication, DNS-based naming and other network information, and a central location for network administration and delegation of authority.
- Kerberos is the default computer network authentication protocol. It allows hosts to prove their identity over a nonsecure network in a secure manner.
- Single sign-on (SSO) allows you to log on once and access multiple related, but independent, software systems without having to log in again.
- A user account enables a user to log on to a computer and domain.
- Local user accounts are stored in the Security Account Manager (SAM) database on the local computer.
- Groups are used to group users and computers together so that when you assign rights and permissions, you can assign them to the entire group rather than to each user individually.
- A right authorizes a user to perform certain actions on a computer, such as logging on to a system interactively or backing up files and directories on a system.

- A permission defines the type of access granted to an object or object attribute.
- Explicit permissions are permissions granted directly to a file or folder.
- Inherited permissions are permissions that are granted to a folder (parent object or container) and then flow into the folder's child objects (subfolders or files inside the parent folder).
- The owner of an object controls how permissions are set on the object and to whom permissions are granted.
- Encryption is the process of converting data into a format that cannot be read by another user. Once a user has encrypted a file, that file automatically remains encrypted when it is stored on disk.
- Decryption is the process of converting data from an encrypted format back to its original format.
- Encryption algorithms can be divided into three classes: symmetric, asymmetric, and hash function.
- Symmetric encryption uses a single key to encrypt and decrypt data. Therefore, it is also referred to as secret-key, single-key, shared-key, and private-key encryption.
- Asymmetric key encryption, also known as public key cryptography, uses two mathematically related keys. One key is used to encrypt the data, while the second is used to decrypt it.
- Different from symmetric and asymmetric algorithms, a hash function is meant as a one-way encryption. That means that after information has been encrypted, it cannot be decrypted.
- Public key infrastructure (PKI) is a system consisting of hardware, software, policies, and procedures that create, manage, distribute, use, store, and revoke digital certificates.
- The most common digital certificate is the X.509 version 3.
- The certificate chain, also known as the certification path, is a list of certificates used to authenticate an entity. It begins with the certificate of the entity and ends with the root CA certificate.
- A digital signature is a mathematical scheme that is used to demonstrate the authenticity of a digital message or document It is also used to prove that the message or document has not been modified.
- When you need to transmit private data over the Internet, you should use SSL over HTTPS (https) to encrypt the data that you're sending. URLs that require an SSL connection start with https: instead of http:.
- IP Security, more commonly known as IPsec, is a suite of protocols that provides a mechanism for data integrity, authentication, and privacy for the Internet Protocol.
- A virtual private network (VPN) links two computers through a wide-area network, such as the Internet.
- Syslog is a standard for logging program messages that can be accessed by devices that would not otherwise have a method for communication.

■ Knowledge Assessment

Multiple Choice

Circle the letter that corresponds to the best answer.

1. Which of the following is not a method for authentication?
   a. Something the user knows
   b. Something the user owns or possesses
   c. Encryption
   d. Something the user is

2. Which of the following is not a biometric device?
   a. Password reader
   b. Retinal scanner
   c. Fingerprint scanner
   d. Face scanner

3. Which of the following services is used for centralized authentication, authorization, and accounting?
   a. VPN
   b. PGP
   c. RADIUS
   d. PKI

4. What is the primary authentication method used on Microsoft Active Directory?
   a. LDAP
   b. Kerberos
   c. NTLAN
   d. SSO

5. The master time keeper and master for password changes in an Active Directory domain is
   a. PDC Emulator
   b. RID
   c. Infrastructure master
   d. Schema master

6. Local user accounts are found in
   a. Active Directory
   b. Registry
   c. SAM
   d. LDAP

7. A(n) _____ authorizes a user to perform certain actions on a computer.
   a. Permission
   b. Encryption algorithm
   c. Authentication protocol
   d. Right

8. Which of the following file systems offers the best security?
   a. FAT
   b. FAT32
   c. NTFS
   d. EFS

9. Which NTFS permission is needed to change attributes and permissions?
   a. Full Control
   b. Modify
   c. Read and Execute
   d. Write

10. Which type of permission is granted directly to a file or folder?
    a. Explicit
    b. Inherited
    c. Effective
    d. Share

11. If you copy a file or folder to a new volume, what permissions will that file or folder have?
    a. The same permissions that it had before.
    b. The same permissions as the target folder.
    c. The same permissions as the source folder.
    d. No permissions at all.

12. Which of the following uses an ACL?
    a. NTFS folder
    b. Active Directory user
    c. Registry key
    d. Login rights

13. Which type of key has one key for encryption and a different key for decryption?
    a. Symmetric
    b. Asymmetric
    c. Hash function
    d. PKI

14. Which infrastructure is used to assign and validate digital certificates?
    a. Asymmetric algorithm
    b. Active Directory
    c. PKI
    d. VPN

15. Which technology is used to encrypt an individual file on an NTFS volume?
    a. BitLocker
    b. BitLocker To Go
    c. PPTP
    d. EFS

Fill in the Blank

Complete the following sentences by writing the correct word or words in the blanks provided.

1. A(n) _____ is a secret numeric password shared between a user and a system that can be used to authenticate the user to the system.

2. A pocket-sized card with embedded integrated circuits that is used for authentication is known as a(n) _____.

3. A device that may give you a second password to log in to a system is a(n) _____.

4. The _____ holds a copy of the centralized database used in Active Directory.

5. By default, your computer clock should not be off more than _____ minutes or you might have problems with Kerberos authentication.

6. A(n) _____ defines the type of access over an object or the properties of an object such as an NTFS file or printer.

7. _____ permissions flow from a parent object to a child object.

8. When you cannot access a folder because someone removed the permissions so that no one can access it, you must take _____ of the folder.

9. The centralized database that holds most of the Windows configuration is known as the _____.

10. To track a user's activities in Windows, you need to enable _____.

Competency Assessment

Scenario 2-1: Understanding the Disadvantages of Biometrics

You are the IT administrator for the Contoso Corporation. Your CIO wants you to investigate the possible use of biometrics for security purposes. The CIO understands what biometrics is and how this technology can be used, but he does not understand the potential disadvantages of using biometrics. What should you tell him?

Scenario 2-2: Limiting Auditing

You are the IT administrator for the Contoso Corporation. Your CIO needs to know when a particular user accessed a certain folder. However, this information is not available because auditing was not enabled. To ensure that this does not happen again in the future, the CIO asks you to enable auditing for everything. How should you respond?

Proficiency Assessment

Scenario 2-3: Looking at NTFS Permissions

Log in as an administrator on a computer running Windows 7 or Windows Server 2008. Create a group called Managers on your computer. Now, create a user account called JSmith and assign it to the Managers group. Next, create another user account called JHamid. Create a folder called SharedTest, and create a text file called test.txt in the SharedTest Folder. Share the folder. Assign Allow Full Control to Everyone. Assign Read and Execute to the Managers group. Log in as JHamid and try to access the \\localhost\SharedTest folder. Then, log in as JSmith and try access the \\localhost\SharedTest folder.

Scenario 2-4: Looking at EFS

Add JHamid to the Managers group you established in the previous exercise. Now, log in as JSmith and encrypt the test.txt file with EFS. Finally, log in as JHamid and try to access the test.txt file.

Workplace Ready

Planning and Maintaining Security

When considering security, you need to look at the entire picture. Security must be planned for from the beginning. Therefore, you need to define what your security goals are, what impact they will have on current access and network applications, and how security measures will affect users. Then, after such measures have been implemented, you must maintain them by constantly monitoring the security of the system, making changes as needed, patching security holes, and constantly reviewing the security logs.

Understanding Security Policies

OBJECTIVE DOMAIN MATRIX

SKILLS/CONCEPTS	MTA EXAM OBJECTIVE	MTA EXAM OBJECTIVE NUMBER
Using Password Policies to Enhance Security	Understand password policies.	2.3

KEY TERMS

account lockout

cracked password

dictionary attack

Group Policy Object (GPO)

keylogger

password

sniffers

strong password

One of the foundations of information security is the protection of networks, systems, and most important of all, data. In fact, the need to protect data is basic to all information security policies, procedures, and processes.

Much of today's data protection is based on the ***password***. Think about your life. You use passwords to secure your voice mail, your ATM access, your email account, your Facebook account, and a host of other things. In order to keep these accounts secure, you need to select strong passwords. In this lesson, we discuss what goes into creating a strong password, as well as how you can configure password settings to ensure that the passwords in your environment stay secure.

■ Using Password Policies to Enhance Security

THE BOTTOM LINE

There are a variety of configuration settings you can use on your system to ensure that your users are required to set and maintain strong passwords. As hard as it may be to believe, when left to their own devices, many users will still select weak passwords when securing their accounts. However, with user education and system controls, you can reduce the risk of weak passwords compromising your data and applications.

CERTIFICATION READY
How do you enforce
stronger passwords for
your organization?
2.3

One basic component of your information security program is ensuring that all employees select and use *strong passwords*. The strength of a password can be determined by looking at the password's length, complexity, and randomness.

Microsoft provides a number of controls that can be used to ensure password security is maintained. These include controls related to:

- Password complexity
- Account lockout
- Password length
- Password history
- Time between password changes
- Enforcement using group policies
- Common attack methods

Using Password Complexity to Make a Stronger Password

Password complexity involves the characters used to make up a password. A complex password uses characters from at least three of the following categories:

- English uppercase characters (A through Z)
- English lowercase characters (a through z)
- Numeric characters (0 through 9)
- Nonalphanumeric characters (!, @, #, $, %, ^, &, etc.)

Microsoft's password complexity settings, when enabled, require characters from three of these categories by default on domain controllers, and the domain can be configured to require this setting for all passwords.

This setting can either be enabled or disabled. There are no additional configurations available.

Of course, even when you enforce password complexity, there is no guarantee that users will not continue to use easily guessable passwords. For example, the password "Summer2010" meets the current complexity guidelines required by the Windows password complexity setting. It's also a terrible password, because it is easily guessable.

Some password selections that should be avoided include words you would find in a dictionary, derivatives of user IDs, and common character sequences such as "123456" or "QWERTY." Likewise, personal details such as spouse's name, license plate number, Social Security number, or date of birth should be avoided. Finally, you should avoid passwords based on proper names, geographical locations, common acronyms, and slang terms.

Some recommended methods for selecting strong passwords include the following:

- **Bump the characters in a word a certain number of letters up or down the alphabet:** For instance, a three-letter shift translation of "AArdvark!!" would yield the password "44DDvhzdvo!!"
- **Create acronyms from words in a song, poem, or other familiar sequence of words:** For example, the phrase "Ask not what you can do for your country?" could yield the password "Anwycdfyc?" Add $$ to the beginning, and you get the strong password $$Anwycdfyc?
- **Combine a number of personal facts like birth dates and favorite colors, foods, etc. with special characters:** This method would yield passwords like "##Yell0w419" or "$^327p!zZ@."

TAKE NOTE *

One of the easiest ways to set a complex password is to start with a dictionary word and use character substitution to make it complex. For example, computer could be changed to C0mput3r.

Using Account Lockout to Prevent Hacking

Account lockout refers to the number of incorrect logon attempts permitted before a system locks an account. Each bad logon attempt is tracked by the bad logon counter, and when the counter exceeds the account lockout threshold, no further logon attempts are permitted. This setting is critical because one of the most common password attacks (discussed later in the lesson) involves repeatedly attempting to log on with guessed passwords.

Microsoft provides three separate settings with respect to account lockout:

- **Account lockout duration:** This setting determines the length of time a lockout will remain in place before another logon attempt can be made. This can be set from 0 to 99,999 minutes. If set to 0, an administrator will need to manually unlock the account; no automatic unlocking will occur.

- **Account lockout threshold:** This setting determines the number of failed logons permitted before account lockout occurs. This can be set from 0 (no account lockouts) to 999 attempts before lockout.

- **Reset account lockout counter after:** This setting determines the period of time, in minutes, that must elapse before the account lockout counter is reset to 0 bad logon attempts. If an account lockout threshold is set, the reset account lockout threshold must be less than or equal to the account lockout duration.

Usually account lockout settings range from three to ten attempts, with account lockout duration and reset account lockout counter after set anywhere from 30 to 60 minutes. Although some users complain when they don't get as many attempts to log in as they need, this is a critical configuration to set to ensure your environment remains secure.

Looking at Password Length

The length of a password is a key component of its strength. Password length is the number of characters used in a password. A password with two characters is considered highly insecure, because there is a very limited set of unique passwords that can be made using two characters. Therefore, a two-character password is considered easy to guess.

On the other side of the spectrum is the 14-character password. Although extremely secure relative to a two-character password, a 14-character password is difficult for most users to remember. When passwords become this long, users often start breaking out the note paper and writing their passwords down, which defeats any security benefits you may have gotten from requiring a 14-character password in the first place.

As these scenarios illustrate, the trick to setting a minimum password length is balancing usability with security. Microsoft permits you to set a minimum password length ranging from one to 14 (a setting of 0 means no password is required, which is never appropriate in a production environment). The generally accepted minimum password length is eight characters.

Using Password History to Enforce Security

Password history is the setting that determines the number of unique passwords that must be used before a password can be re-used. This setting prevents users from recycling the same passwords through a system. The longer the period of time a password is used, the greater the chances it can be compromised.

Microsoft allows you to set the password history value between 0 and 24. Ten is a fairly common setting in standard environments, although Windows Server 2008 defaults to 24 on domain controllers.

Setting the Time between Password Changes

The final password setting you should be familiar with is the time between password changes. This setting actually consists of two settings:

- **Minimum Password Age:** The minimum password age setting controls how many days users must wait before they can reset their password. This setting can be a value from one to 998 days. If set to 0, passwords can be changed immediately. Although this seems to be a fairly innocent setting, too low a value could allow users to defeat your password history settings. For example, if you set this value to 0 and your password history is set to 10, all users have to do is reset their password 10 times in a row, and then they can go back to their original password. This setting must be set to a lower value than the maximum password age, unless the maximum password age is set to 0, which means passwords never expire. Ten days or greater is usually a good setting, although this can vary widely depending on administrator preferences.

- **Maximum Password Age:** The maximum password age setting controls the maximum period of time that can elapse before you are forced to reset your password. This setting can range from one to 999 days, or it can be set to 0 if you never want passwords to expire. A general rule for this setting is 90 days for user accounts; although for administrative accounts, it's generally a good idea to reset passwords more frequently. In high-security areas, 30 days is not an uncommon setting.

We have discussed the different settings you can use to ensure the best password security for your environment. Now, let's look at how to review those settings on a Windows 7 workstation.

 REVIEW THE PASSWORD SETTINGS ON A WINDOWS 7 WORKSTATION

GET READY. Before you begin these steps, be sure to launch the **Local Security Policy** snap-in from the **Administrative Tools** menu (see Figure 3-1).

Figure 3-1

Local Security Policy window

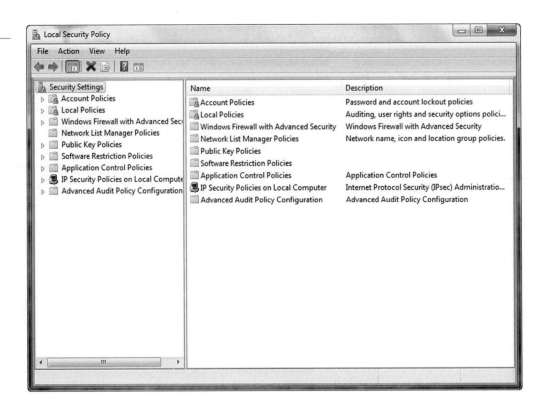

1. In the **Local Security Policy** snap-in, click on **Account Policies**.

2. Click on **Password Policy**. You should see the password settings we've discussed in the right window. See Figure 3-2.

Figure 3-2

Password Policy security settings

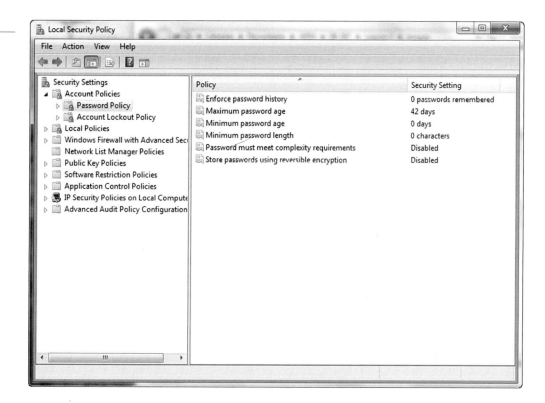

3. Click on each of the password settings (see Figures 3-3, 3-4, 3-5, 3-6, and 3-7 for the different settings).

Figure 3-3

Enforce password history

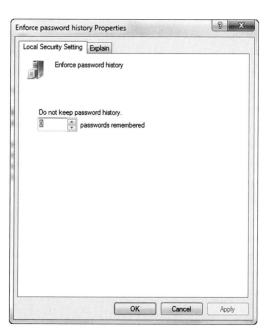

Figure 3-4

Maximum password age

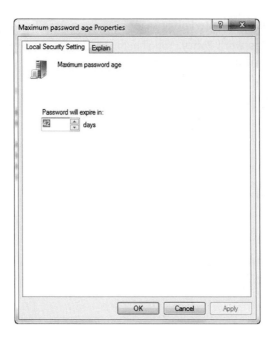

Figure 3-5

Minimum password age

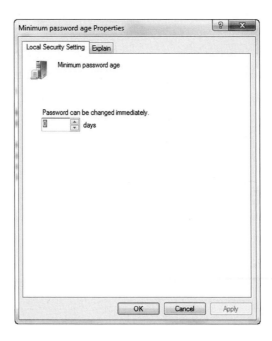

Figure 3-6

Minimum password length

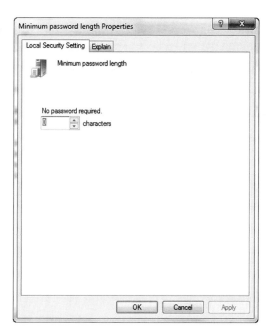

Figure 3-7

Enforcing password complexity

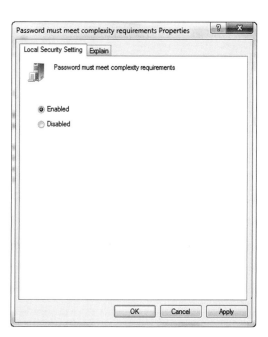

4. Click on **Account Lockout Policy**. You should see the account lockout settings we've discussed in the right window. See Figure 3-8.

Figure 3-8

Account Lockout Policy settings

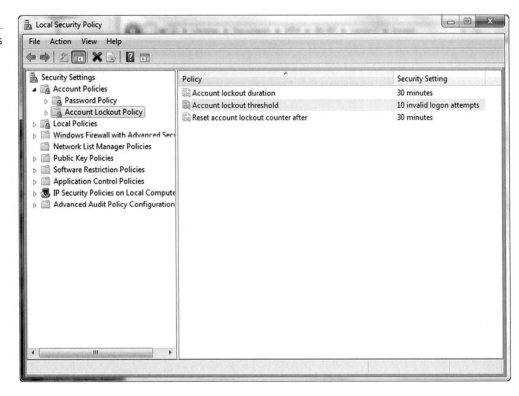

5. Click on each of the account lockout settings as discussed above (see Figures 3-9, 3-10, and 3-11 for the different settings).

Figure 3-9

Account lockout threshold

Figure 3-10

Account lockout duration

Figure 3-11

Reset account lockout timer

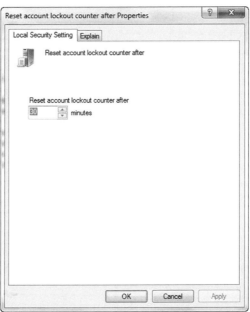

The password settings for a Windows 2008 domain are configured differently than for a stand-alone host or client. In this example, we are reviewing current password settings. We'll look at changing these settings using a Group Policy Object (GPO) in the next section.

Now that we have looked at setting password policies on a local client, let's take a look at how Group Policies can be used to set these properties for the members of a domain.

Using Password Group Policies to Enforce Security

Before we look at using Group Policies to enforce password settings, we should describe exactly what a Group Policy (also known as a Group Policy Object) is.

A *Group Policy Object (GPO)* is a set of rules that allow an administrator granular control over the configuration of objects in Active Directory (AD), including user accounts, operating systems, applications, and other AD objects. GPOs are used for centralized management and configuration of the Active Directory environment.

Now that you have a better idea of what a GPO is, let's look at how you can use one to enforce password controls in Active Directory.

USE A GROUP POLICY TO ENFORCE PASSWORD CONTROLS ON DOMAIN SYSTEMS

GET READY. Before you begin these steps, be sure to launch the **Active Directory Users and Computers** snap-in from the **Administrative Tools** menu.

1. Right-click the root container for the domain and select **Properties**.
2. In the **Properties** dialog box for the domain, click the **Group Policy** tab.
3. Click **New** to create a new GPO in the root container. Type "**Password Policy**" as the name of the new policy, and then click **Close**.
4. Right-click the root container for the domain, and then click **Properties**.
5. In the **Properties** dialog box, click the **Group Policy** tab, and then select your newly created GPO (named Password Policy.)
6. Click **Up** to move your new GPO to the top of the list.
7. Click **Edit** to open the **Group Policy Object Editor** for the GPO you just created.
8. Under **Computer Configuration**, navigate to the **Windows Settings\Security Settings\Account Policies\Password Policy** folder.
9. From here, you can set the policies as we did in the earlier exercise. Open each policy in turn, change the setting, and click **OK** to return to the main dialog box.
10. Once you have configured the settings as desired, close the **Group Policy Object Editor**.
11. Click **OK** to close the domain properties dialog box.
12. Exit **Active Directory Users and Computers**.

You have now set a GPO to enforce password settings. This process works great with Windows Server 2003. However, with Windows Server 2008, the most current release of the Windows Server operating system, setting these policies requires a slightly different process.

In particular, Windows Server 2008 permits you to store what Microsoft calls password group policies. These policies allow you to set different password policies on different containers in the Active Directory. In order to support this new functionality, Windows Server 2008 includes two new object classes:

- Password Settings Container
- Password Settings Object

The Password Settings Container (PSC) is created by default under the System container in the domain. You can view it by using the Active Directory Users and Computers snap-in, but you will need to enable the advanced features to get to it. The PSC stores the Password Settings Objects (PSOs) for the domain.

If no fine-grained password policies are configured, the Default Domain Policy, also accessible through the Active Directory Users and Computers snap-in, applies to all accounts in the domain.

Let's take a look at how to modify the Default Domain Policy to achieve an implementation that is similar to the use of the GPO in earlier versions of Active Directory.

 USE THE DEFAULT DOMAIN POLICY TO ENFORCE PASSWORD CONTROLS ON DOMAIN SYSTEMS

GET READY. Before you begin these steps, be sure to launch the **Active Directory Users and Computers** snap-in with the **Advanced Features** enabled from the **Administrative Tools** menu.

1. Expand the domain to show the default folders.
2. Double-click **System**. The list of default objects under the System container should be visible.

3. Right-click the **Default Domain Policy** and select **Properties**. The **Default Domain Policy Properties** dialog box will open (See Figure 3-12).

Figure 3-12

Default Domain Policy
Properties Object tab

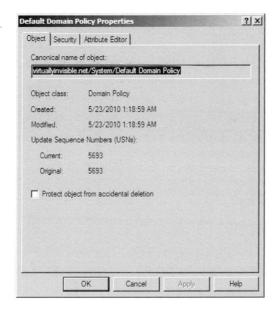

4. Click on the **Attribute Editor** tab, and scroll down to the **Password Attributes** (see Figure 3-13).

Figure 3-13

Default Domain Policy
Properties Attribute Editor tab

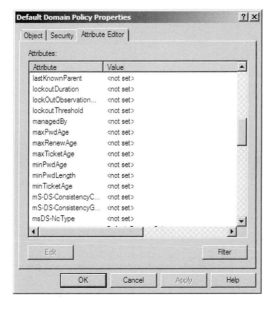

5. Double-click the attribute you want to change.

6. When you have completed your desired changes, click **OK** to close the **Default Domain Policy Properties** dialog box.

7. Exit **Active Directory Users and Computers**.

TAKE NOTE *

The new functionality of Windows Server 2008 provides significant benefits to experienced Active Directory administrators, but it can create significant complexity for someone new to AD. Make changes with caution.

Now that you know some ways to set password attributes on the client, both in a Windows Server 2003 Active Directory and in the current version of Active Directory, we need to discuss some of the most common attack methods you might encounter in the real world.

Understanding Common Attack Methods

Passwords have long been recognized as one of the weak links in many security programs. Although tokens, smart cards, and biometrics are gaining traction in the business world for securing key systems and data, a significant amount of confidential and private data is still being secured with passwords. Passwords are considered a weak link for two main reasons.

First, you are completely reliant on users in the selection of passwords. Even though many users will select strong passwords in line with your standards, and even though you have some tools to enforce password attributes like complexity and minimum length, there will still be users who continue to select weak passwords. Attackers are aware of this and will try to exploit those individuals.

Second, even strong passwords are vulnerable to attack through a variety of different mechanisms.

EXAMINING DICTIONARY AND BRUTE FORCE ATTACKS

A *dictionary attack* uses a dictionary containing an extensive list of potential passwords that the attacker then tries in conjunction with a user ID in an attempt to guess the appropriate password. This is known as a dictionary attack because the earliest versions of this attack actually used lists of words from the dictionary as the basis of their login attempts. Today, custom dictionaries with likely passwords are available for download from the Internet, along with applications that can use these possible passwords against your systems.

Another, more crude type of attack—called a brute force attack—doesn't rely on lists of passwords, but rather tries all possible combinations of permitted character types. Although this type of attack was historically considered ineffective, improvements in processor and network performance have made it more useful, although not nearly as effective as a dictionary attack.

These types of attacks tend to be most successful when a password's length is seven characters or less. Each additional character adds a significant number of possible passwords. These attacks are often successful because users sometimes use common words with the first letter capitalized and then append a number to meet the complexity guidelines. These are the easiest passwords for users to remember, but they are also the easiest for an attacker to compromise.

The Account Lockout settings discussed earlier in the lesson are a critical defense against this type of attack, because an Account Lockout will either slow or even stop a brute force attack in its tracks after the configured number of incorrect logon attempts is reached.

LOOKING AT PHYSICAL ATTACKS

Anytime your computer can be physically accessed by an attacker, that computer is at risk. Physical attacks on your computer can completely bypass almost all security mechanisms, such as by capturing the passwords and other critical data directly from the keyboard when a software or hardware *keylogger* is used. In fact, if your encryption key passes through a keylogger, you might find that even your encrypted data is jeopardized.

Some other physical attacks may include the use of a hidden camera to tape your keystrokes, or even the removal and duplication (or direct theft) of your hard drive. Although not specifically a password attack, if attackers remove your hard drive, they can frequently bypass password controls by mounting the drive remotely and accessing your data directly from the drive, without an intervening operating system.

Lesson 1 contains more details on keylogging.

EXAMINING LEAKED AND SHARED PASSWORDS

Another challenge you'll encounter when dealing with users in an office environment is leaked or shared passwords. Users tend to trust their co-workers. After all, everyone works for the same company, and in many cases, they have access to similar company information. As a result, users can easily be convinced to share their passwords with co-workers who feel they "need" this information. This practice is especially problematic in environments with high turnover, because there is no way to tell who in the last crop of terminated employees still has a friend's user ID and password and thus has continued access to the network.

Even if users don't deliberately provide their password to another employee, the casual work environment frequently makes it easy for employees to watch as their co-workers key in their user IDs and passwords.

Finally, spouses, children, and other relatives may end up with access to your computing environment because of their close relationship with your employees.

User awareness is the best way to combat this type of attack. Providing users with a greater understanding of the risks and impact of these types of behaviors can go a long way in keeping passwords under the control of only authorized users. In addition, the minimum and maximum password age settings, as well as the password history setting, can help mitigate this risk. Here, even if someone obtains a password he or she shouldn't have, when the maximum password age limit is hit, it will force a reset of all passwords, including shared ones.

LOOKING AT CRACKED PASSWORDS

A *cracked password* frequently relies on more than just a password attack. In a password crack attack, the attacker gets access to an encrypted password file from a workstation or server. Once he or she has access, the attacker starts running password cracking tools against the file, with an eye toward breaking as many passwords as possible and leveraging them to further compromise the company's network and systems.

Passwords that are stored in an encrypted state are harder to break than passwords that are stored in clear text or in a hashed state. However, with today's computing power, even encrypted password stores are being compromised by password cracking attacks.

If you ever become aware that your password store has been compromised, you need to have all employees with an account on the compromised system change their passwords immediately.

You can also use the same tools that potential attackers might use to audit the security of your password stores. Trying to crack your own password file is a fairly common practice, as it not only allows you to test the security of your password store, but if any passwords are compromised and/or weak, it gives you the ability to have users change them to more secure passwords.

EXAMINING NETWORK AND WIRELESS SNIFFERS

If an attacker can access your internal network, your wireless network, or even an Internet access point used by your employees, then he or she has the ability to use a specialized tool known as a sniffer to try to intercept unencrypted passwords. Although applications have gotten much better in recent years, there are still a number of them that pass sensitive information like passwords across networks in clear text—which means this information can be read by anyone with the ability to view data as it traverses the network.

Sniffers are specially designed software (and in some cases hardware) applications that capture network packets as they traverse a network, displaying them for the attacker. Sniffers are valid forms of test equipment, used to identify network and application issues, but the technology has been rapidly co-opted by attackers as an easy way to grab logon credentials.

In addition to sniffers that are used to attack wired networks, there are now sniffers that have the ability to capture wireless data as well. Whenever you are connected to your business wireless, perhaps while at the local coffee shop or even while attending a meeting at a hotel, you are potentially at risk of having your data literally pulled out of the air and made available to an attacker. The use of encryption remains the best mechanism for combating this type of attack.

Another area of concern with sniffers is wireless keyboards. At its core, a wireless keyboard is a broadcast technology that sends keystrokes from the keyboard to a receiver connected to the computer. If you can get a receiver tuned to the same frequency close enough to the computer, you can capture every keystroke entered into the wireless keyboard—without needing to install a keylogger. Most wireless keyboards now support additional security, such as encrypted connections, but they are still broadcasting all information that the user types, so as long as people continue to enter the majority of their data via keyboard, this will be a significant potential source for attackers to exploit. In fact, many companies only permit their employees to use wired keyboards in order to mitigate this risk.

X REF

Sniffing is discussed in more detail in Lesson 4.

LOOKING AT GUESSED PASSWORDS

Although not as prevalent an issue as it was in years past, the possibility still exists that someone could sit down at your computer and guess your password. As we have seen in countless movies, an attacker may be familiar with the person whose system they are trying to compromise, or they may look around and see a postcard from a trip or pictures of an employee's kids with their names listed and ascertain a password from these items. Indeed, if a user does not follow corporate rules requiring a strong, not easily guessable password, but instead selects a password based on a spouse's, child's, or pet's name and birthday, an attacker could more easily guess the password and access the employee's data.

That being said, this type of attack is almost never seen these days. With the widespread availability of password cracking tools, the type of individual targeting required to guess someone's password is seldom worth the effort. It is generally much easier to leverage an attack using one of the other methods currently available. Typically, only co-workers or close friends will try to guess a user's password.

SKILL SUMMARY

> **IN THIS LESSON YOU LEARNED:**
>
> - The strength of a password can be determined by looking at the password's length, complexity, and randomness.
> - A complex password uses characters from at least three of the following categories: uppercase, lowercase, numeric characters, and nonalphanumeric characters.
> - Account lockout refers to the number of incorrect logon attempts permitted before a system will lock an account.
> - The Minimum Password Age setting controls how many days users must wait before they can reset their password.
> - The Maximum Password Age setting controls the maximum period of time that can elapse before users are forced to reset their password.
> - A Group Policy Object (GPO) is a set of rules that allow an administrator granular control over the configuration of objects in Active Directory (AD), including user accounts, operating systems, applications, and other AD objects.
> - Passwords have long been recognized as one of the weak links in many security programs.
> - During a dictionary attack, the attacker tries an extensive list of potential passwords in conjunction with a user ID to try to guess the appropriate password.

- Brute force attacks try all possible combinations of permitted character types in an attempt to determine a user's password.

- Physical attacks on a computer can completely bypass almost all security mechanisms, such as by capturing passwords and other critical data directly from a keyboard when a software or hardware keylogger is used.

- In a password crack attack, attackers get access to an encrypted password file from a workstation or server. Once they have access to this file, attackers start running password cracking tools against it.

- If an attacker can gain access to your internal network, your wireless network, or even an Internet access point used by your employees, he or she has the ability to use a specialized tool known as a sniffer to intercept unencrypted passwords.

- Although not as prevalent an issue as it was in years past, the possibility still exists that someone could sit down at your computer and guess your password.

■ Knowledge Assessment

Multiple Choice

Circle the letter or letters that correspond to the best answer or answers.

1. Which of the following are not valid password controls? (Choose all that apply.)
   a. Minimum Password Age
   b. Maximum Password Age
   c. Maximum Password Length
   d. Account Lockout Threshold
   e. Password History

2. Which of the following would be an acceptable password on a Windows 7 Professional system with Password Complexity enabled and Minimum Password Length set to eight? (Choose all that apply.)
   a. Summer2010
   b. $$Thx17
   c. ^^RGood4U
   d. Password
   e. St@rTr3k

3. What is the maximum setting for Minimum Password Age?
   a. 14
   b. 999
   c. 998
   d. 256

4. You are setting up your first secure Windows 7 Professional workstation and you are setting the password history. What are the minimum and maximum settings you can use? (Choose the best answer.)
   a. 0, 14
   b. 1, 14
   c. 0, 24
   d. 1, 24
   e. 0, 998

5. Which of the following are common types of password attacks? (Choose two answers)
   a. Cracking
   b. Man in the middle
   c. Smurf
   d. Spoofing
   e. Brute force

6. One form of brute force password attack uses an extensive list of predefined passwords. What is this form of brute force attack called? (Choose the best answer.)
   a. Bible attack
   b. Cracking attack
   c. Guessing attack
   d. Dictionary attack

7. As the Chief Security Officer for a small medical records processing company, you suspect that a competitor will be attacking your network soon. Having worked in the business for a while, you're pretty sure that this competitor will try to run a dictionary attack against one of your Windows application servers. You want to be sure your competitor can't get into the server using this attack method. Which setting should you adjust in order to ensure this attack has a limited chance at success? (Choose the best answer.)
   a. Minimum Password Length
   b. Account Lockout Threshold
   c. Password History
   d. Maximum Password Age

8. You are the head of the corporate security department, and the Microsoft team has asked you for some assistance in setting the password controls on their new stand-alone server. Which Administrative Tool should you use to configure these settings?
   a. Active Directory Users and Computers
   b. Computer Management
   c. Security Service
   d. Local Security Policy

9. What are the two new features introduced in Windows Server 2008 that permit the use of fine-grained password policies? (Choose all that apply.)
   a. Global Policy Object
   b. Password Settings Container
   c. Password Settings Object
   d. Password Policy

10. Why would you use a minimum password age?
   a. To ensure that someone does not guess a password
   b. To stop someone from trying over and over to guess a password
   c. To make sure a user does not reset a password multiple times until he or she can reuse his or her original password
   d. To automatically reset a password

Fill in the Blank

1. A set of rules that allows an administrator granular control over the configuration of objects in Active Directory (AD), including user accounts, operating systems, applications, and other AD objects, is known as a(n) _____.

2. The number of incorrect logon attempts permitted before a system will lock an account is known as the _____.

3. The setting that determines the number of unique passwords that must be used before a password can be re-used is the _____.

4. The type of attack that uses an extensive list of potential passwords is known as a(n) _____.

5. When you use special software to read data as it is broadcast on a network, you are _____ the network.

6. The _____ needs to be less than or equal to the Account Lockout Duration.

7. The highest setting that Account Lockout Duration can use is _____.

8. In a Windows Server 2008 Active Directory, the _____ automatically applies in the event you have not set a fine-grained password policy.

9. The three configuration settings for account lockout are _____, _____ , and _____.

10. A _____ account is one type of account you can configure so that the password does not expire.

■ Competency Assessment

Scenario 3-1: Understanding Long Passwords

a. Let's say you have a PIN that is four digits long. Each digit can be 0, 1, 2, 3, 4, 5, 6, 7, 8, or 9, giving you a total of 10 possible digits. How many different PINs are possible?

b. Let's say you have a four-letter password, and each character in the password must be a lowercase letter (a–z). There are 26 letters in the alphabet. How many different passwords are possible?

c. Let's say you have a six-letter password, and each character in the password must be a lowercase letter (a–z). How many different combinations are possible?

d. Let's say you have an eight-letter password, and each character in the password must be a lowercase letter (a–z). How many different combinations are possible?

e. Let's say you have an eight-letter password, and each character in the password must be either a lowercase letter (a–z) or an uppercase letter (A–Z). How many different combinations are possible?

f. Let's say you have an eight-letter password, and each character in the password must be a lowercase letter (a–z), an uppercase letter (A–Z), a digit (0–9), or a special character (~`!@#$%^&*()_-+={[}]|\:;"'<,>.? or /). How many different combinations are possible?

Scenario 3-2: Changing Passwords

Imagine that you work for the Contoso Corporation. Your CIO tells you that he just got a message on his computer saying that he has to change his password. He wants to know why he must not only use such a relatively long password, but also why he must change that password on a regular basis. What should you tell him?

■ Proficiency Assessment

Scenario 3-3: Managing Users

Log in to a computer running Windows 7 and create an account for John Adams (JAdams) using the Control Panel. Then add JAdams to the Administrator group. Set the password for JAdams to Password01. Verify the groups that JAdams is a member of using the Computer Management Control.

Scenario 3-4: Configuring a Local Security Policy

On a computer running Windows 7, open Group Policy Management to access the Local Group Policy. View the Password Policy and Account Lockout Policy.

 Workplace Ready

Understanding Group Policies

Group Policies is one of the most powerful features included with Active Directory. Besides being used to configure password policies and account lockout policies, it can be used to assign user rights that define what an individual can do on a computer. It can also be used to install software, prevent software from being installed, lock down a computer, standardize a working environment, and preconfigure Windows. When you look deeper in Group Policies, you will see that there are literally thousands of settings.

Understanding Network Security

OBJECTIVE DOMAIN MATRIX

SKILLS/CONCEPTS	MTA EXAM OBJECTIVE	MTA EXAM OBJECTIVE NUMBER
Using Dedicated Firewalls to Protect a Network	Understand dedicated firewalls.	3.1
Controlling Access with Network Access Protection (NAP)	Understand Network Access Protection (NAP).	3.2
Using Isolation to Protect a Network	Understand network isolation.	3.3
Protecting Data with Protocol Security	Understand protocol security.	3.4
Securing Wireless Networks	Understand wireless security.	1.4

KEY TERMS

application-level firewall

circuit-level firewall

DMZ (demilitarized zone)

DNS Security Extensions (DNSsec)

DNS poisoning

DNS spoofing

firewall

honey net

honeypot

host firewall

intrusion detection systems (IDS)

intrusion prevention systems (IPS)

MAC address

Network Access Protection (NAP)

network firewall

Open Systems Interconnect (OSI)

padded cell

personal firewall

Secure Content Management (SCM)

spoofing

stateful inspection

Unified Threat Management (UTM)

Traditionally, when building an information security infrastructure, the first point of focus was the network. As soon as networks began interconnecting, it was obvious that the network offered the main vector of attack. In other words, it was the primary way to get to an organization's information from the outside.

At this point, the driving philosophy around network protection was reminiscent of the castles of old. According to this mindset, the best way to secure your network was to build strong walls, dig moats, and control access to the castle through the main gate. In network terms, this meant deploying multiple layers of firewalls, then controlling who could enter the network with firewall rules, access controls, and demilitarized zones (DMZs). This practice is known as securing the perimeter, or defense in depth.

This model worked quite well until the next round of technological evolution in the late 1990s, when the concept of the virtual private network (VPN) was introduced. VPNs allowed companies to securely extend their network across untrusted networks like the Internet, but this also impacted the perimeter of the network. Next came wireless network technologies, literally moving the perimeter that required protection into the air and offering additional challenges to the layered security model.

The good news is that as network technologies have evolved and securing a networks' perimeter has become more challenging, the security technologies available for addressing these challenges have evolved as well. In this lesson, we will discuss such security solutions and how they can be used to address the challenges you will encounter.

■ Using Dedicated Firewalls to Protect a Network

THE BOTTOM LINE

Even today, firewalls remain the foundation of network security technology. There are a number of options, types, and technologies associated with selecting, implementing, and maintaining firewalls in your network. There are also a number of drivers to help you determine the proper solution for your organization.

CERTIFICATION READY
Where would most companies place their dedicated firewall?
3.1

One of the first things that comes to mind when people talk about information security is the firewall. Firewalls have long been the foundation of an organization's network security infrastructure. But what exactly is a firewall?

A *firewall* is a system that is designed to protect a computer or a computer network from network-based attacks. A firewall does this by filtering the data packets that are traversing the network. A typical perimeter firewall is implemented with two (or more) network connections (see Figure 4-1), namely:

- A connection to the network being protected; and
- A connection to an external network.

Figure 4-1

A firewall implementation

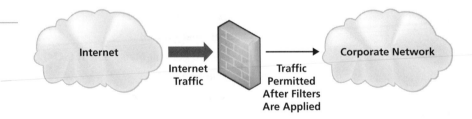

There are numerous variations on this model, but ultimately, all firewalls protect hosts on one network from hosts on another network.

Firewalls are used to divide and isolate networking areas for an organization. For example, one of the most common uses of a firewall would be to divide the network of your organization (internal network) from the external network (Internet). The internal network may also be referred to as clean, secure, and local while the external network may be referred to as dirty, unsecure, and remote. They all reference the same model, but occasionally, you may find you need to translate a particular term into terminology you are familiar with.

In today's networks, you'll find firewalls used for a number of purposes beyond just securing the perimeter. For instance, many corporate networks are divided into zones secured by firewalls. Thus, you may find that your organization's firewalls are not only securing Internet and extranet connections, but also creating secure zones for your financial systems, securing your research and development servers, or perhaps even securing the production network from the development and test networks.

Given the widely varying uses for firewalls in today's networks, there are a variety of different firewall types. But before we get into a discussion of the different types of firewalls, we need to discuss the OSI model.

Understanding the OSI Model

Any discussion about network security requires an understanding of the ***Open Systems Interconnect (OSI)*** reference model. The OSI model is a conceptual model, created by the International Organization for Standardization (ISO) in 1978 and revised in 1984, to describe a network architecture that allows the passage of data between computer systems. Although never fully utilized as a model for a protocol, the OSI model is nonetheless the standard for discussing how networking works.

As shown in Figure 4-2, the OSI model is built in the same way it is usually discussed, from bottom to top. The seven layers of this model are as follows: physical, data link, network, transport, session, presentation, and application. Here, the physical layer is referred to as layer 1, the data link layer as layer 2, and so on. This is important to remember because you will frequently hear routers referred to as "layer 3 devices" or specific types of firewalls described as "layer 7 devices." This nomenclature refers to where on the OSI model a device interacts. Accordingly, it is important that you are familiar with the high-level concept of the OSI model and what occurs at each layer.

Figure 4-2

The seven-layer OSI model

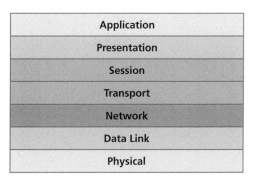

| Application |
| Presentation |
| Session |
| Transport |
| Network |
| Data Link |
| Physical |

Each layer of the OSI model has its own specific function. The following sections describe the function of each layer, starting with the physical layer and working upward.

PHYSICAL LAYER (LAYER 1)

The physical layer of the OSI model is used to define the physical characteristics of the network, including the following specifications:

- **Media:** Cabling types, voltage, signal frequency, speed, bandwidth, etc.
- **Hardware:** Type of connector, type of network interface card, etc.
- **Topology:** The topology used in the network, such as ring, mesh, star, or bus

DATA LINK LAYER (LAYER 2)

The data link layer connects the data layer to the physical layer so that data can be transmitted across the network. The data link layer handles error detection, error correction, and hardware addressing (i.e., the address of a network interface card).

The data link layer is broken into two sublayers:

- **Media Access Control (MAC) sublayer:** The MAC address is defined at this layer. The *MAC address* is the physical or hardware address burned into each NIC (for example, 96-4C-E5-48-78-C7). The MAC sublayer also controls access to the underlying network media.

- **Logical Link Control (LLC) sublayer:** The LLC layer is the layer responsible for the error and flow control mechanisms of the data link layer. The LLC layer is specified in the IEEE 802.2 standard.

TAKE NOTE ✳

The IEEE 802.x standards define a variety of networking technologies. For example, 802.1x defines a standard for wireless security. Similarly, Ethernet is defined by the IEEE 802.3 standard.

NETWORK LAYER (LAYER 3)

The network layer is primarily responsible for routing. This layer defines the mechanisms that allow data to be passed from one network to another. To be clear, this layer doesn't specify how the data is passed; rather, it defines the mechanisms that permit this passage. How the data is passed is defined by the routing protocols (which are discussed in more detail later in the lesson.) As a result, a router is typically known as a layer 3 device.

TAKE NOTE ✳

It's important to remember that in addition to routing (allowing traffic to select the best path), the network layer of the OSI model specifies one other critical function: addressing. In the case of TCP/IP, this is the layer where IP addresses are specified. Although the data link layer uses hard-coded MAC addresses to communicate on the physical layer, network protocols use software-configured addresses and routing protocols to communicate across the network.

TRANSPORT LAYER (LAYER 4)

The transport layer does exactly what its name implies: It provides the mechanisms for carrying data across a network. This layer uses three main mechanisms to accomplish this task:

- **Segmentation:** When, for example, you download an MP3 file from your favorite music site, you are dealing with a large block of data. In order for this file to get from the music site to your PC, it needs to be broken down into smaller, more manageable blocks so the network can handle it. This process is called segmentation, and the transport layer performs this function.

- **Service addressing:** Network protocols (TCP/IP, for example) provide a number of network services, and these services are identified by ports. The transport layer ensures that when data traverses the network, it is passed to the right service and the right port.

- **Error checking:** Transport layer protocols also perform error checking on data and ensure that information is sent or received correctly.

The protocols you will see operating at the transport layer come in two types:

- **Connection oriented:** A connection-oriented protocol (such as Transmission Control Protocol [TCP]) requires an end-to-end connection between hosts before data can be transmitted. You can think of this like a telephone call. When making a call, you can't start speaking to the person at the other end of the line until you have successfully connected to that person.

- **Connectionless:** A connectionless protocol (such as the User Datagram Protocol [UDP]) allows for the transmission of data without requiring that a connection is already established. Connectionless protocols rely on the network to ensure the proper delivery of data from one host to another. You can think of a connectionless protocol like sending an email. Obviously, you don't have to connect directly to the recipient before sending an email; instead, you type and address your message, then click send. Here, you rely on the network—and not an existing connection—to ensure the email gets to the addressee.

The transport layer has an additional responsibility in the OSI model: handling flow control of data. Flow control determines how the receiving device accepts the data transmissions. There are two common methods of flow control:

- **Buffering:** Buffering flow control temporarily stores data in a buffer and waits for the destination device to become available. Buffering can be problematic if the sending device is able to transmit data much faster than the receiving device is able to receive it. Too high a transmit rate can overload a buffer, which has a limited size, causing data loss.

- **Windowing:** In a windowing environment, data segments are grouped together, and when sent, they require only one acknowledgment. Here, the sending and receiving devices agree to the size of the window (i.e., the number of segments that can be sent at one time). In some cases, the window size is agreed to when the connection is established; in others, the window size varies based on network congestion and device resources. These types of windows are referred to as sliding windows. Windowing improves network performance by reducing the number of acknowledgements that need to be sent between devices.

TAKE NOTE *

If you are familiar with PC hardware, you may recognize these two flow control methods. They are the same methods used for flow control in a PC when moving data into and out of the different types of data storage, including hard drives, cache, and RAM.

SESSION LAYER (LAYER 5)

The session layer is responsible for data synchronization between the applications on the sending device and the receiving device. This layer establishes, maintains, and breaks sessions between the two devices. While the transport layer is responsible for connections between the two devices, it is the session layer that is actually responsible for transferring the data between the two devices.

PRESENTATION LAYER (LAYER 6)

The presentation layer converts application layer data into a format that can be transmitted across a network. Data formatted for transport across a network is not always natively readable by applications. Some common data formats that are converted by the presentation layer include the following:

- Graphics files
- Text and data files
- Music and video files

The presentation layer is also the layer in which encryption and decryption of data takes place.

APPLICATION LAYER (LAYER 7)

Finally, at the top of the OSI model is the application layer. This layer takes data from the user and passes that data to the lower layers of the OSI model for transport. Responses are then passed up through the layers and displayed to the user.

> **TAKE NOTE ✳**
>
> It's important to remember that the application layer of the OSI model is not the actual application you see on your computer. Rather, the application layer is used to define how the applications running on your computer can take advantage of the network service. For example, if you wanted to print a document to a network printer, your word processing application would take the file information and pass it to the application layer, which would then pass it down the other layers in the model so that it could be transmitted to the printer. Of course, there are applications (software programs) that may use the network service or application that runs at application layer services, like web browsers.

Although the OSI model provides a framework to categorize technology, this model is not fully implemented on today's networks. Instead, today's networks follow a simplified model that usually consists of the following four layers:

- **Link layer:** This is the lowest layer of the TCP/IP model and is designed to be hardware independent. It is responsible for linking to the hardware networking technology, and it transmits data. TCP/IP has been implemented on top of virtually any hardware networking technology in existence.
- **Internet layer:** This layer is responsible for connecting multiple networks together and for routing packets between networks.
- **Transport layer:** This layer is responsible for end-to-end message transfer capabilities independent of the underlying network. It also handles error control, segmentation, flow control, congestion control, and application addressing (port numbers).
- **Application layer:** The term "application layer" refers to higher-level network protocols and services, such as SMTP or FTP.

Now that you have an understanding of the OSI model, we can discuss various networking technologies and their impact on your information security program.

Examining Hardware Firewalls and Their Characteristics

In today's network environment, the vast majority of production firewalls are hardware based. A hardware firewall is a firewall that runs on a dedicated platform specifically designed, optimized, and hardened (the process of securing a system) to run the firewall application software.

Although there are a variety of types of firewalls, each with varying characteristics, all firewalls share some basic functions. For one, all firewalls filter traffic based on a set of configured rules. Generally, these rules are based on information contained in the data packets that are traveling across the network. In particular, the header information contained in those data packets provides the firewall with the information it needs to properly apply the rules. These rules are generally defined by a company's security policies and business requirements.

Although it is possible to configure a firewall to permit all traffic and only block specific traffic based on rules, virtually all firewalls work according to the deny-all permit-specific philosophy. This means that the firewall will, by default, deny all traffic, so any traffic permitted to traverse the firewall must be explicitly configured in the firewall's rules.

TAKE NOTE *

Don't get too hung up on the definitions of firewall types. Instead, seek to understand the functionality of each type. What you call different types of firewalls is not as important as knowing how these firewalls function.

There are a variety of firewall types, and depending on who is doing the defining, you may even find that different people define firewall types in different ways. The key is to understand the basics, because outside of passing the certification test, you will generally not be called upon to identify firewall types in your day-to-day duties.

LOOKING AT PACKET FILTERING

The first type of firewall is known as a packet filtering firewall. This type of firewall is considered first generation because the earliest firewalls functioned as packet filters. As discussed, the primary purpose of a firewall is to filter traffic. Accordingly, and as its name suggests, a packet filtering firewall inspects the data packets that attempt to traverse it, and based on the rules that have been defined on the firewall, it allows or denies each packet as appropriate.

One of the very first versions of this type of firewall was the packet filtering router. Routers have the ability to do some rudimentary packet filtering, such as permitting all outbound traffic while denying all inbound traffic, or blocking specific protocols from passing through the router, such as telnet or ftp.

Different from routers, firewalls improve packet filtering by increasing granular control. For example, you might configure a packet filtering firewall to block web browsing from the Internet except to your company's website, while at the same time permitting outbound web traffic from your internal network to the Internet. Or you could set up a rule that drops any ping requests unless they originate from a network team member's workstation.

When you are configuring a packet filtering firewall rule, you will generally use one or more of the following TCP/IP attributes:

- Source IP addresses
- Destination IP addresses
- IP protocol (telnet, ftp, http, https, etc.)
- Source TCP and UDP ports (e.g., the http protocol runs on TCP port 80)
- Destination TCP and UDP ports
- The inbound firewall network interface
- The outbound firewall network interface

Some of the more common protocols and ports you will encounter in a production network include the following:

- FTP (file transfer)   20/tcp and 21/tcp
- Telnet (terminal login)   23/tcp
- DNS   53/udp and 53/tcp
- HTTP (web)   80/tcp
- HTTPS (web)   443/tcp
- SMTP (email)   25/tcp
- POP3 (email)   110/tcp
- IMAP3 (email)   220/tcp
- IMAP4 (email)   143/tcp
- LDAP (directory services)   389/tcp
- SQL server   1433/tcp
- RDP (terminal services)   3389/tcp

This is not a comprehensive list, as there are thousands of different protocols and ports, but these are the most common protocols you will see when configuring rules on a packet filtering firewall. For a comprehensive list of protocols and ports, visit http://www.iana.org/assignments/port-numbers.

LOOKING AT CIRCUIT-LEVEL FIREWALLS

Circuit-level firewalls are typically considered second-generation firewall technology. They work in a similar fashion to packet-filtering firewalls, but they operate at the transport and session layers of the OSI model.

Instead of analyzing each individual packet, a circuit-level firewall monitors TCP/IP sessions by monitoring the TCP handshaking between packets to validate the session. Traffic is filtered based on specified session rules and may be restricted to authorized computers only. When the session is established, the firewall maintains a table of valid connections and lets data pass through when session information matches an entry in the table. When the session is terminated, the table entry is removed and the circuit is closed. One unique feature of circuit-level firewalls is that sessions that cross this type of firewall appear to originate from that firewall. This allows the internal network to be hidden from the public network.

A circuit-level firewall is also known as a transparent proxy, because (as mentioned) all sessions appear to originate from the firewall. Circuit-level firewalls are almost always used in conjunction with other types of firewalls, as they are only able to permit sessions from authorized computers. Additional granularity is typically required in most production environments.

LOOKING AT APPLICATION-LEVEL FIREWALLS

Application-level firewalls (also known as proxy servers) work by performing a deep inspection of application data as it traverses the firewall. Rules are set by analyzing client requests and application responses, then enforcing correct application behavior. Application-level firewalls can block malicious activity, log user activity, provide content filtering, and even protect against spam and viruses. Microsoft Internet Security and Acceleration Server is an example of an application-level firewall.

Now for the downside—deep inspection of application data is a resource-intensive activity, and significant processing power may be required to reduce the chances that the firewall will negatively impact network performance. The deeper the inspection, the higher the resource requirements and the higher the possibility of a detrimental effect on network performance. Thus, when you deploy an application-level firewall, it is important that you size it appropriately. Cutting corners on processors and RAM on your application-level firewall is an excellent formula for creating unhappy users, and it is always a better idea to go a little more powerful than your immediate needs. Remember to always plan for growth. Network utilization seldom decreases over time. You usually don't want to go back to management in a year to fund an upgrade.

One capability available on some application-level firewalls that can offset the negative performance effects of deep inspection is the addition of caching. Caching allows the firewall to store commonly downloaded data and provide it in response to requests from a user rather than having to retrieve the data from the Internet. Most web browsers have this capability for local storage of commonly used pages; a caching firewall extends this capability to all users on the network. For example, if fifty employees all read the front page of the online version of the *Wall Street Journal* when they come into the office, the firewall will cache the first visit to the site, then serve the stored page to the next forty-nine visitors.

Caching was a much more effective technology during the early days of the Internet, when most of the content was static. In recent years, with the advent of customizable views, mashups, and interactive content, the effectiveness of caching has become more and more limited.

LOOKING AT STATEFUL MULTILEVEL FIREWALLS

Stateful multilevel firewalls are designed to provide the best features of both packet filtering and application-level firewalls. This type of firewall provides network-level packet filtering and is also capable of recognizing and processing application-level data. When configured correctly, these firewalls can provide the highest level of security of all the firewall types discussed here; however, they are typically the most expensive firewalls. In addition, with all of their available features, they can also be very complex to configure and maintain.

USING UNIFIED THREAT MANAGEMENT AND SECURE CONTENT MANAGEMENT DEVICES

To make your network the most secure, you need to implement a comprehensive solution that goes beyond the normal firewall. Unified Threat Management (UTM) consists of multiple security function including a comprehensive firewall, intrusion prevention, antivirus gateway, antispam filtering, content filtering, and reporting. You should also have a redundant solution that includes load balancing to protect yourself if a device fails. You could even combine an enterprise level firewall with a *Secure Content Management (SCM)* appliance. An SCM appliance specializes in content and threat analysis by integrating different functions and features including antivirus, anti-spam, and content filtering.

Using Hardware Firewalls versus Software Firewalls

Before we can consider when it's appropriate to utilize a hardware firewall instead of a software firewall, we need to look at what is meant by the term "software firewall." There are two basic types of software firewall:

- *Host firewall:* This type of software firewall is installed on a host and used to protect the host from network-based attacks. One example of this type of application is the Windows firewall included with recent versions of Microsoft operating systems. Host firewalls are also known as *personal firewalls*.

- *Network firewall:* This category of software firewall consists of applications that are installed on servers used to protect network segments from other network segments. These types of firewalls offer similar functionality to hardware firewalls. The most popular network firewalls are those produced by Cisco.

The one circumstance in which it clearly doesn't make sense to use a hardware firewall is to protect a single host. If you need to protect only a single host, the best solution is to install a software firewall on the host with a specific set of rules based on what you're trying to protect. If the host is part of a larger network, which is almost always the case, then any network firewalls deployed on the network will also protect the host.

Host firewalls aside, there are a variety of factors that will impact your decision of whether to use a hardware solution or a software solution to protect your network. Many of these factors are related to some of the challenges associated with software firewalls. They include the following:

- **Host hardware:** Software firewalls run on the server's general-purpose hardware. This can lead to bottlenecks (including processor, memory, or network bottlenecks), especially if the hardware isn't sized appropriately to address the traffic requirements associated with running a firewall application.

- **Host operating system:** Although both hardware and software firewalls run operating systems, a hardware firewall runs a hardened operating system, providing a smaller attack surface than an unhardened operating system. In order to match the security level of the hardened OS provided by a hardware firewall, a software firewall server needs to be similarly hardened. This can require specialized expertise and additional investments in both time and resources. As a result, most software firewalls have larger attack surfaces than their hardware counterparts.

- **Other applications:** Software firewalls must compete for resources with any other processes running on the host. In contrast, a hardware firewall has dedicated hardware resources that are not shared with any other service. As a result, when using a software firewall, you may find that you need additional hardware to match the performance of a hardware firewall because of the added resource requirements.

- **Availability/stability:** One potential issue associated with using a software firewall is that its reliability is tied to the reliability of the underlying operating system and associated hardware. Although the hardware components in a host will generally be as reliable as the components found in a hardware firewall, they are not always available in a redundant configuration, as hardware firewalls are. Operating systems have come a long way in terms of stability, but a general-purpose operating system such as what you would use with a software firewall is typically not as stable as the hardened operating system used on a hardware firewall.

Despite all the potential challenges associated with software firewalls, there are still a couple of compelling reasons to use software firewalls. First, they are very cost effective. Second, they are generally less complex to install and support than their hardware counterparts.

Therefore, in a medium to large network environment in which performance, availability, and reliability are critical, a hardware firewall is the best solution. Indeed, you will find hardware firewalls in virtually every enterprise network. In contrast, if you have a small network, are trying to keep costs down, or are trying to secure a single host, then using a software firewall may be the right answer.

Using Stateful versus Stateless Inspection

As previously discussed, the most basic firewall systems work by filtering packets. A packet filtering firewall inspects data packets as they attempt to traverse it and, based on the rules that have been defined on the firewall, either allows or denies each packet. The firewall doesn't consider any other information related to the packets when determining which packets are permitted to cross the firewall and which aren't. This type of data packet inspection is known as stateless inspection.

In stateless inspection, the data traversing the firewall are examined for information such as the following:

- The IP address of the sending device
- The IP address of the receiving device
- The type of packet (TCP, UDP, etc.)
- The port number

Stateful inspection takes packet filtering to the next level. In addition to examining the header information of the packets traversing the firewall, a stateful inspection firewall considers other factors when determining whether traffic should be permitted across the firewall. Stateful inspection also determines whether a packet is part of an existing session, and that information can be used to decide whether to permit or deny a packet. The existing session is referred to as the state, which frequently occurs at layer 4 (the transport layer) of the OSI model. Many of today's stateful inspection firewalls can also track communications across layers 5 through 7 as well.

Stateful inspection may sound relatively easy, but it's actually a very complex process, which is why stateful inspection firewalls are typically more expensive and more challenging to configure. A stateful inspection firewall keeps track of all current sessions in a state table stored in memory. In other words, when you initiate a connection to the MSN website to check today's headlines, the firewall stores the information regarding your session in a table. The same is done for every other connection occurring across the firewall. Then, as each packet reaches the firewall, it is analyzed to determine whether it is part of an existing session (state). If it is, and if the session is permitted based on the current firewall rules, then the packet is passed. In contrast, if the packet is not part of an existing session and is not being used to initiate a permitted session, it is dropped.

Another benefit of stateful inspection is that once a session is established, the firewall manages access based on sessions rather than on packets. This permits a simpler set of firewall rules when compared to traditional packet filtering firewalls. A packet filtering firewall requires a rule for each authorized packet. Therefore, if you want to permit a connection between Host A and Host B across a packet filtering firewall, you need a rule that permits packets from Host A to Host B, as well as another rule that permits packets from Host B to Host A. In comparison, when using a stateful inspection firewall, you can define a rule permitting a connection from Host A to Host B, and then the firewall's state table management will automatically allow the return traffic.

Stateful inspection firewalls make excellent perimeter firewalls for protecting an internal network from the Internet, for protecting DMZ-based hosts (discussed in more detail later in this lesson) from the Internet, and for protecting extranets from connections to customers, vendors, or business partners.

■ Controlling Access with Network Access Protection (NAP)

THE BOTTOM LINE

One of the problems that many security programs struggle with is how to ensure that the computers attached to the network are compliant with the organization's security policies. Companies want to be sure that computers that are fully patched, are running up-to-date antivirus software, and belong to the organization before they are allowed to connect to the network. The challenge is finding a mechanism that permits the network to check each system before it connects. As the solution to this problem, Microsoft has developed Network Access Protection as part of Windows Server 2008.

CERTIFICATION READY
How can you make sure that all computers on your network have an up-to-date antivirus package and current security patches from Microsoft?
3.2

Recognizing the need for administrators to have more granular control over what systems connect to a network, Microsoft introduced *Network Access Protection (NAP)* as part of the Windows Server 2008 operating system. NAP is a solution that allows administrators a more powerful way to control access to network resources. NAP's controls are based on the client computer's identity and whether that computer complies with the configured network governance policies.

NAP is a complex set of controls, a full discussion of which could easily fill this entire lesson or even this entire book. Therefore, for the purposes of this section, we will only be examining NAP at a high level, discussing its purpose, components, and requirements.

Understanding the Purpose of NAP

NAP allows network administrators to define highly granular levels of network access based on who a client is, which groups the client belongs to, and how compliant the client is based on NAP policy. If a client is not compliant, NAP provides a mechanism to automatically bring the client into compliance. Then, once the client is compliant and all issues have been corrected, NAP will dynamically increase the client's level of network access.

NAP has three distinct components:

- **Health state validation:** In order for NAP to validate the health state of a computer, the administrator must first define health requirement policies. Then, when the computer tries to connect to the network, system health agents (SHAs) and system health validators (SHVs) validate the computer's configuration against the health requirement policy. In addition to defining health requirement policies, administrators must also define what action to take if a computer is not compliant. NAP can be configured to monitor only; here, the results of the system health check are logged for later analysis. If NAP is configured for limited access, computers that do not comply with health requirement policies will have their access limited to a restricted network. Generally, this would involve access to a remediation server so that the computer's issues can be corrected. In contrast, computers that comply with the health requirement policies will be granted unlimited network access.

TAKE NOTE*

If you are going to deploy NAP in your environment, be sure to spend some time running in monitor-only mode. This will allow you to get a better understanding of the impact of the limited access policy if/when you implement it. Although security is important, it's a good idea to roll out new security capabilities with as little user impact as possible.

- **Health policy compliance:** Administrators can enforce compliance with health requirement policies by configuring NAP to automatically update noncompliant computers with missing software updates or configuration changes. It is important to understand that these compliance changes are performed using configuration management software, not NAP natively. When NAP is configured for monitoring only, noncompliant computers have access to the network so that they can be updated with required updates or configuration changes. In comparison, when NAP is configured in limited access mode, noncompliant computers have limited access until the required updates and configuration changes are completed. In this case, the resources required to update the system should be included in the parts of the network the computer can access. Whether NAP is configured for monitoring or limited access, any NAP-compatible computers can be brought into compliance automatically. For computers that cannot support NAP (older versions of Windows, non-Windows operating systems, etc.), administrators can define exceptions that still allow the computers access to the network.

- **Limited access mode:** The final component that NAP provides to protect a network is limited access mode. This mode permits administrators to protect their networks by limiting the access of noncompliant computers. Noncompliant computers can be limited based on time (how long they can stay connected) or by what portions of the network they can access. If configured for limited access, it's recommended that this access include the resources needed to bring the computer into compliance. Then, after the computer is brought into compliance, NAP can open its access dynamically, without requiring a reboot or reauthentication.

Looking at How NAP Works

There are a variety of components used to make NAP work, including system health agents (SHAs) and system health validators (SHVs). SHAs run on the client computer and report the computer's status to the SHVs, which are running on the network and manage the NAP configuration.

These components provide health state tracking and compliance validation. They are the foundation of the NAP service because they allow NAP to determine what action needs to be taken based on a computer's configuration.

Client operating systems that have a Windows Security Health Validator SHA to monitor Windows Security Center settings include the following:

- Windows Vista Business
- Windows Vista Enterprise
- Windows Vista Ultimate
- Windows 7 Home Premium
- Windows 7 Professional
- Windows 7 Ultimate
- Windows XP Service Pack 3

Windows Server 2008 includes a corresponding Windows Security Health Validator SHV. Although currently leveraged largely by Microsoft, NAP is extensible and has an API that allows any vendor to provide its own SHAs and SHVs to interoperate with NAP.

The other major part of the NAP puzzle is the enforcement piece. With NAP, enforcement clients (ECs) and enforcement servers (ESs) perform this function. These components require health state validation, and if a computer is not compliant, they enforce limited network access using the Network Policy Server (NPS), which is a component in Windows Server 2008.

NPS is the RADIUS (Remote Authentication Dial-In User Service) server and proxy service in Windows Server 2008. When NPS functions as a RADIUS server, it provides authentication, authorization, and accounting (AAA) services for network access. When used for authentication and authorization, NPS interacts with the Active Directory to verify user or computer credentials, as well as to obtain user or computer account properties when a computer attempts an 802.1x-authenticated connection or a VPN connection.

NPS also acts as a NAP health policy server. In particular, administrators define system health requirements in the form of health policies on the NPS server, and the server then evaluates health state information provided by NAP clients to determine whether the clients comply. When a client is determined to be out of compliance, the NPS server offers the set of remediation actions that must be carried out by the NAP client to become compliant.

The role of NPS as an AAA server is independent from its role as a NAP health policy server. These roles can be used separately or combined as needed.

NPS also allows the Windows Server 2008 host to act as the health policy server, enforcing limited access in the following ways:

- **IPsec enforcement:** IPsec enforcement requires that the connecting client be configured to run IPsec before it can connect to other hosts. This is the most stringent of the various limited access mechanisms, because the client computer cannot communicate with anything until it is configured for IPsec communications. IPsec enforcement allows you to enforce anything the Windows IPsec client can be configured for. You can require IPsec communications with other compliant computers on a per-IP address or per-port number basis. This is a highly secure configuration due to the fact that IPsec encrypts all data traversing the network. In fact, you'll rarely see this configuration of NAP unless you're working in a high-security network environment that encrypts all network traffic.

- **802.1x enforcement:** 802.1x enforcement requires that the connecting client be compliant to obtain full access through an 802.1x-authenticated network connection. Here, the client must not only be able to successfully authenticate using 802.1x—it must also comply with the active health policy. The health policy is enforced every time the client attempts to connect to the network and authenticate with 802.1x. For noncompliant computers, network access is limited through a restricted access profile placed on the network device. The restricted profile can specify packet filters or force the computer to join a restricted VLAN. It's important to remember that 802.1x enforcement will also actively monitor the health status of the connected client, and if the client becomes noncompliant, it will apply the restricted access profile to the connection.

TAKE NOTE*

802.1x is an authentication protocol used to secure LANs from client connections. 802.1x authentication involves three parties: a client (also known as the supplicant), a network device (also known as the authenticator), and an authentication server. When the client wants to connect to the network, it makes a request to the network device. The network device then forwards that request to the authentication server using RADIUS. The authentication server next determines whether the client device is permitted on the network. If it's permitted, then the network device allows it to connect.

- **VPN enforcement:** VPN enforcement requires that a computer be compliant in order to obtain unlimited network access through a remote access VPN connection. This can be a huge benefit for organizations with large numbers of remote employees. One of the major challenges facing a company with many remote users is ensuring that these users' computers remain fully patched, are running up-to-date antivirus software, and are securely configured. NAP solves this issue with VPN enforcement. Noncompliant computers receive network access that is restricted by IP packet filters applied by the

VPN server. As with 802.1x enforcement, VPN enforcement enforces health policy requirements every time a computer attempts to use a remote access VPN connection to connect to the network. VPN enforcement also actively monitors the health status of the connected client, and if the client becomes noncompliant, it will apply the restricted access profile to the connection.

- **DHCP enforcement:** DHCP enforcement requires that a computer be compliant with the health policy in order to obtain an unlimited-access IPv4 address configuration from a DHCP server. For noncompliant computers, network access is limited by an IPv4 address configuration that allows access to only a restricted network. DHCP enforcement enforces health policy requirements every time a DHCP client attempts to lease or renew an IP address configuration. As with the other modes of limited access, DHCP enforcement also actively monitors the health status of the NAP client and renews the IPv4 address configuration for access only to the restricted network if the client becomes noncompliant.

The last major element of your NAP installation is the remediation servers. These servers, which are not a formal component of NAP (there are no acronyms associated with the remediation servers), consist of the servers, services, or other resources that a noncompliant computer can use to become compliant. Of course, in order for a noncompliant computer to use remediation servers, these servers must be available as part of the limited access granted to the computer.

A remediation server might contain the latest software updates and virus signatures, could be a web server for requesting 802.1x credentials, or might even be a web server with instructions on how to configure IPsec to connect to the network. The makeup of your remediation servers is specific to your environment and your health policy. An SHA can communicate with a remediation server directly, or it can instead use installed client software to remediate issues.

Examining the Requirements for NAP

As previously mentioned, a number of different Microsoft operating systems support NAP, including the following:

- Windows Server 2008 or Windows Server 2008 R2
- Windows Vista Business
- Windows Vista Enterprise
- Windows Vista Ultimate
- Windows 7 Home Premium
- Windows 7 Professional
- Windows 7 Ultimate
- Windows XP Service Pack 3

However, there are a number of additional components you may need in order to successfully implement NAP. These include:

- Active Directory Domain Controller
- Active Directory-based Certificate Authority
- System Health Agents
- System Health Validators
- RADIUS server
- Enforcement clients
- Enforcement servers

- Network Policy Server
- 802.1x network devices
- VPN server
- DHCP server
- Remediation server

Not every NAP implementation will require all these components, but you should be aware that you might need them depending on why and how you are deploying NAP in your organization.

■ Using Isolation to Protect a Network

THE BOTTOM LINE

In addition to protecting the perimeter, you can use a number of other techniques to guard the computing resources on your internal network. These technologies allow you to isolate portions of your network, provide a special use for your firewalls, or even supplement the security provided by your firewalls. VLANs and routing are network technologies that can help you segregate your network into security zones. You can deploy technologies like Honeypots to help distract attackers from the important portions of your network, and firewalls can also play a part if you need to create DMZs on your network. VPNs, NAT, server isolation, and domain isolation are some additional concepts you can use to secure your network.

CERTIFICATION READY
What would you use to isolate your subnet with all of your servers from the rest of the network?
3.3

Understanding Virtual LANs

Before we can discuss what a virtual LAN is, we need to quickly review the concept of Local Area Networks (LANs). A LAN is a network of hosts covering a small physical area, like an office, a floor in a building, or a small group of buildings. LANs are used to connect multiple hosts. These LANs are then connected to other LANs using a router, which (as discussed) is a layer 3 device.

One of the challenges associated with LANs as they grow larger is that each device on the LAN broadcasts traffic onto the LAN. Although these broadcasts will not cross a router, if there are enough hosts, the aggregate broadcast traffic can saturate a network. One solution is to deploy more routers as a way to divide the network into more manageable segments. However, routers add latency to network traffic, and they require a routing protocol (discussed in the next section) for traffic to find its way from one part of the network to another.

Accordingly, virtual LANs (VLANs) were developed as an alternate solution to deploying multiple routers. VLANs are logical network segments used to create separate broadcast domains, but they still allow the devices on the VLAN to communicate at layer 2 without requiring a router. VLANs are created by switches, and traffic between VLANs is switched not routed, which creates a much faster network connection because there is no need for involvement of a routing protocol. Even though the hosts are logically separated, the traffic between these hosts is switched directly as if the hosts were on the same LAN segment.

VLANs provide a number of benefits over routed networks, including the following:

- Higher performance on medium or large LANs due to reduced broadcast traffic
- Better organization of devices on the network for easier management
- Additional security because devices can be put on their own VLAN

There are several different ways to assign hosts to VLANs. These methods are as follows:

- **VLAN membership by port:** Because the ports on a switch are defined as belonging to a specific VLAN, any device that is plugged into a port is assigned to the corresponding VLAN. For example, a thirty-two port switch might have ports 1–4 assigned to VLAN1, ports 5–16 assigned to VLAN2, and ports 17–32 assigned to VLAN3. Although this seems like a straightforward method for organizing ports, it can be problematic if you work in an environment in which users change office locations frequently. For example, if you've assigned the ports in one section of cubicles to the sales department and two weeks later, management decides to move the department to the other side of the building, you will need to reconfigure the switch to support this move. However, in a relatively static environment, this model works well.

- **VLAN membership by MAC address:** With this model, membership in a VLAN is based on the MAC address of the host. When the VLAN is set up on the switch, the hosts are assigned based on their MAC address. Thus, when a workstation moves to another location and connects to a different switch port, the switch automatically assigns the host to the appropriate VLAN based on the workstation's MAC address. Because the MAC address is generally hard coded into the host's NIC, this model is generally more usable in an environment in which hosts move. One downside to this model is that it requires more initial work to set up because you need to get all the MAC addresses from the hosts and associate them with the appropriate VLANs.

- **Membership by IP subnet address:** In this type of VLAN association, membership is based on the layer 3 header. The switch reads the layer 3 IP address and associates the address range with the appropriate VLAN. Even though the switch accesses layer 3 information in the header, the VLAN assignment is still done at layer 2 of OSI model and no routing takes place. This model is also conducive to environments in which there are frequent user moves. Performance may be affected because the switch needs to read the layer 3 header to determine which VLAN to assign the host to. This is generally not an issue with today's switch technologies, but it is good to be aware of the additional overhead associated with this model.

- **Membership by protocol:** VLANs can also be organized based on protocol. This was a useful solution when many LANs ran multiple network protocols, but with the current dominance of TCP/IP in virtually every network, this model is almost never used anymore.

The next question to think about is: How do VLANs help with security? In short, there are two basic ways to leverage a VLAN in support of security.

First, because a VLAN is logical separation, traffic on one VLAN is not directly accessible to hosts on another VLAN. However, this is of minimal use as there are now techniques called VLAN hopping that can provide access to traffic on other VLANs.

The second use for VLANs from a security perspective is that they allow you to better organize your hosts for assigning access permissions. This technique is used in conjunction with firewalls or access control lists. For example, if you have a section of your building that your administrators sit in, you can create a VLAN for that area and give it access through your firewalls so that these employees can access all sections of the network. Meanwhile, the sales department might be on a VLAN that has its access restricted to the sales application servers, with access to the HR and finance applications blocked.

Understanding Routing

Routing takes place one step up the OSI model from a VLAN—in other words, at layer 3. Recall that routing is the process of forwarding a packet based on the packet's destination address. At each step in the packet's route across the network, a decision must be made about where to forward the packet. To make these decisions, the IP layer consults a routing table stored in the memory of the routing device. Routing table entries are created by default when TCP/IP initializes, and additional entries are added either manually by a system administrator or automatically through communication with routers.

But what exactly is a router? Previously, we defined routing as the process of forwarding a packet based on the packet's destination address. Thus, in its simplest form, a router is any device that forwards packets from one interface to another. This is a very simple description for a very complex process.

Routers come in two basic types—software and hardware. A software router is a computer running an operating system and multiple services, including a routing service. For example, Windows Server 2008 supports routing. Some benefits of using a software router are as follows:

- **Tight integration with the OS:** The routing service is frequently integrated with the operating system and other services.
- **Consistent/easier user interface:** No retraining is required on a new interface/operating system—the routing functions are configured through the standard user interface.
- **Low cost:** If you are adding routing to an existing server, you do not have to pay for dedicated hardware. This reduces the overall cost, although if you were to dedicate a software router for routing only, any cost savings would be negligible.
- **Flexibility:** Software routers allow you to configure and run multiple services on a single platform.

When would you use a software router? Typically, you will find software routers in small offices that are looking for an inexpensive, easy-to-manage solution. Another circumstance in which you might use a software router is between two LAN segments where traffic requirements are expected to be low. An example of this might be a lab segment where you want to isolate the lab hosts but do not want to invest in a dedicated hardware router.

Although there are benefits to using software routers, there are also some pretty significant drawbacks when compared to hardware routers. These include the following:

- **Slow performance:** Due to the additional overhead associated with the operating system and any additional running services, software routers are typically slower than hardware routers.
- **Lower reliability:** Any software router has the potential for issues with the operating system and other running services, as well as for problems with the greater number of hardware components as compared to a hardware router. As a result, software routers are typically less reliable than hardware routers.
- **Limited scalability:** When scaling a software router to multiple high-speed interfaces, you are subject to the limitations of the computer hardware. Because most PC-based servers are not designed to route multiple high-speed network interface cards, software routers will generally not scale as easily or as large as hardware routers. Also, adding additional services like access control lists or firewall services will impact a software router's performance to a greater degree than a comparable hardware router.
- **Limited protocol support:** Software routers typically do not support anywhere near the number of routing protocols that a hardware router does. For example, Windows Server 2008 is limited to the IP routing protocol RIP, and it does not presently support any of the more advanced IP-based routing protocols like BGP4.

You now understand what a software router entails, but what about a hardware router? In short, a hardware router is a dedicated hardware device whose main function is to route packets. This description is not as accurate now as it was in years past, however, because many of today's hardware routers are multifunction devices—for instance, they may include VPN,

DHCP, firewall, caching, or perhaps even intrusion detection services. The benefits of hardware routers (as compared to software routers) include the following:

- **High performance:** Hardware routers run on custom-built, single-purpose hardware platforms, with highly optimized hardware and operating systems.
- **High reliability:** Hardware routers are typically more reliable than their software counterparts, due in large part to the limited software capabilities and dedicated hardware. A hardware router typically has higher modularity than a software router. Hardware routers can also be deployed in pairs so that one router will take over if the other fails. Although this is theoretically possible with a software router, it is very seldom done.
- **Wide routing protocol support:** Hardware routers can typically be configured to support any routing protocol from RIP to OSPF to BGP, as long as you purchase the appropriate functions. They also support a greater number of routing algorithms than software routers. In a larger network environment, this can be critical.

As with anything, hardware routers have their drawbacks, including the following:

- **High cost:** Typically, hardware routers are dedicated platforms, which usually makes them more expensive than software routers that also provide other services. This line is blurring as additional features become available on hardware routers. That being said, a small router can be relatively inexpensive.
- **Lower user friendliness:** Hardware routers are typically configured using a Secure Shell (SSH) connection and are managed through a command-line interface. Although there are graphical tools for managing routers, a lot of router configuration is still done through the command line using an extremely complex list of commands. Thus, an experienced router support engineer can configure or troubleshoot a hardware router without too much difficulty, but for someone new to routers, there is a steep learning curve.
- **Greater complexity:** Although an individual hardware router may not actually be much more complex than its software-based counterpart, as you scale to large networks, a hardware router environment can rapidly become extremely complicated. This issue would also apply to software routers, but software routers are not as common in the real world. In most network environments, hardware routers are used almost exclusively, and software routers are reserved for only the smallest networks or locations.

EXAMINING HOW ROUTING WORKS

When a router receives a packet that must be forwarded to a destination host, the router has to make a decision. In particular, it needs to determine whether it can deliver the packet directly to the destination host, or whether it needs to forward the packet to another router. To make this decision, the router examines the destination network address. If the router has an interface that is connected to the same network as the destination host, it can deliver the packet directly. Where it gets interesting is when the router is not connected to the same network as the destination host—here, the router must determine the best route to the destination host so it can forward the packet correctly.

When a router needs to forward a packet to another router, it uses the information in its routing tables to choose the best path for the packet. Which router to forward the packet to is determined by a number of variables pertaining to the network path to the destination host, including the number of hops, the cost of each hop, and so on. This database is stored in the router's memory to ensure the lookup process is performed very quickly.

TAKE NOTE *

Just because there is a route to a destination doesn't mean there is also a route back. Although this is not a common problem in networks with dynamic routing enabled, it can occur, particularly if you are working in a heavily firewalled network environment.

As the packet travels across the network toward its destination, each router along the way makes a decision about where to forward the packet by consulting its routing table. Moreover, when the destination host sends a reply packet, it is possible that this packet may not travel back to the original sender via the same route. The route taken by the reply packet depends on the metrics of each path along the return route. In other words, the way to the destination host may not be the best path back to the sending host.

The information in a routing table can be generated in one of two ways. The first method is to manually configure the routing table with the routes for each destination network. This is known as static routing. Static routing is more suited to small environments in which the amount of information to configure is small and the overhead of dynamic routing is unacceptable. Static routers do not scale well to large or frequently changing networks because of the requirement for manual administration.

The second method for generating routing table information is to make use of a dynamic routing protocol. Because dynamic routing protocols are quite a bit more complex than static routing, we need to take a more in-depth look at this subject.

A general definition of "protocol" is an agreed-upon method for exchanging data between two devices. Accordingly, a routing protocol defines the method for exchanging routing information between two routing devices—and a dynamic routing protocol involves the exchange of routing information that is automatically built and maintained in a routing table. In other words, when you are using a dynamic routing protocol, routing information is exchanged between routers and used to update the information stored in each device's routing table. This can be done either periodically (at scheduled intervals) or on demand. If set up correctly at the outset, dynamic routers require little administration, outside of ensuring that software updates are applied in a timely fashion. Because they learn routing information dynamically and have the ability to route around failures when the network architecture supports it, dynamic routers are generally used in large network environments in which static routing would be impractical.

TAKE NOTE*

Don't forget: Routers need to be patched, too! Because they run an operating system, routers have security and functionality updates that must be applied.

LOOKING AT ROUTING PROTOCOLS

Routing protocols are based either on a distance vector or a link state algorithm. The differences between the two methods relate to when routing information is exchanged, what information is sent during this exchange, and how quickly the protocol can route around outages when the network topology supports it. Path selection involves apply a routing metric to multiple routes in order to select the best route. Some of the metrics used are bandwidth, network delay, hop count, path cost, load, reliability, and communication costs. (The hop count is the number of routers traversed by a packet between its source and destination.)

Distance vector-based routing protocols require that each router inform its neighbors of its routing table. This is done by sending the entire routing table when the router boots, and then sending it again at scheduled intervals. Each router takes the updates from its neighboring routers and then updates its own routing table based on this information. Using the information from these updates, a router can build a network map in its routing table, and it can then use this map to determine hop counts for each network entry in the routing table. RIP is one example of a distance vector-based routing protocol that is supported by Windows Server 2008.

Routing updates sent using a distance vector-based routing protocol are unacknowledged and unsynchronized, which is one of the drawbacks of these protocols. Some other drawbacks of this type of routing protocol include the following:

• **High overhead:** Because every router on the network sends its entire routing table when it sends an update, distance vector-based protocols produce very large routing tables. This adds overhead to the router memory needed to store the tables, as well as the router processing power needed to maintain these tables. Large routing tables can also hamper an administrator trying to determine the source of an issue when problems arise.

- **Lack of scalability:** Distance vector-based networks are limited to 15 hops (router traversals) for any given route. In a large network (like the Internet), it is very easy to have network segments that are greater than 15 hops away—and such segments would be unreachable in a distance vector-based network.

- **Intensive bandwith utilization:** Distance vector-based protocols require that routers exchange their entire routing table whenever they are updated. On a large network with large routing tables, these updates can utilize significant amounts of bandwidth, especially across smaller WAN connections or demand dial links.

- **Long convergence time:** Convergence is the amount of time it takes for a routing algorithm to detect and route around a network failure. Distance vector-based protocols typically have longer convergence times than link state-based protocols (described later in the lesson).

- **Routing loop issues:** Distance vector-based protocols can also suffer from routing loop issues when there are multiple paths to a network. A routing loop is when a packet is sent back and forth between two networks or across multiple networks where the packet is eventually sent back to the network that sent it. Since it is a loop, the packet never gets to its destination. If one or more mechanisms are not in place to deal with routing loop issues and packets that are caught in a routing loop are not dropped, your network would eventually be congested as it deals with the lost packets.

- **Count to infinity issues:** Count to infinity issues occur when there is a network outage and the routing algorithm cannot calculate a new router. Here, one router will broadcast a route and increment the hop count for the router, then a second router will broadcast the same route to the first router, also incrementing the hop count, and so on, until the route metric (hop count) reaches 16 and the route is discarded.

Thankfully, some distance vector-based routing protocols have additional mechanisms that allow them to avoid count to infinity issues, as well as to improve convergence. These mechanisms are as follows:

- **Split horizon:** The split horizon mechanism prevents routes from being broadcast out the interface they were received from. Split horizon eliminates count to infinity and routing loops during convergence in single-path internetworks and reduces the chances of count to infinity in multipath internetworks.

- **Split horizon with poison reverse:** The split horizon with poison reverse mechanism allows routes to be broadcast back to the interface they were received from, but they are announced with a hop count of 16, which indicates that the network is unreachable (in other words, the route has been poisoned and is unusable through that interface).

- **Triggered updates:** Triggered updates allow a router to announce changes in metric values almost immediately, rather than waiting for the next periodic announcement. The trigger is a change to a metric in an entry in the routing table. For example, networks that become unavailable can be announced with a hop count of 16 through a triggered update. If triggered updates were sent by all routers immediately, each triggered update could cause a cascade of broadcast traffic across the IP internetwork.

The advantages of distance-vector routing are that it requires little maintenance and is easy to configure, making it popular in small network environments.

Link state routing—the second type of routing protocol—was designed to overcome the disadvantages of distance vector routing. Routers that use link state routing protocols learn about their network environment by "meeting" their neighboring routers. This is done through a "hello" packet, which tells the neighboring router what networks the first router can reach. Once this introduction is complete, the neighboring router will send the new network information to each of its neighboring routers using a link state advertisement. Open Shortest Path First (OSPF) is an example of a link state routing protocol. The neighboring routers copy the contents of the packet and forward the link state advertisement to each attached network, except for the network the link state advertisement was received on. This is known as flooding.

A router that uses a link state routing protocol builds a tree, or map, of shortest paths using itself as the root. This tree is based on all the link state advertisements seen, and it contains the route to each destination in the network. Once this tree is built, routing information is sent only when changes to the network occur, instead of periodically as with distance vector-based protocols.

There are a number of advantages to the link state method, especially when compared to distance vector-based routing protocols. Some advantages include the following:

- **Smaller routing tables:** Because the router only maintains a table of link states, rather than a copy of every route on the network, it is able to maintain much smaller routing tables.
- **High scalability:** Link state protocols do not suffer from the 16-hop issue that distance vector-based protocols do, so they are able to scale to much larger networks.
- **More efficient use of network bandwidth:** Because link state information is not exchanged after the network has converged, routing updates do not consume precious bandwidth unless there is an outage that forces the network to reconverge.
- **Faster convergence:** Link state routing protocols converge faster than distance vector-based protocols because updates are sent as soon as a change to the network occurs, instead of having to wait for the periodic updates used in distance vector-based protocols.

One disadvantage of link state protocols is that they are more complex to understand and configure than distance vector protocols. They also require additional processing power on the router, due to the need to calculate the routing tree.

Routing can be a key component of network security because it lets you determine which parts of a network can be accessed by other parts of the network. For example, if you have a business partner connection to a third-party network, the third-party network will need to have routing information in order to access any systems that you have put on your extranet DMZ. Although a firewall is the best way to secure this connection, you can add an additional layer of security by restricting the routing available to the third party. In other words, if you only tell the third party's network the routes to the extranet, it will not be able to send packets to any other parts of your network where it should not have access.

Looking at Intrusion Detection and Intrusion Prevention Systems

Two other technologies available to secure networks are *intrusion detection systems (IDSs)* and *intrusion prevention systems (IPSs)*. An IDS is a solution designed to detect unauthorized user activities, attacks, and network compromises. An intrusion prevention system (IPS) is similar to an IDS, except that in addition to detecting and alerting, an IPS can also take action to prevent a breach from occurring.

There are two main types of IDS/IPSs:

- **Network based:** A network-based IDS (NIDS) monitors network traffic using sensors that are located at key locations within the network, often in the demilitarized zone (DMZ) or at network borders. These sensors capture all network traffic and analyze the contents of individual packets for malicious traffic. A NIDS accesses network traffic by connecting to a hub, network switch configured for port mirroring, or network tap.
- **Host based:** A host-based IDS (HIDS) generally has a software agent that acts as the sensor. This agent monitors all activity of the host on which it is installed, including monitoring the file system, logs, and kernel to identify and report suspicious behavior. A HIDS is typically deployed to safeguard the host on which it is installed.

There are two common deployment methodologies used when placing an IDS/IPS to protect a network from the Internet. Each has its own advantages and disadvantages:

- **Unfiltered:** An unfiltered IDS/IPS installation examines the raw Internet data stream before it crosses the firewall. This provides the highest amount of visibility for detecting attacks, but it also means that there is a significantly larger volume of data to be monitored and a higher possibility of false positives. There is also a chance that during periods of high traffic, the IDS/IPS might not be able to process all the packets, so attacks may be missed.

- **Screened:** A screened IDS/IPS solution monitors only that traffic that gets through the screening firewall. The advantage to this model is it dramatically reduces the amount of information that needs to be monitored, thereby also reducing the chances of false positives and lost packets during high traffic volumes. However, there is a loss of visibility with this model because you cannot see attacks on the screening firewall.

TAKE NOTE *

Historically, IDSs and IPSs have been used to secure Internet connections, because these connections typically present the largest threat to a network. However, with the interconnectivity of networks beyond the Internet and the threat of insider attacks, it may make sense to deploy an IDS or IPS in strategic locations on your internal network. You should especially consider doing so if your internal network has connections to third-party networks, such as those of customers, vendors, or business partners.

Looking at Honeypots

Honeypots, honey nets, and padded cells are complementary technologies to IDS/IPS deployments. A *honeypot* is a trap for hackers; it is designed to distract hackers from real targets, detect new vulnerabilities and exploits, and learn about the identity of attackers. A *honey net* is a collection of honeypots used to present an attacker with an even more realistic attack environment. Finally, a *padded cell* is a system that waits for an IDS to detect an attacker and then transfers the attacker to a special host where he or she cannot do any damage to the production environment. These are all related technologies, and each can be used to add an additional layer to your security infrastructure.

As previously mentioned, a honeypot is a valuable surveillance and early warning tool. However, "honeypot" is also a generic term used to describe anything that would attract an attacker. Thus, although the term usually refers to a host running special software for detecting and analyzing attacks, it can sometimes refer to other things, such as files, data records, or even unused IP address space.

There are a variety of different types of honeypots, including the following:

- **Production:** A production honeypot is a relatively easy solution to deploy. It is used to distract attackers from potentially vulnerable production systems and is relatively simple to use. Production honeypots typically capture limited information, and they can generally be found in corporate networks. This type of honeypot is typically used as an additional early warning system that enhances an IDS/IPS system.

- **Research:** A research honeypot is more complex than a production honeypot and is more difficult to deploy and maintain. This type of honeypot captures extensive information, which can then be used to develop attack signatures, identify new attack techniques and vulnerabilities, and develop a better understanding of an attacker's mindset. Research honeypots are used primarily for research by universities, the military, or other government organizations.

When deploying a honeypot, you should ensure that the associated server contains no production information and is not being used for production purposes. This ensures that your production data is secure—and, because there is no legitimate reason for traffic or activity on the system, you can safely assume that any activity that occurs on the honeypot is malicious activity.

You should be aware, however, that honeypots can create risks to your environment. Because you are essentially using a honeypot as bait for an attacker, you are actually luring attackers into your network environment. As a result, you need to be absolutely certain that all honeypots are isolated from your production environment. If they are not, an attacker may be able to jump from a honeypot to your production environment and compromise critical systems or infrastructure. It's somewhat like trying to lure a bear to an adjoining campsite to keep them away from yours—there's always a chance the bear may find your campsite anyway.

One area in which honeypots are especially useful is in the battle against spam. One challenge associated with spam and spam filtering is that the spammers are constantly changing the techniques they use to bypass spam filters. They also have a variety of techniques for harvesting email addresses from websites for inclusion in their spam target lists. As a result, the people who develop spam filters spend much of their time working to identify these techniques and to develop new filters to combat them. Honeypots are an essential component of this fight, and there are two types of honeypots that can be used to combat spam:

- **Email address honeypot:** Any email address that is dedicated to receiving spam for analysis can be considered a spam honeypot. An example of this technique is Project Honey Pot, a distributed, open-source project that uses honeypot pages installed on websites around the world in conjunction with uniquely tagged email addresses for analyzing not only spam delivery, but also email address harvesting techniques.

- **Email open relay honeypot:** Email open relays are servers whose job is to relay messages from mail server to mail server. If you have ever used POP3 or IMAP to send email through your personal ISP, you have used a mail relay server. In some instances, these servers are set up so they do not need credentials to send email, which is a significant prize for spammers because it allows them to relay millions of spam emails anonymously. Setting up a honeypot that appears to be an open relay can potentially reveal a spammer's IP address and provide bulk spam capture. This allows for in-depth analysis of the spammer's techniques, response URLs and email addresses, and other valuable information.

Although these are all extremely exciting technologies, they are deployed in very few corporate environments. Instead, these technologies are primarily used by educational institutions and security research firms. Corporate information security professionals are so busy securing their environment from attacks that they don't spend a lot of time researching attack patterns. As long as an attack doesn't succeed, these professionals are satisfied. Still, in high-security environments in which there is extensive Internet-based activity and data that requires additional layers of security, honeypots may be part of the layered security defense.

Looking at DMZs

When most people hear the term **DMZ** (short for **demilitarized zone**), images of barbed wire and machine gun emplacements come to mind. Although not entirely accurate in the scope of information security, this vision is not that far from reality. In computer networking, a DMZ is a firewall configuration used to secure hosts on a network segment. In most DMZs, the hosts on the DMZ are connected behind a firewall that is connected to a public network like the Internet. Another common configuration is to have the firewall connected to an extranet that has connections to customers, vendors, or business partners. DMZs are designed to provide access to systems without jeopardizing the internal network.

There are two typical DMZ configurations you may encounter in production environments:

- **Sandwich DMZ:** In a sandwich DMZ model (see Figure 4-3), there is both an outer firewall and an inner firewall. The outer firewall secures the DMZ network segment from the external (insecure) network. Servers that are meant to be accessed from the external network (like the Internet) have the appropriate rules configured to permit secure access. The inner firewall is then used to add an additional layer of security between the servers on the DMZ and the internal (secure) network. The main benefit of this model is that in the event that the outer firewall and/or a server on the DMZ is compromised, there is an additional layer of firewall security protecting the internal network. Ideally, the outer and inner firewalls are from different vendors in order to ensure that the same exploit cannot be used to compromise both. The major drawbacks of this model are that it is more complex to implement and maintain, it is more expensive because of the extra firewall, and if you have different firewall vendors, you'll need additional training for your staff.

Figure 4-3

Sandwich DMZ

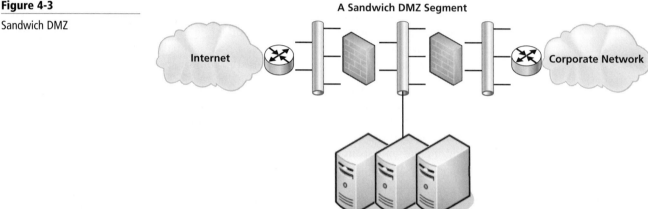

A Sandwich DMZ Segment

- **Single firewall DMZ:** In a single firewall DMZ (see Figure 4-4), the DMZ is an additional network connection from the firewall. This leaves you with an external network connection, an internal network connection, and a DMZ network connection all connected to the same firewall. Although this architecture still allows the firewall to control access to DMZ resources, if the firewall is compromised, access to the internal network may be breached. This model is less expensive than the sandwich model, but it does not provide as high a level of security.

Figure 4-4

Single firewall DMZ

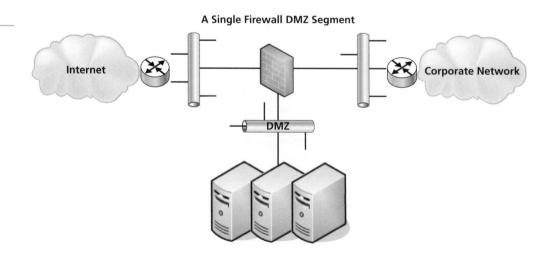

A Single Firewall DMZ Segment

Now that you understand the architecture of a DMZ, you should also understand what types of servers and services you might place on a DMZ. Some of the most common include the following:

- **Web servers:** Web servers are the most common servers found in DMZ networks. Accessed using HTTP over port 80 or HTTPS over port 443 for secure access, web servers are commonly Internet-accessible. In fact, the next time you access a web server on the Internet, you can count on the fact that it is hosted on a DMZ somewhere. Web servers add an additional layer of complexity due to the fact that many web applications need to communicate with an internal database or databases to provide some specialized services. These databases often contain sensitive information, so you should not place them on the DMZ because you do not want them to be accessed from the insecure network (the Internet). An example of this might be an e-commerce application. When you reach a seller's website, the catalog data—including product descriptions, prices, and availability—are contained in the database (sometimes referred to as the back end database). If the database server also contains critical information like Social Security numbers, financial information, or credit card data, you may want to add an application firewall between the web server and the database server. Although this increases the cost and complexity of your solution, it adds an extra layer of security to protect the database.

- **Email relay servers:** Email servers are another type of server that needs to be accessed from the Internet. In the early years of computer networking, it was not unusual for email to be restricted to an organization's corporate network. However, once companies and individuals were increasingly connected to the Internet, the ability to send and receive email from other companies became critical to business success. By placing your email relay servers, which communicate on port 25, on a DMZ, they can receive email from the Internet and then relay it securely to mail servers on the internal network. Spam filtering capabilities are frequently included on these relay servers.

- **Proxy servers:** Proxy servers are used to proxy or act as an intermediary for user requests from the internal network to the Internet, and they are usually used to retrieve website information. These servers can be placed on a DMZ to provide additional security for web browsing. Some proxy servers will filter content (including inappropriate websites), add virus protection and antispyware security, and even improve performance by caching web requests.

- **Reverse proxy servers:** Reverse proxy servers are used to provide secure access to internal applications from an insecure network. Although these servers have largely been replaced by VPN technologies, they are still sometimes used to provide employees access to web-based email servers on the internal network, provide access to internal web applications, and in some cases, even provide secure terminal services connections to an internal network.

Understanding Network Address Translation (NAT)

Network Address Translation (NAT) is a technique used to modify the network address information of a host while traffic is traversing a router or firewall. This technique hides the network information of a private network while still permitting traffic to be transferred across a public network like the Internet.

NAT was originally created as a workaround for IP addressing issues. Recall that the Internet relies on the TCP/IP protocol suite for communications between hosts. A critical component of this protocol suite is IP addressing. In the early days of the Internet, when the TCP/IP protocol and related addressing was being developed, the 32-bit addressing scheme (known as IPv4) was considered more than adequate for any potential network growth. Technically, there were 4,294,967,296 unique addresses available using a 32-bit address, and even discounting the reserved ranges, there were still over 3 billion possible addresses. At the time, that was enough to provide an address for every person on the planet, including children. Unfortunately, the designers of this addressing scheme dramatically underestimated the explosive growth of the Internet, as well as the widespread adoption of TCP/IP in business and home networks—both of which threatened to exhaust the pool of IPv4 IP addresses. Without unique addresses, the Internet would be unable to successfully route TCP/IP traffic. NAT was the resulting solution for maintaining Internet functionality given the limited number of IP addresses available.

Today, one practical use for NAT is that it allows you to use one set of IP addresses on the internal LAN and a second set of IP addresses for the Internet connection. There is a device (usually a router or firewall) located between the two networks that provides NAT services, managing the translation of internal addresses to external addresses. This allows companies to use large numbers of unregistered internal addresses while only needing a fraction of that number of addresses on the Internet, thus conserving the addresses. This permits the reuse of addresses within private networks while ensuring that the addresses used on the Internet remain unique.

TAKE NOTE*

Network Address Translation (NAT) is supported under Windows Server 2008 by the Routing and Remote Access Service.

The long-term solution for the address issue is IPv6 or Internet Protocol Version 6, the next generation protocol for the Internet. This protocol is designed to offer several advantages over IPv4, including support for addresses that are 128 bits long. This permits 2^{128} unique IPv6 addresses, or over 340 trillion addresses. However, adoption of IPv6 has been slow, in large part due to the successful use of NAT and proxy servers to conserve the number of IPv4 addresses currently used on the Internet.

Today, there are two main types of NAT:

- **Static NAT:** Static NAT maps an unregistered IP address on the private network to a registered IP address on the public network, using a one-to-one basis. This method is used when the translated device needs to be accessible from the public network. For example, a web server on your DMZ network might have an unregistered address of 10.20.30.40 that is translated by a NAT-capable device to an Internet-facing address of 12.4.4.234. Thus, a user trying to connect to that website can enter 12.4.4.234, and the router or firewall at the other end will translate that address to 10.20.30.40 when the packet reaches it. This version of NAT is typically used in conjunction with DMZs or extranet networks.

- **Dynamic NAT:** Dynamic NAT maps an unregistered IP address on the private network to a registered IP address that is selected by the routing device providing the NAT service from a pool of registered addresses. This method is most commonly used when a large number of systems on the internal network need to access the Internet, but they don't have the requirement for a static address. Here, a workstation's address is translated to the next available registered address in the pool as soon as it initiates a connection to the public network.

There are two major security implications associated with the use of NAT. First, NAT can be used to hide private network addresses, which makes it more difficult for an attacker to successfully penetrate a private network. The addresses that are visible to an Internet-based attacker are the NAT addresses typically stored on the firewall, which should be one of the more secure devices on your network.

NAT also presents a unique issue when working with the IPsec protocol (discussed in more detail later in the lesson). Early implementations of IPsec did not support NAT, so the IPsec protocol could not be used when NAT was enabled in an environment. NAT traversal capability was added in later versions of the IPsec protocol, but IPsec still requires that some special steps be taken in order to work successfully with NAT.

Understanding Virtual Private Networks (VPNs)

VPN (Virtual Private Network) is a technology that uses encrypted tunnels to create secure connections across public networks like the Internet. There are a variety of uses for this technology, but three of the most common are shown in Figure 4-5.

Figure 4-5

Uses for VPN technology

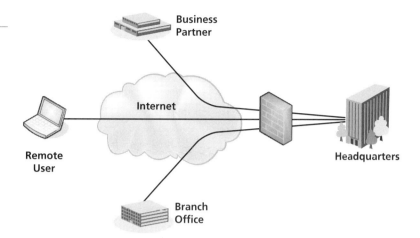

VPNs are commonly used by remote employees for access to the internal network, to create secure network-to-network connections for branch offices or business partner connections, or even to create secure host-to-host connections for additional security and isolation on an internal network. VPNs utilize encryption and authentication to provide confidentiality, integrity, and privacy protection for data.

Remote access VPNs were first introduced in the late 1990s and were initially used in conjunction with modems to provide more secure, more flexible connectivity to corporate networks. All that was required was a dial-up Internet connection and a VPN client, and you could connect to a corporate network over an encrypted connection. Shortly thereafter, with the advent of high-speed Internet connections, the use of VPN technologies exploded. It was now possible in some cases to get a faster connection at home via high-speed Internet than in a branch office via typical dedicated network connections. This technology also allows businesses to migrate from expensive dedicated network connections to less expensive Internet-based VPN connections.

The first standards-based VPNs were based on the IPsec protocol. IPsec-based VPNs quickly overtook some of the proprietary-based VPNs that were the first products marketed.

Understanding Internet Protocol Security (IPsec)

Internet Protocol Security (IPsec) is a standards-based protocol suite designed specifically for securing Internet Protocol (IP) communications. It is also a component of IPv6, the next generation of the IP protocol. IPsec authenticates and encrypts each IP packet in an IP data stream. In addition, IPsec has protocols that can be used to establish mutual authentication and cryptographic keys negotiation during a session. IPsec operates at the network layer of the OSI model.

IPsec was designed to provide interoperable, high-quality, cryptographically based security for IPv4 and IPv6. Today, it offers a comprehensive set of security services, including the following:

- Access control
- Connectionless data integrity checking
- Data origin authentication
- Replay detection and rejection
- Confidentiality using encryption
- Traffic flow confidentiality

TAKE NOTE *

Why do layers matter? The fact that IPsec operates at layer 3 of the OSI model means that it can be used to encrypt any traffic in layers 4 through 7 of the model. In practical terms, this means that IPsec can be used to encrypt any application traffic.

The IPsec protocol has three major components:

- **Authentication Header (AH):** AH provides integrity protection for packet headers, data, and user authentication. It can optionally provide replay protection and access protection. AH cannot encrypt any portion of packets. For AH to work in conjunction with NAT, the IP protocol number 51 needs to be allowed across the firewall.

- **Encapsulating Security Payload (ESP):** ESP provides authenticity, integrity, and confidentiality protection of data packets. Unlike AH, ESP cannot protect packet headers—it protects the data only. For ESP to work in conjunction with NAT, the IP protocol number 50 needs to be allowed across the firewall.

- **Internet Key Exchange (IKE):** IKE is used to negotiate, create, and manage security associations (SA), which means that it is the protocol that establishes the secure communication channel to network hosts. For IKE to work in conjunction with NAT, the User Datagram Protocol (UDP) port 500 needs to be allowed across the firewall.

IPsec can be used in two different modes:

- **Transport mode (host-to-host):** In transport mode, only the data packet payload is encapsulated. Because the packet header is left intact, the original routing information is used to transmit the data from sender to recipient. When used in conjunction with AH, this mode cannot be used in a NAT environment because the encryption of the header is not compatible with the translated addressing.

- **Tunnel mode (gateway-to-gateway or gateway-to-host):** In tunnel mode, the IP packet is entirely encapsulated and given a new header. The host/gateway specified in the new IP header decapsulates the packet. This is the mode used to secure traffic for a remote access VPN connection from the remote host to the VPN concentrator on the internal network. This is also the mode used to secure site-to-site IPsec connections.

Using Other VPN Protocols

Although IPsec is considered the predominant protocol associated with VPNs, there are other protocols that can also be used to build VPNs or provide VPN-like connectivity.

USING SECURE SOCKETS LAYER (SSL) AND TRANSPORT LAYER SECURITY (TLS)

One of the key VPN protocols used today is SSL/TLS, which is the main alternative to IPsec for implementing a VPN solution.

The SSL protocol standard was originally proposed as a standard by Netscape. Although this protocol is widely used to secure websites, it has since been formalized in the IETF standard known as Transport Layer Security (TLS). The SSL/TLS protocol provides a method for secure client/server communications across a network and prevents eavesdropping and tampering with data in transit. SSL/TLS also provides endpoint authentication and communications confidentiality through the use of encryption.

If you have ever connected to a website using HTTPS, the secure version of HTTP web browsing, you have used the SSL protocol. This protocol provides 128-bit encryption, and it is currently the leading security mechanism for protecting web traffic on banking, e-commerce, email, and essentially any other secure websites you might encounter. In typical end user/browser usage, SSL/TLS authentication is one way. Here, only the server is authenticated when the client compares the information entered to access a server to information on the SSL certificate on the server (the client knows the server's identity), but not vice versa (the client remains unauthenticated or anonymous). However, SSL/TLS can also perform bidirectional authentication by using client-based certificates. This is particularly useful when this protocol is used to access a protected network because it adds an additional layer of authentication to the access.

As discussed in the section on IPsec, a VPN creates a secure tunnel through a public network like the Internet. Although SSL VPNs still leverage the concept of tunneling, they create their tunnels differently than IPsec. An SSL VPN establishes connectivity using the SSL protocol. IPsec works at layer 3 of the OSI model, while SSH functions at layers 4 and 5. SSL VPNs can also encapsulate information at layers 6 and 7, which makes SSL VPNs very flexible.

One additional feature of an SSL VPN is that it usually connects using a web browser, whereas an IPsec VPN generally requires that client software be installed on the remote system.

SSL VPNs are predominantly used for remote access VPN connections in which a client is connecting to applications on an internal network, as opposed to site-to-site connections in which two gateways are used to connect disparate private networks across the Internet.

Some benefits of SSL/TLS VPNs over IPsec VPNs include the following:

- **Lower cost:** Because an SSL VPN is typically clientless, you don't have the costs of rolling out, supporting, and updating client software.
- **Platform independence:** Because access to an SSL VPN is granted through the standard SSL interface, which is a component of virtually every web browser, virtually any OS that runs a browser is supported.
- **Increased client flexibility:** As a general rule, IPsec clients are generally installed only on corporate systems. In comparison, due to their additional flexibility, SSL VPNs can be configured to allow access from a variety of clients, including corporate systems, home systems, customer or supplier systems, or even kiosk machines in libraries or Internet cafes. This wider access can greatly increase employee satisfaction.
- **NAT support:** Historically, Network Address Translation (NAT) has caused issues with IPSec VPNs. Virtually all IPsec vendors have created workarounds for this issue. Still, with an SSL VPN, you don't have these issues because SSL works at a higher layer than IPsec.
- **Granular access control:** Depending on your environment, this could be considered either a benefit or a drawback. SSL VPNs require a greater granularity of access than a typical IPsec VPN. In particular, instead of creating a tunnel from the host to the internal network, SSL VPNs require that each resource that is accessed be explicitly defined. The upside is unless you have explicitly defined a resource, an SSL VPN user cannot access it, which offers security benefits. However, in a complex environment, this could add significant overhead to your VPN support.
- **Fewer firewall rules are required:** In order to access an IPsec gateway across a firewall, you need to open several ports to support the individual protocols for authentication and the tunnel. With an SSL VPN, you only need to open port 443, which is generally easy to do due to the prevalence of the HTTPS protocol.

EXAMINING SECURE SHELL (SSH)

Secure Shell (SSH) is a protocol for secure remote login and other secure network services over a network. SSH can be used for a number of applications across multiple platforms, including UNIX, Microsoft Windows, Apple Mac, and Linux. Some of the applications supported with SSH include the following:

- Secure logins
- Secure remote command executions
- Secure file transfers
- Secure backups, copying, and mirroring of files
- Creating VPN connections (when used in conjunction with the OpenSSH server and client)

The SSH protocol consists of three major components:

- **Transport layer protocol:** This provides server authentication, confidentiality, and integrity with perfect forward secrecy.
- **User authentication protocol:** This provides authentication of the client to the server.
- **Connection protocol:** This multiplexes the encrypted tunnel into several logical channels.

Now that we've looked at some of the protocols you can use to secure traffic across a network, and usually across public networks like the Internet, let's look at a technique for providing additional security on your internal network.

Looking at Server and Domain Isolation

Security professionals are constantly being asked by businesses to allow greater resource access to facilitate business requirements. Although wider and easier access to resources can increase the production of a business, it also presents significant security challenges. The risks of virus attack, rogue users and devices, and unauthorized access to sensitive information associated with unauthorized or unmanaged devices are enough to keep any information security professional awake at night.

One example of this might be a developer's workstation. Many developers feel they have unique requirements in order to do their job, and as a result, they may run custom configurations, unsupported operating systems, and/or open source applications, and they may not participate in the corporate patch and configuration management programs. Since these computers will have to be connected to an organization's network to access internal resources, and these workstations may give you additional security challenges, server and domain isolation gives you some additional security options.

TAKE NOTE*

If you want to leverage isolation in your environment, be sure to take the time to plan appropriately. This can be a complex implementation, and you must understand your needs before you start enabling protocols.

Server and domain isolation is a solution based on IPsec and Microsoft Active Directory that enables administrators to dynamically segment their Windows environment into more secure and isolated logical networks. These logical networks are segmented based on policy and can be accomplished without needing to deploy firewalls, implement VLANs, or make other changes on the network. Internal servers and domains can be secured through the use of authentication and encryption. This creates an additional layer of policy-driven protection, and it provides another alternative to the security controls previously discussed in this lesson.

Server and domain isolation should not be confused with Network Access Protection (NAP). NAP focuses on ensuring that the clients that attach to the network are configured appropriately and authorized. In comparison, server and domain isolation creates logical security zones within the network and controls who can access them. Both are viable security solutions, but they have very different goals and use very different technologies to secure the environment. In a high-security setting, you may want to deploy both technologies to ensure the protection of your network and data.

Figure 4-6 provides an example of server and domain isolation in which the isolated network can only be accessed by computers with the appropriate IPsec and Active Directory configuration.

Figure 4-6

Server and domain isolation

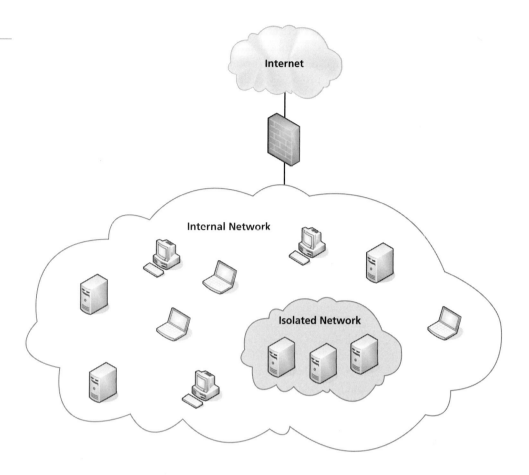

How does the isolation process work? In short, authentication to the isolated environment is based on a computer's machine credentials. The machine credentials can be an Active Directory-issued Kerberos ticket, or it can be an X.509 certificate automatically distributed to the computer by a Group Policy. Once the machine has authenticated, the associated isolation policies are enforced by the built-in IPsec functionality in Windows.

Here, it's important to recall that IPsec supports two modes. Tunnel mode is the most frequently used mode, because it supports the widely used remote access and site-to-site VPN solutions that are becoming ubiquitous in the corporate world. Transport mode is used for server and domain isolation because it is the mode that supports secure host-to-host communications.

■ Protecting Data with Protocol Security

THE BOTTOM LINE

In this lesson, we have discussed a number of security protocols, such as IPsec, SSL/TLS, and SSH. In this section, we are going to look at several additional protocols that can be used to secure your data. This includes an examination of protocol spoofing, network sniffing, and some other common attack methods you might encounter when working to secure a corporate computing environment.

One of the more challenging topics for any information security professional to tackle is the idea of protocol security. This has long been the area of networking professionals, and although there is an obvious overlap between networking and information security, understanding protocol security can be a real challenge for information security professionals both new and old. In order to develop an appreciation of exactly how network protocols can impact security, we need to start our discussion with a look at tunneling.

Understanding Tunneling

Tunneling is defined as the encapsulation of one network protocol within another. Tunneling can be used to route an unsupported protocol across a network, or to securely route traffic across an insecure network. VPNs employ a form of tunneling when data is encapsulated in the IPsec protocol.

One example of tunneling that is used to move unsupported traffic across a network is the Generic Routing Encapsulation (GRE) protocol. GRE is an IP-based protocol frequently used to carry packets from unroutable IP addresses across an IP network.

In order to understand why the GRE protocol is used, we need to discuss IPv4 addressing. One component of the IPv4 addressing scheme is a set of addresses known as either private or reserved address ranges. These ranges include 10.0.0.0 through 10.255.255.255, 172.16.0.0 through 176.31.255.255, and 192.168.0.0 through 192.168.255.255. These ranges were assigned to help delay the exhaustion of all available IPv4 IP addresses, and they are typically used for both home and office networks where there is not a requirement for the addresses to be routed across a public network like the Internet. These networks generally use NAT to permit Internet access.

Another area where these addresses are used is for lab/development networks in an enterprise environment. Sometimes there is a requirement to route traffic from one lab/development network to another, but because these networks use private addresses, they may not be routable across the enterprise network. This is when GRE becomes useful. Traffic between the labs can be encapsulated in a GRE tunnel, which can be routed over the enterprise network without requiring readdressing.

PPTP (Point-to-Point Tunneling Protocol) is a proprietary VPN protocol originally developed by the PPTP Forum, a group of vendors that included Ascend Communications, Microsoft Corporation, 3Com, ECI Telematics, and U.S. Robotics. PPTP was designed as an extension of the Point-to-Point Protocol (PPP) to allow PPP to be tunneled through an IP network. At one time, PPTP was the most widely used VPN protocol, but the release of IPSec had a significant effect on PPTP's use.

Another tunneling protocol that was once widely used is L2TP (Layer 2 Tunneling Protocol), which combined the best features of PPTP and the L2F (Layer Two Forwarding) protocol, which was an early competing protocol for PPTP developed by Cisco Systems. Like PPTP, L2TP was designed as an extension of PPP to allow PPP to be tunneled through an IP network. L2TP support was first included in a Microsoft server product with the release of Windows Server 2000. Prior to Windows Server 2000, PPTP was the only supported protocol. A number of hardware VPN vendors, including Cisco, also supported the L2TP protocol.

Using DNS Security Extensions (DNSSEC)

If you have ever connected to a website by name, you have used the Domain Name System (DNS). DNS is a service used on the Internet for resolving fully qualified domain names (FQDN) to their actual Internet Protocol (IP) addresses using a distributed network of name servers. Here, you enter a server name (such as www.espn.com), and DNS ensures your connection is directed to the proper servers. Although this service is largely invisible to end users, DNS is a critical element of how the Internet functions.

Let's say you want to check the scores from your favorite sport using ESPN's website. Before DNS, when you asked, "What's the address of ESPN's website?" the answer might be 199.181.132.250. If you are like most people, you'd remember that number for less than 30 seconds, so you would probably never find those sports scores. In contrast, with DNS, you can simply tell your computer to go to www.espn.com, and the DNS infrastructure of the Internet will translate this name to the correct address. In other words, DNA is much like a phone book: You put in a name, and it gives you the correct number.

However, DNS was developed during the early years of the Internet, when functionality was the goal, not security. As a result, DNS was built without security. In recent years, this lack of security has been exploited with forged DNS data, which, among other things, redirects connections to malicious websites. Say you type in the address of your bank, and shortly thereafter, it appears you have reached your destination. You enter your user ID and password to access your account, but you can't log in. Now, say that one month later, you find out your account has been emptied. What happened was that your initial connection was the result of a bad DNS entry. Instead of connecting to your bank's website, you connected to a clever duplicate that captured your login information and let the bad guys steal your savings.

Thankfully, **DNS Security Extensions (DNSSEC)** adds security provisions to DNS so that computers can verify they have been directed to proper servers. This new standard was published in March 2005 and is slowly being adopted across the Internet. DNSSEC provides authentication and integrity checking on DNS lookups, ensuring that outgoing Internet traffic is always sent to the correct server. This removes the issue of forged DNS data because there is no way to forge the appropriate authentication. This not only addresses the problem of website redirection, but it also reduces some of the challenges associated with spam and use of faked mail domains.

DNSSEC provides authentication and integrity checking through the use of public key encryption. The domain name structure provides a hierarchy of authenticated keys, creating a chain of trust from the root of the DNS hierarchy to the domain being queried. DNSSEC addresses many of the most problematic security issues associated with the Internet's core infrastructure, but it comes at a significant cost. As with any large-scale public key implementation, rolling DNSSEC out to the entire Internet will be an enormously complex, resource-intensive project. There are also challenges associated with maintaining the web of trust created by using public keys on a scale this large.

Looking at Protocol Spoofing

Another area of concern with respect to protocols is the concept of protocol *spoofing*. The word "spoof" can be used to refer to a hoax. Accordingly, protocol spoofing is the misuse of a network protocol to perpetrate a hoax on a host or a network device. Some common forms of protocol spoofing are as follows:

- **ARP spoofing:** ARP (Address Resolution Protocol) spoofing (also called ARP poisoning) is an attack on the protocol used to determine a device's hardware address (MAC address) on the network when you have its IP address. This is critical for proper delivery of network data once the data has reached the proper LAN segment. An ARP spoofing attack occurs when an attacker modifies the network's ARP caches and takes over the IP address of the victim host. This permits the attacker to receive any data intended for the original host.

- *DNS spoofing:* DNS spoofing occurs when an attacker is able to intercept a DNS request and respond to the request before the DNS server is able to. As a result, the victim host is directed to the wrong website, where additional malicious activities can take place. This attack is frequently used in conjunction with network sniffing, which is discussed in the next section.

- **IP address spoofing:** In an IP address spoofing attack, the attacker creates IP packets with a forged source IP address to either conceal the identity of the attacking host or impersonate the identity of a victim host. This type of attack was very popular in the early days of packet analysis firewalls. Here an attacker would spoof an internal IP address from outside a firewall, and if not configured correctly, the firewall would permit the attacker access to the internal network.

It is important to note that the term "protocol spoofing" also has another definition within the computing arena. In particular, the term is sometimes used to represent a technique associated with data compression and employed to improve network throughput and performance. Although a valuable tool in the appropriate circumstances, this form of protocol spoofing does not have any information security implications.

Utilizing Network Sniffing

Network sniffing is a type of network analysis that is useful for administrators responsible for maintaining networks and identifying network issues. It involves connecting a device to a network with the appropriate software to allow access to the details of the packets that are traversing the network. Figure 4-7 shows an example of Wireshark, a commonly used open source network sniffing tool.

Figure 4-7

Wireshark

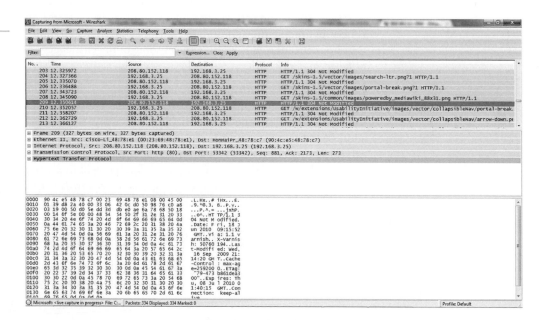

As you can see in the figure, this tool reveals a significant amount of information about the packet being analyzed. To a network administrator with an in-depth understanding of networking, this information can be used to identify application issues, network latency, and a variety of other network errors. Unfortunately, to an attacker with similar skills, the information offered by network sniffing provides equally valuable data that can be used for attack purposes. For example, any data sent in clear text (i.e., not encrypted) can generally be read directly from the network. In the early days of the Internet, this was a significant amount of traffic. Back then, reading passwords from data packets was a trivial exercise. Today, however, with the widespread use of encryption through secure websites and the use of VPNs for remote access, the risks presented by network sniffing are slightly mitigated because attackers can no longer read the data contents of a packet. Nonetheless, attackers can still obtain important information about data packets that can be useful in attacks.

It is important to be aware that a network sniffer can only see traffic that crosses the port that it is connected to. Therefore, a sniffer placed on the LAN in a branch office cannot capture traffic from the headquarters network. And, in a switched environment that leverages VLANs, the amount of traffic passing any one port can be limited. The ports that offer the most information are the ingress/egress points to the network, where all the traffic from the subnet is concentrated. This means an attacker cannot directly capture traffic from your network, but that doesn't mean you're safe. For instance, a system on your internal network that is infected by a virus can end up running a network sniffer and providing the captured traffic to a remote host.

Another security challenge associated with network sniffers is that they are passive devices. Unless an attacker has made modifications to a network to access more information, it is almost impossible to detect a network sniffer. In fact, there could be a network sniffer on a network node beyond your internal network that could be capturing packets about your Internet access. In this circumstance, you don't even have access to the network infrastructure to look for changes.

You also need to be aware that wireless networks are particularly susceptible to network sniffing attacks, due to the lack of a port requirement. Once connected to a wireless network, an attacker has access to all the traffic on that network. That's why it's an excellent idea to only use encrypted connections for anything you do on a wireless network beyond general web browsing.

Understanding Common NETWORK Attack Methods

We have covered the information security challenges associated with computer networking throughout this lesson. The final piece of the network security puzzle is understanding the types of attacks you can expect to see as you work to protect computer networks. Although no list of attack methods can ever be complete, if only because attackers are constantly coming up with new types of attacks, this list covers the most common categories:

> **TAKE NOTE***
>
> A botnet is a distributed network of computers that have been compromised by malicious software and are under the control of an attacker.

- **Denial of service/distributed denial of service (DoS/DDoS) attacks:** The goal of a denial of service attack is to flood the network that is being attacked with overwhelming amounts of traffic, thereby shutting down network infrastructure like a router or firewall. Because the attacker isn't interested in receiving responses to his or her attack packets, DoS attacks are ideal opportunities for using spoofed addresses. Spoofed addresses are more difficult to filter because each spoofed packet appears to come from a different address, thus hiding the true source of the attack. This makes backtracking the attack extremely difficult. The new wrinkle to the DoS is the distributed DoS, which leverages botnets to generate DoS attacks from multiple sources. Not only does this make the attack more difficult to defend against, as multiple computers can generate significantly more traffic than a single computer, but it also makes it much more difficult to track down the source of the attack.

- **IP spoofing to bypass network security:** As previously discussed, IP spoofing is the modification of data packets so that data packets from an attacking computer appear to be from a trusted computer. By appearing as a trusted computer, the attacker is able to bypass network security measures, like packet filters or other solutions that rely on IP addresses for authentication. Using this method of attack on a remote system can be extremely difficult, because the attacker must modify thousands of packets in order to successfully complete the attack. This type of attack generally works best when there are trust relationships between machines. For example, it is not uncommon in some environments to have UNIX hosts on a corporate network that trust each other. In such instances, once a user successfully authenticates to one host, he or she is automatically trusted on the other hosts and does not need a user ID or password to get into the system. If an attacker can successfully spoof a connection from a trusted machine, he or she may be able to access the target machine without an authentication. Identifying the trusted machine is frequently accomplished via network sniffing.

- **Man in the middle attacks:** A man in the middle attack is a type of attack in which the attacker breaks into the communication between the endpoints of a network connection. Once the attacker has broken into the communication stream, he or she can intercept the data being transferred or even inject false information into the data stream. These types of attacks are frequently used to intercept both HTTP and HTTPS connections. Systems that are connected to a wireless network are especially susceptible to this form of attack.

- **Back door attack:** Back door attacks are attacks against an opening left in a functional piece of software that allows access into a system or software application without the owner's knowledge. Many times, these back doors were left by the application developers, but current code testing has dramatically reduced the number of back doors found in commercial software. A more common version of this attack occurs when system administrators create system accounts that they can use in the event they are asked to leave a company. Thus, as an information security professional, one of your goals should be to validate all system accounts belonging to employees at least once a year.

- *DNS poisoning:* A DNS poisoning attack is an attack against the cached information on your DNS server. When a DNS request is made, the result of the request is cached on the DNS server so that subsequent requests for the same server can be returned more quickly, without requiring lookup by an external DNS server. Unfortunately, these cache files are not particularly secure, and attackers can target these files to insert a bogus IP address for a specific server entry into a cache. When this occurs, any host making a request for that site from the poisoned DNS server will be directed to the wrong site. The bogus entry in the cache will remain until the cache expires and is refreshed.

- **Replay attack:** A replay attack occurs when an attacker is able to capture an intact data stream from a network using a network sniffer, modify certain components of the data stream, and then replay the traffic back to the network to complete the attack. For example, an attacker could capture a session in which a purchase is being made, modify the delivery address, and replay the traffic to place an order that would be delivered to his or her address.

- **Weak encryption keys:** An attack against weak encryption keys successfully occurs when the keys have a value that permits encryption to be broken. Once this happens, the attacker is able to access the data that is supposed to be encrypted. Probably the most high-profile example of this attack was the weakness exploited in the Wired Equivalent Privacy (WEP) security standard used in conjunction with wireless networks. Intended to be used to secure wireless networks, WEP keys were found to be weak, and they could be broken if 5 to 10 MB of wireless traffic could be captured. This traffic could then be run through one of many tools published by the hacker community, and the result would be the WEP key, which permits an attacker to read the information protected with WEP. This is another example of an attack that relies on a network sniffer to be successful.

- **Social engineering:** Social engineering attacks occur when an attacker contacts an employee of an organization and tries to extract useful information from that person. This information may later be used to help pull off a different attack. With social engineering, the attacker usually tries to appear as harmless or respectful as possible. Generally, he or she will ask a number of questions in an attempt to identify possible avenues to exploit during an attack. If an attacker does not receive sufficient information from one employee, he or she may reach out to several others until he or she has sufficient information for the next phase of an attack.

- **Software vulnerability attack:** This category of attack exploits a known or unknown vulnerability in an operating system or application to perform malicious activities. This is probably one of the most common avenues for attack, and it is used frequently by viruses and worms. A solid patch management practice is the best defense against this type of attack, especially if coupled with a vulnerability management program.

- **Buffer overflow attack:** A buffer overflow attack exploits poorly written code by injecting data into variable fields and leveraging the response to access information in the application. This attack is made possible when the application developer doesn't limit or check the size of the data being entered in an application field. When data that is too long for the field is entered, it creates an error that can be exploited by the attacker to perform malicious actions against the application.

- **Remote code execution attack:** Remote code execution attacks are commonly run against web applications. When an application is improperly coded, an attacker is able to run arbitrary, system-level code through the application and use the results to access data or perform other unintended actions against the application or application server.

- **SQL injection attack:** SQL injection attacks are one of the oldest attacks against web applications using the SQL Server database application. In this type of attack, control characters are entered into the web application, and depending on the configuration of the database server, the attack results can range from retrieval of information from the web server's database to allowing the execution of code or even full access to the server. This attack relies on database weaknesses as well as coding weaknesses.

- **Cross-site scripting attack (sometimes abbreviated as an XSS attack):** Cross-site scripting attacks are by far the most common and potentially the most dangerous current attack method employed against web users. These attacks allow hackers to bypass the security mechanisms provided by a web browser. By injecting malicious scripts into web pages and getting users to execute them, an attacker can gain elevated access privileges to sensitive page content, session cookies, and a variety of other information maintained by the browser.

Other attack methods include the password cracking, dictionary attack and brute force attacks, which were covered in Lesson 3.

The final component of network security you must be familiar with is wireless security.

■ Securing Wireless Networks

THE BOTTOM LINE

Wireless LANs have become one of the most popular forms of network access, rapidly spreading through homes, to business, to public access wireless hotspots like the ones you find in a Starbucks or McDonald's. Wireless networks offer a great deal of convenience, but this convenience must be balanced against the security implications of a network that is not contained by the walls of your building. In this section, we discuss those implications and describe some of the techniques you can use to secure a wireless network, including encryption keys, SSID, and MAC address filters.

CERTIFICATION READY
What methods can you use to secure a wireless network?
1.4

A wireless LAN (WLAN) allows users to connect to a network while remaining mobile. Although this gives users easy access to a network from areas like conference rooms, offices, lunch rooms, and other areas where wired connections don't exist, it also gives potential attackers similarly easy access to the network. Many corporate wireless networks can actually be accessed by anyone with a laptop and wireless card. If you have ever used a wireless connection in a neighborhood, you may have noticed that your computer sees wireless networks other than the one you are connecting to. Businesses have the same issues as your neighbors: They are broadcasting their network to anyone within range. In fact, with specialized antennas, wireless networks can be accessed from surprisingly long distances, and if you're not careful, that access may occur without your knowledge.

In the early days of wireless networks, implementing this technology was easy, but securing it was not. As a result, there were battles between users who wanted the ease of access and increased mobility that wireless promised and security personnel who were acutely aware of the risks that wireless networking introduced. As a result, most corporations had strict policies prohibiting the use of wireless to directly access internal networks, frequently requiring users to use VPNs to connect from the production wireless network to the internal network. As a result, some users would install wireless access points under their desks and hope that no one from security would notice. Attackers would then drive around office parks looking for these unsecured access points so that they could breach the perimeters of corporate networks and attack unprotected internal networks. Corporate security organizations would also perform similar exercises in the hopes of finding rogue wireless connections before attackers did. Today, however, with some of the new security capabilities available with wireless networks, it is now possible to securely offer wireless access to internal networks, reducing both the frequency of rogue access points, as well as the number of resources needed to find and shut down those access points.

Another capability sometimes discussed when deploying wireless networks is ensuring the wireless access point radio strength is tuned appropriately. Although there is some ability to tune a wireless signal to reduce the risk of unauthorized users, it is not a good idea to rely on this method as your first line of defense when trying to keep your network secure. Frequently, what you will find is that you negatively impact usability far more than you improve security.

Using Service Set Identifier (SSID)

The most basic component of a wireless network is the Service Set Identifier (SSID). An SSID is defined in the IEE 802.11 standard as a name for the WLAN. It does not provide any inherent security capabilities, although specifying the SSID of the WLAN you want to connect to will ensure that you connect to the correct WLAN.

Although there aren't any specific security capabilities associated with an SSID, there are definitely some security considerations you should take into account:

- **Choose your own SSID:** The first thing you need to do when setting up a WLAN is to choose a unique SSID. Each WLAN access point comes with a default SSID set. If you use the default, there is a risk that one of your neighbors will also use the default, causing confusion and conflicts. Therefore, be sure to select your own unique yet easy to remember SSID.

- **Naming conventions:** Now that you have chosen an SSID, there are some measures you can take to make it a little more challenging for an attacker to identify the owner of your WLAN. It is generally not a good idea for corporations to broadcast the fact that they are the owner of a particular wireless network. Selecting SSIDs based on company name, company product lines, or anything else that might allow an attacker to confirm who owns the WLAN should thus be avoided. Instead, select an SSID that your employees can remember but that doesn't invite attacks. Things like city names, sports, mythological characters, or other generic SSID names are generally safe choices.

- **Turn off your SSID:** Your SSID is used to identify your WLAN and permit computers to connect to it. If you broadcast this information, then client systems can search for available wireless networks, and the name of your WLAN will appear in the list. With just a few clicks, you can connect to the WLAN. Although extremely convenient for authorized users, broadcasting an SSID makes it equally easy for attackers to connect in the same way. To prevent this from happening, you can turn off the SSID broadcast for your network, rendering it essentially invisible to casual wireless network browsers. The problem with doing this is twofold, however. First, it makes it more difficult for authorized users to connect to the network, and second, any attacker who is trying to get in through your wireless network will most likely have a wireless sniffer, which will show him or her the SSID of your WLAN whether it's broadcast or not, because this information is in the wireless packets. In this case, it's generally wise to select ease of use over hiding your SSID (i.e., security through obscurity).

Now, let's look at some techniques for securing a WLAN.

Understanding Keys

The best available mechanism for securing a WLAN is to use authentication and encryption. WLANs offer three key-based security mechanisms for this purpose.

EXAMINING WIRED EQUIVALENCY PRIVACY (WEP)

The very first security capability available to WLAN users was WEP (Wired Equivalency Privacy). WEP was included as part of the original IEEE 802.11 standard and intended to provide privacy. Widely recommended in the early days of WLAN use, WEP rapidly fell out of favor when a flaw with the encryption mechanism was discovered. This flaw makes it relatively easy for an attacker to crack the encryption and access the wireless network, so WEP is generally only used if no other solution is available or if the WLAN is being used with older devices or devices (like PDAs or handheld games) that require WEP.

One of the other challenges associated with WEP was the confusing mix of keys used by vendors. Some vendors implemented the keys in HEX, some used ASCII characters, and some just used passphrases. Depending on the version of WEP, the length of the keys could also vary. This was particularly problematic for home users who wanted to use equipment from multiple vendors. Consumers often ended up with equipment that wouldn't support WEP in the same way.

EXAMINING WI-FI PROTECTED ACCESS (WPA) AND WI-FI PROTECTED ACCESS VERSION 2 (WPA2)

Wi-Fi Protected Access (WPA) was designed as the interim successor to WEP. The WPA protocol implements the majority of the IEEE 802.11i standard, which was included in the updated WLAN standard. WPA features a new security protocol, Temporal Key Integrity Protocol (TKIP), which although related to WEP to ensure backwards compatibility, adds new features to help address the issues associated with WEP. Unfortunately, because TKIP uses the same underlying mechanism as WEP, it is also vulnerable to a number of similar attacks—although the possibility of attack is significantly less than with WEP.

Wi-Fi Protected Access Version 2 (WPA2) is the standards-based version of WPA, except WPA2 implements all of the IEEE 802.11i standards.

WPA/WPA2 functions in two modes:

- **Shared-key WPA:** In shared-key WPA, a passphrase is configured and entered on both the client and the wireless network. This is similar to how WEP works, but the protection of the WPA passphrase is much more secure due to the use of strong encryption with automatic rekeying. This mode is generally meant for home users.

- **IEEE 802.1x:** In 802.1x mode, WPA/WPA2 uses an external authentication server coupled with the EAP (Extensible Authentication Protocol) standard to enable strong authentication for connection to the WLAN. A typical authentication process includes the following steps:

  1. **Initialization:** Upon detection of a host, the port on the switch is enabled and set to the "unauthorized" state. Only 802.1x traffic is allowed while the port is in this state.

  2. **Initiation:** The host that is trying to connect to the WLAN next transmits EAP-Request Identity frames to a special layer 2 address on the local network segment. This is known as the authenticator. The authenticator then forwards the packets to a RADIUS authentication server.

3. **Negotiation:** The authentication server sends a reply to the authenticator. The authenticator then transmits the packets to the connecting host. These packets are used to negotiate the EAP authentication method.

4. **Authentication:** If the authentication server and connecting host agree on the EAP authentication method, then the connecting host is authenticated. If authentication is successful, the authenticator sets the port to the "authorized" state and normal traffic is allowed. If it is unsuccessful, the port remains in the "unauthorized" state and the host is not able to connect.

Use of 802.1x authentication to secure a WLAN is generally reserved for large corporate environments where there are sufficient resources to support the additional servers and support required by this mode of operation. IEEE 802.1x authentication, particularly when used in conjunction with a token-based authentication solution, permits a very secure WLAN implementation.

Utilizing MAC Filters

As discussed earlier in this lesson, a MAC address is the unique hardware address of a network adapter. This information can be used to control what systems are able to connect to a WLAN through the use of MAC filters. By turning MAC filtering on, you can limit network access to only permitted systems by entering the MAC address information into the MAC filters. The table of permitted MAC addresses is maintained by the wireless access points.

Considering Pros and Cons of Specific Security Types

Now that we have discussed the different security mechanisms available when working with WLANs, let's consider some of the advantages and disadvantages of each:

- **WEP:** WEP is a solution that, although better than no security at all, is not particularly secure. The vulnerabilities within the WEP encryption scheme make it very easy to crack. WEP will keep your neighbors from connecting to your home WLAN, but it will not slow a determined attacker.

- **WPA/WPA2:** WPA/WPA2 is the best security method for both home and corporate WLAN security. In pre-shared key mode, WPA/WPA2 can secure a WLAN with a passcode that is shared by the clients and wireless access points. As long as a secure passcode is selected, this is a very secure solution for small networks. For corporate networks, where additional authentication infrastructure can be purchased, the 802.1x security available within WPA/WPA2 permits a more secure WLAN implementation. The downside to this approach is that it is more expensive and significantly more complex that the other solution. This method also requires significantly higher support because user accounts need to be maintained, additional servers need to be supported, and troubleshooting is more challenging. Nonetheless, these challenges can be overcome with a well designed, redundant architecture for the WLAN.

- **MAC address filtering:** MAC address filtering is a good solution for a home or small office environment, but it has significant challenges as the number of permitted devices grows. Manually maintaining a table of MAC addresses becomes a significant challenge when you get above 10 to 20 devices, especially in dynamic environments where systems are being purchased and decommissioned regularly. Any changes to the list of permitted devices requires updating the MAC address filtering table, which is generally a manual process. Another issue with MAC address filtering is that MAC addresses can be "spoofed" by someone with sufficient knowledge or the ability to perform an Internet search for a tool to change a MAC address. If hackers are able to get the MAC address of an authorized system, they can reset their MAC address to that address and thus gain access to a WLAN. MAC address filters are a good solution for small, static environments like a home or a small office. Although they will not stop a determined attacker, they are one more impediment to ensure that only a truly motivated attacker will attempt to bypass them.

The good news when reviewing available security mechanisms for wireless networks is that there are solutions available for just about any situation. In the early days of wireless, WLANs offered great convenience for users but no security for protecting a company's network. Deploying wireless access was as easy as buying an inexpensive wireless access point and plugging it into the network. As a result, security departments were forced to dedicate resources to tracking down rogue wireless access points. Fortunately, there are now multiple tools that you can use to identify rogue access points. So, while the issue certainly still exists, it is not as prevalent as it was in years past.

SKILL SUMMARY

IN THIS LESSON YOU LEARNED:

- A firewall is a system that is designed to protect a computer or a computer network from network-based attacks. A firewall does this by filtering the data packets that are traversing the network.

- Firewalls that are based on packet filtering inspect data packets as they attempt to traverse the firewall. Based on rudimentary rules, these firewalls permit all outbound traffic while denying all inbound traffic or blocking specific protocols, like telnet or ftp, from passing through the router.

- Instead of analyzing each individual packet, a circuit-level firewall monitors TCP/IP sessions by monitoring the TCP handshaking between packets to validate a session.

- Application-level firewalls (also known as proxy servers) work by performing a deep inspection of application data as it traverses the firewall. Rules are set by analyzing client requests and application responses, and correct application behavior is then enforced.

- Stateful multilevel firewalls are designed to provide the best features of both packet filtering and application-level firewalls.

- Network Access Protection (NAP) gives administrators a more powerful way to control access to network resources. NAP controls are based on a client computer's identity and whether the computer complies with the configured network governance policies.

- Virtual LANs (VLANs) were developed as an alternate solution to deploying multiple routers. VLANs are logical network segments used to create separate broadcast domains while still allowing the devices on the VLANs to communicate at layer 2 without a router.

- An intrusion detection system (IDS) is a solution designed to detect unauthorized user activities, attacks, and network compromises.

- An intrusion prevention system (IPS) is similar to an IDS, except that in addition to detecting and alerting, an IPS can also take action to prevent a breach from occurring.

- Honeypots, honey nets, and padded cells are complementary technologies to IDS/IPS deployments. A honeypot is a trap for hackers.

- A DMZ is a firewall configuration used to secure hosts on a network segment. In most DMZs, the hosts on the DMZ are connected behind a firewall that is connected to a public network like the Internet.

- Network Address Translation (NAT) is a technique used to modify the network address information of a host while traffic is traversing a router or firewall. This technique hides the network information of a private network while allowing traffic to be transferred across a public network like the Internet.

- DNS Security Extensions (DNSSEC) adds security provisions to DNS so that computers can verify that they have been directed to the proper servers.

- Protocol spoofing is the misuse of a network protocol to perpetrate a hoax on a host or a network device.

- A denial of service (DoS) attack floods the target network with overwhelming amounts of traffic, shutting down network infrastructure like routers or firewalls.

- A man in the middle attack occurs when an attacker breaks into the communication between the endpoints of a network connection. Once the attacker has broken into the communication stream, he or she can intercept the data being transferred or even inject false information into the data stream.

- Back door attacks are attacks against an opening left in a functional piece of software that allows access into a system or software application without the owner's knowledge.

- A DNS poisoning attack is an attack against the cached information on a DNS server.

- A replay attack occurs when an attacker is able to capture an intact data stream from a network using a network sniffer, modify certain components of the data stream, and then replay the traffic back to the network to complete the attack.

- A buffer overflow attack exploits poorly written code by injecting data into variable fields and leveraging the response to access information in the application.

- SQL injection attacks are one of the oldest types of attacks against web applications using the SQL Server database application.

- A wireless LAN (WLAN) allows users to connect to a network while mobile.

- The Service Set Identifier (SSID) is the name for a WLAN. A connecting host must know a WLAN's SSID to connect.

- Wired Equivalency Privacy (WEP) is an older wireless encryption protocol that rapidly fell out of favor when a flaw with its encryption mechanism was found.

- Wi-Fi Protected Access (WPA) was designed as the interim successor to WEP.

- Wi-Fi Protected Access Version 2 (WPA2) is the standards-based version of WPA. Unlike WPA, WPA2 implements all of the IEEE 802.11i standards.

- A MAC address is the unique hardware address of a network adapter.

- By turning MAC filtering on, you can limit network access to only permitted systems by entering the MAC address information into the MAC filters.

■ Knowledge Assessment

Multiple Choice

Circle the letter or letters that correspond to the best answer or answers.

1. Which of the following elements and issues should be considered when deciding whether to use a software or hardware firewall? (Choose all that apply.)
   a. Host operating system
   b. Application conflicts
   c. Operating system version
   d. Firewall service efficiency
   e. Stability

2. Which of the following are layers of the OSI model? (Choose all that apply.)
   a. Physical
   b. Control
   c. Application
   d. Network
   e. Encryption

3. At which layer of the OSI model does routing occur?
   a. Physical
   b. Data link
   c. Transport
   d. Session
   e. Network

4. Which of the following are valid firewall types? (Choose the best answer.)
   a. Virtual
   b. Network
   c. Packet filtering
   d. IPsec
   e. Application

5. Which of the following pieces of information are typically examined by a stateful inspection firewall?
   a. IP address of the sending host
   b. IP address of the receiving host
   c. IP address of the router
   d. Data packet type
   e. Data packet size

6. What is the purpose of NAP? (Choose the best answer.)
   a. NAP translates private IP addresses to Internet-routable IP addresses.
   b. NAP permits a firewall to perform deep inspection on packets.
   c. NAP provides a mechanism to perform network analysis on captured packets.
   d. NAP controls what systems are permitted to connect to a network.

7. An attack that relies on having a user execute a malicious script embedded in a web page is which kind of attack? (Choose the best answer.)
   a. Man in the middle
   b. Brute force
   c. Cross-site scripting
   d. SQL injection

8. You have just purchased a new wireless access point for your small computer services company, and you want to ensure that only your systems are able to connect to the wireless network. To that end, you enable MAC address filtering and put the MAC addresses of all your computers in the permitted table. At what layer of the OSI model does this filtering occur?
   a. Physical
   b. Data link
   c. Network
   d. Transport
   e. Session

9. You are the Information Security Officer for a medium-sized manufacturing company, and your sales team has just deployed a new e-commerce application to allow for the direct sale of your products to your customers. To secure this application, you are deploying an application firewall. At what layer of the OSI model does this filtering occur? (Select all answers that apply.)
   a. Physical
   b. Data link
   c. Network
   d. Presentation
   e. Application

10. Which of the following are components of Network Access Protection? (Choose all that apply.)
    a. MAC address compliance
    b. Health policy compliance
    c. Limited access mode
    d. IP address mode
    e. Health state validation

11. Which of the following are password-based attacks? (Choose all that apply.)
    a. Replay attacks
    b. Network sniffer attacks
    c. Brute force attacks
    d. Man in the middle attacks
    e. Dictionary attacks

12. What type of attack relies on the attacker tricking the sending host into thinking his or her system is the receiving host, and the receiving host into thinking his or her system is the sending host? (Choose the best answer.)
    a. Replay attack
    b. Brute force attack
    c. Man in the middle attack
    d. Cross-site scripting attack
    e. SQL injection attack

13. Which of the following systems cannot participate in a NAP implementation? (Choose all that apply.)
    a. Windows 7 Home
    b. Windows 7 Home Premium
    c. Windows XP Service Pack 2
    d. Windows Vista Ultimate
    e. Windows 7 Professional

14. Which of the following are common uses for a VPN?
    a. Remote access
    b. Server isolation
    c. Intrusion detection
    d. Extranet connections
    e. Domain isolation

15. Which of the following are common types of routing protocols? (Choose all that apply.)
    a. Link vector
    b. Dynamic link
    c. Distance link
    d. Distance vector
    e. Link state

Fill in the Blank

1. You are a network administrator, and you have just been put in charge of registering your company's domain name and setting up the DNS so that people on the Internet can get to your website. Here, _____ can be used to ensure that your DNS entries are not poisoned by an attacker.

2. The two most common protocols you can use to create a VPN are _____ and _____.

3. The three common types of protocol spoofing are _____, _____, and _____.

4. The type of attack that relies on a weakness in an operating system or an application is known as a(n) _____.

5. An attack that relies on access to a physical LAN segment is known as a(n) _____ attack.

6. An attack that records a stream of data, modifies it, and then resends it is known as a(n) _____ attack.

7. The two common types of Network Address Translation are _____ and _____.

8. If you are setting up a WLAN in a corporate environment and you want to use 802.1x and a RADIUS server to secure the connections, you need to use _____ keys.

9. The four mechanisms used by NAP to restrict network access and enforce policies are _____, _____, _____, and _____.

10. A(n) _____ can be deployed to distract an attacker from the critical systems on your network.

■ Competency Assessment

Scenario 4-1: Using Windows Firewall

You work for the ABC Corporation. You need to tell a user how to open the Windows Firewall console on a computer running Windows 7 and create a Windows Firewall inbound rule that allows Internet Explorer to communicate over ports 80 and 443. What steps must this user follow?

Scenario 4-2: Looking at a Routing Table

You work for the Contoso Corporation, where you have a computer running Windows 7. Execute the commands necessary to display the current routes. Now, add a route to the 10.24.57.0 network using the 192.168.50.1 gateway, and display the routes to confirm it has been added. Finally, delete the new route.

■ Proficiency Assessment

Scenario 4-3: Sniffing Packets

You've decided that you want to develop a better understanding of packets and how they operate. Therefore, you choose to use a protocol sniffer provided by Microsoft called Network Monitor to analyze these packets. When you look at the packets, you want to identify the four main parts that make up most of them. What steps would you take to do this?

Scenario 4-4: Looking at Ports

You are talking with the CIO of your company. One of the programs she needs access to is on a server that is on the DMZ using the following protocols:

Secure Shell (SSH)

Network News Transfer Protocol

Simple Network Management Protocol

NetBIOS Session Service

Network Time Protocol

The CIO wants to know what a port is and what ports are involved with these protocols. What should you tell her?

Workplace Ready

Defense in Depth

Recall from Lesson 1 that the concept of defense in depth involves providing multiple layers of security to defend your assets. This ensures that if an attacker breaches one layer of your defenses, you still have additional layers to keep him or her out of the critical areas of your environment. To use access control, you must establish physical security that prevents individuals from getting direct access to your servers without going through the network. You should also have firewalls and routers that limit access over the network. You can then use host firewalls, User Account Control, and other components to protect the server itself.

Besides looking at access control, keep in mind the need for authentication, authorization, and accounting. To protect network resources, you still need to establish a system that allows access based on authentication and authorization. And to ensure that a security breach has not occurred, you must also have established accounting measures that are reviewed regularly.

Protecting the Server and Client

OBJECTIVE DOMAIN MATRIX

SKILLS/CONCEPTS	MTA EXAM OBJECTIVE	MTA EXAM OBJECTIVE NUMBER
Protecting the Client Computer	Understand client protection.	4.1
Protecting Your Computer from Malware	Understand malware.	2.6
Protecting Your Email	Understand email protection.	4.2
Protecting Your Server	Understand server protection.	4.3
Securing Internet Explorer	Understand Internet security.	1.3

KEY TERMS

Adware

backdoor

Bayesian filter

content zones

cookie

malicious software (malware)

Microsoft Baseline Security Analyzer (MBSA)

offline files

pharming

phishing

pop-up window

rootkit

Sender Policy Framework (SPF)

spam

spyware

Trojan horse

User Account Control (UAC)

virus

virus hoax

Windows Defender

Windows Firewall

Windows Server Update Server (WSUS)

Windows updates

worm

Say that you are talking to your company's CIO about your network security. In particular, you are trying to explain to him that you have established a multilayer approach to security. You have firewalls and other devices protecting the network borders to your organization. You also have protection configured for the servers and the clients. This way, if a hacker bypasses the external security layer, he or she will need to break through another layer to get to the network resources and confidential information.

■ Protecting the Client Computer

THE BOTTOM LINE

Users utilize client computers to connect to servers and network applications. Because these client computers are connected to an organization's network, they must be protected.

CERTIFICATION READY
What does it take to secure a client computer?
4.1

If you have been working with computers for much time, you know that protecting a client computer can be quite complicated. Most of these computers will run a Windows operating system, and even within a single organization, you will have a wide range of software applications and network services. Since the computer is how users usually connect to an organization's network, it is important that the client computers are kept secure from malware and intrusion.

Protecting Your Computer from Malware

Malicious software, sometimes called malware, is software that is designed to infiltrate or affect a computer system without the owner's informed consent. The term "malware" is usually associated with viruses, worms, Trojan horses, spyware, rootkits, and dishonest adware. As a network administrator or computer technician, you need to know how to identify malware, how to remove it, and how to protect a computer from it.

CERTIFICATION READY
Do you know how a buffer overflow is exploited?
2.6

LOOKING AT TYPES OF MALWARE

Because it is now quite common for computers to be connected to the Internet, there are more opportunities than ever before for your organization's computers to be infected by malware. Indeed, over the last few years, a staggering amount of malware has been produced. As a security professional, you are responsible for protecting your organization's computers against infection. Furthermore, if a computer on your network does somehow happen to get infected by malware, you must make sure this infection does not spread to other computers.

Many early forms of malware were written as experiments or pranks. Most of the time, they were intended to be harmless or merely annoying. However, as time passed, malware increasingly became a tool for vandalism or compromising private information. Today, malware can even be used to launch denial of service (DoS) attacks against other systems, networks, or websites, causing those systems to have performance problems or become inaccessible.

As mentioned before, malware can be divided into several categories, including the following:

- Viruses
- Worms
- Trojan horses
- Spyware and dishonest adware
- Rootkits
- Backdoors

A computer *virus* is a program that can copy itself and infect a computer without the user's consent or knowledge. Early viruses were usually some form of executable code that was hidden in the boot sector of a disk or as an executable file (e.g., a filename with a .exe or .com extension). Later, as macro languages began to be used in software applications (such as word processors and spreadsheet programs), virus creators seized upon this technology, embedding malicious macros in documents of various types. Unfortunately, because macro code is automatically executed when a document is opened, these documents can infect other files and cause a wide range of problems on affected computer systems. Today, websites also pose a virus threat, as they can be written in various programming and scripting languages and may include executable programs. Therefore, whenever you access the Internet, your system is under constant threat of infection.

A *worm* is a self-replicating program that copies itself to other computers on a network without any user intervention. Unlike a virus, a worm does not corrupt or modify files on the target computer. Instead, it consumes bandwidth and processor and memory resources, slowing the system down or causing it to be unusable. Worms usually spread via security holes in operating systems or TCP/IP software implementations.

Trojan horses derive their name from the Trojan horse story in Greek mythology. In short, a *Trojan horse* is an executable program that appears as a desirable or useful program. Because it appears to be desirable or useful, users are tricked into loading and executing the program on their systems. After the program is loaded, it might cause a user's computer to become unusable, or it might bypass the user's system security, allowing his or her private information (including passwords, credit card numbers, and Social Security number) to be accessible by an outside party. In some cases, a Trojan horse may even execute adware.

Spyware is a type of malware that is installed on a computer to collect a user's personal information or details about his or her browsing habits, often without the user's knowledge. Spyware can also install additional software, redirect your web browser to other sites, or change your home page. One example of spyware is the keylogger, which records every key a user presses. When a keylogger is installed on your system, whenever you type in credit card numbers, Social Security numbers, or passwords, that information is recorded and eventually sent to or read by someone without your knowledge. (It should be noted that not all keyloggers are bad, however, as some corporations use them to monitor their corporate users.)

Adware is any software package that automatically plays, displays, or downloads advertisements to a computer after the software is installed or while the application is being used. Although adware may not necessarily be bad, it is often used with ill intent.

A *rootkit* is a software or hardware device designed to gain administrator-level control over a computer system without being detected. Rootkits can target the BIOS, hypervisor, boot loader, kernel, or less commonly, libraries or applications.

A *backdoor* is a program that gives someone remote, unauthorized control of a system or initiates an unauthorized task. Some backdoors are installed by viruses or other forms of malware. Other backdoors may be created by programs on commercial applications or with a customized application made for an organization.

Viruses and worms often exploit what is known as a buffer overflow. In all application programs including Windows itself, there are buffers that hold data. These buffers have a fixed size. If too much data is sent to these buffers, a buffer overflow occurs. Depending on the data sent to the overflow, a hacker may be able to use the overflow to send passwords to himself or herself, alter system files, install backdoors, or cause errors on a computer. When patches are released to fix a potential buffer overflow, the patch adds code to check the length of data sent to the buffer to make sure that it does not overflow.

IDENTIFYING MALWARE

The first step in removing malware is detecting that you have it. Sometimes, it is easy to see that you are infected with malware. Other times, you may never know that you have it. Some common symptoms of malware include the following:

- Poor system performance
- Unusually low levels of available memory
- Poor performance while connected to the Internet
- Decreased response rates
- Longer start-up times
- Instances in which your browser closes unexpectedly or stops responding

- Changes in your browser's default home or default search pages
- Unexpected pop-up advertising windows
- Addition of unexpected toolbars to your browser
- Instances in which unexpected programs automatically start
- Inability to start a program
- Malfunctions in Windows components or other programs
- Missing programs or files
- Unusual messages or displays on your monitor
- Unusual sounds or music played at random times
- Creation and/or installation of unknown programs or files
- Appearance of unknown browser add-ins
- Corrupted files
- Unexpected changes in file sizes

Of course, to see these symptoms, you may need to actively look for them. For example, when your Windows machine becomes slow, you might start Task Manager to view processor and memory utilization. You could then look at the ongoing processes to see which process is using the greatest amount of processor and memory resources. You might also review the processes and services in memory (again, you can use Task Manager). In addition, you could use the System Configuration. Of course, to be able to determine which processes and services are rogue, you need to have a baseline of what processes and services are currently running on your healthy system for comparison purposes. Finally, to detect malware, you should use an up-to-date antivirus program and an up-to-date antispyware package, which together can scan your entire system and look for malware in real time as you open files and access websites.

With the many tools attackers can now use to deliver malware, it is easy to see the importance of protecting your computer from all types of malware threats. Of course, when protecting yourself, a little common sense can go a long way.

USING SECURITY UPDATES AND ANTIVIRUS SOFTWARE FOR CLIENTS

Some viruses, worms, rootkits, spyware, and adware gain access to a system by exploiting security holes in Windows, Internet Explorer, Microsoft Office, or some other software package. Therefore, the first step you should take to protect yourself against malware is to keep your system up to date with the latest service packs, security patches, and other critical fixes.

The second step in protecting your computer from malware is to use an up-to-date antivirus software package. In addition, if your antivirus software does not include an antispyware component, you should install an antispyware software package. Then, you should be sure to perform a full system scan with your antivirus software at least once a week.

Windows Defender is a software product from Microsoft that is intended to prevent, remove, and quarantine spyware in Microsoft Windows. This program will help protect your computer against pop-ups, slow performance, and security threats caused by spyware and other unwanted software by detecting and removing known spyware from your computer. Windows Defender features real-time protection, a monitoring system that recommends actions against spyware as soon as it's detected, and minimal interruptions to help you stay productive. Of course, as with any antivirus package, you must keep Windows Defender up to date.

For Windows XP, Windows Defender can be downloaded from the following website: http://www.microsoft.com/windows/products/winfamily/defender/default.mspx

USING COMMON SENSE WITH MALWARE

To avoid malware, it's also important to use common sense. Therefore, you should always follow these steps:

1. Don't install unknown software or software from an unreputable source.
2. Don't open strange email attachments.

3. Don't click on hyperlinks from unknown people when you don't know what the links are supposed to do. This applies not just to hyperlinks sent via email, but also hyperlinks sent using instant messaging services.

4. If your email client supports auto launch, turn it off. Otherwise, you might automatically activate a computer virus just by opening an email.

5. Don't visit questionable websites, especially porn sites or sites that allow you to download pirated software, music, or video.

6. If your web browser alerts you that a particular site is known for hosting malware, pay attention to this warning.

7. When surfing the Internet, if you encounter browser pop-ups that tell you that you need to download the newest driver or check your system for viruses, proceed with caution.

8. Don't forget to perform regular backups. That way, if you get a virus and lose any data, you can restore your system from your backup.

REMOVING MALWARE

Whenever you start seeing any of the symptoms listed earlier in this lesson, you should quickly move to detect and (if necessary) remove any malware present on your system. Again, the first step in removing malware is to run an antivirus software package and perform a full scan. If you don't already have antivirus software, this is a good time to purchase it. If you cannot download this software with your computer, try downloading it on another machine, then copying it to an optical disk (such as a CD or DVD) or a thumb drive to transfer it to your system. If the software finds malware and removes it, you should reboot your computer and run the program yet again to be sure your system is clean. If the program keeps finding different malware after reboot, you should continue repeating the process until your machine is clean.

Microsoft offers Microsoft Security Essentials (MSE), a free antivirus software product that provides protection from malware including viruses, rootkits, spyware, and Trojan horses. To download MSE, visit the following website:

http://www.microsoft.com/security_essentials/

If your antivirus software package keeps finding the same malware over and over again, you need to be sure that you're not accessing a disk or other device that keeps infecting your system. You may also need to reboot Windows in safe mode and try another scan. If you have the option to do so, you can also try booting from a CD or DVD and running the scan.

If your software can't remove a particular virus, do a little research on the Internet. Often, you can find step-by-step instructions for removing malware, including deleting files and keys in the registry. Of course, be sure that the instructions are from a reliable source and that you follow them precisely.

Remember, if your antivirus package does not have an antispyware component, you should install a separate antispyware package to check for spyware. You can also use Windows Defender.

Microsoft also offers the Microsoft Windows Malicious Software Removal Tool, which checks computers running Windows for infections by specific, prevalent malware. Microsoft releases an updated version of this tool on the second Tuesday of each month, and as needed to respond to security incidents. The tool is available from Microsoft Update, Windows Update, and the Microsoft Download Center.

Finally, don't forget to use the following tools when trying to remove unknown malware:

- Use Task Manager to view and stop unknown processes and to stop unknown or questionable services.
- Use the Services MMC to stop unknown or questionable services.

TAKE NOTE *
Although this list may be common knowledge for IT personnel, all users should receive frequent reminders and awareness training to help protect your network.

TAKE NOTE *
Be sure that your antivirus software is up to date. If it is not current, it will not be able to detect newer viruses.

TAKE NOTE *
If you've purchased an antivirus software package and are having trouble removing malware, don't be afraid to contact the software company for assistance.

TAKE NOTE *
Because some malware has keylogging capabilities, you may want to update your login information for your online accounts whenever you find and remove any malware.

- Use System Configuration to disable unknown or questionable services and startup programs.
- In Internet Explorer, be sure to disable any unknown or questionable add-ins.

EXAMINING A VIRUS HOAX

A *virus hoax* is a message warning the recipient of a nonexistent computer virus threat, usually sent as a chain email that tells the recipient to forward it to everyone he or she knows. This is a form of social engineering that plays on people's ignorance and fear. Some hoaxes may tell people to delete key system files that make their system work properly. Others may advise you to download software from the Internet to protect against the supposed virus, when in reality, the downloaded software is some form of malware. Antivirus specialists agree that recipients should always delete virus hoaxes when they receive them, instead of forwarding them.

Utilizing Windows Updates

After installing Windows, you should check to see whether Microsoft has released any *Windows updates*, including fixes, patches, service packs, and updated device drivers. If so, you should apply them to your Windows system. By adding fixes and patches, you'll keep Windows stable and secure. Be aware that in some instances, Microsoft will release several fixes or patches together in the form of a service pack or cumulative package.

One way to keep Windows up to date is to use the Windows Update program. This program scans your system to determine what updates and fixes your system needs. You then have the opportunity to select, download, and install each update. See Figure 5-1.

Figure 5-1

Windows Update

For corporations, you can also use *Windows Server Update Service (WSUS)* or System Center Configuration Manager (SCCM) to keep your systems updated. The advantage of using one of these two systems is that it allows you to test the patch, schedule the updates, and prioritize client updates. Once you determine a patch is safe, you can enable it for deployment.

Microsoft routinely releases security updates on the second Tuesday of each month, commonly known as "Patch Tuesday." Most other updates are released as needed; these are known as "out of band" updates. Because computers are often used as production systems, you should test any updates to make sure they do not cause problems for you. Although Microsoft performs intensive testing, occasionally problems do occur, either as a bug or as a compatibility issue with third-party software. Therefore, always be sure you have a good backup of your system and data files before you install patches so that you have a back-out plan if necessary.

Microsoft classifies updates as Important, Recommended, or Optional:

- **Important updates:** These updates offer significant benefits, such as improved security, privacy, and reliability. They should be installed as they become available and can be installed automatically with Windows Update.
- **Recommended updates:** These updates address noncritical problems or help enhance your computing experience. Although these updates do not address fundamental issues with your computer or Windows software, they can offer meaningful improvements.
- **Optional updates:** These include updates, drivers, or new software from Microsoft to enhance your computing experience. You need to install these manually.

Depending on the type of update, Windows Update can deliver the following:

- **Security updates:** A security update is a broadly released fix for a product-specific security-related vulnerability. Security vulnerabilities are rated based on their severity, which is indicated in the Microsoft security bulletin as critical, important, moderate, or low.
- **Critical updates:** A critical update is a broadly released fix for a specific problem addressing a critical, nonsecurity related bug.
- **Service packs:** A service pack is a tested, cumulative set of hotfixes, security updates, critical updates, and updates, as well as additional fixes for problems found internally since the release of the product. Service packs might also contain a limited number of customer-requested design changes or features. After an operating system is released, many corporations consider the first service pack as the time when the operating system has matured enough to be used throughout the organization.

Not all updates can be retrieved through Windows Update. Sometimes, Microsoft may offer the fix for a specific problem in the form of a hotfix or cumulative patch that you can install. A hotfix is a single, cumulative package that includes one or more files that are used to address a problem in a software product, such as a software bug. Typically, hotfixes are made to address a specific customer situation, and they often have not gone through the same extensive testing as patches retrieved through Windows Updates.

For small environments, you can configure your system to run Auto Update to ensure that critical, security, and compatibility updates are made available for installation automatically without significantly affecting your regular use of the Internet. Auto Update works in the background when you are connected to the Internet to identify when new updates are available and to download them to your computer. When a download is complete, you are notified and prompted to install the update. At this point, you can install the update, get more details about what is included in the update, or let Windows remind you about the update at a later time. Some updates require you to reboot, but some do not.

To change your Windows Update settings, click the Change settings option in the left pane of the Windows Update window. See Figure 5-2. Here, you can specify which types of updates you want to download and install automatically, or you can disable Windows Update all together. You can also specify whether Windows Update will check for updates for other Microsoft products and/or install any other software Microsoft recommends.

Figure 5-2

Changing Windows Update settings

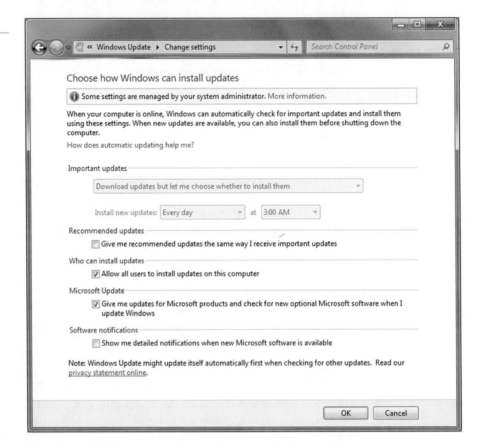

If Windows Update fails to retrieve any updates, you should check your proxy settings in Internet Explorer to see whether the program can get through your proxy server (if any) or firewall. You should also check to see whether you can access the Internet, such as by going to http://www.microsoft.com.

To see all updates that have been installed, click View Update History on the main screen of Windows Update. If you suspect a problem with a specific update, you can then click Installed Updates at the top of the screen to open the Control Panel's programs. From there, you will see all installed programs and updates. If the option is available, you can then remove the update.

Utilizing User Account Control

> **_User Account Control (UAC)_** is a feature that started with Windows Vista and is included with Windows 7. UAC helps prevent unauthorized changes to your computer—and in doing so, it helps protect your system from malware.

If you are logged in as an administrator, UAC asks you for permission before performing actions that could potentially affect your computer's operation or change settings that affect other users. Similarly, if you are logged in as a standard user, UAC will ask you for an administrator password before taking such actions. Because UAC is designed to prevent unauthorized changes—especially those made by malicious software that you may not know you are running—you need to read these warnings carefully, making sure that the action or program that's about to start is one you intended to start.

As a standard user, in Windows 7, you can do the following without administrative permissions or rights:

- Install updates from Windows Update
- Install drivers from Windows Update or drivers that are included with the operating system
- View Windows settings
- Pair Bluetooth devices with a computer
- Reset the network adapter and perform other network diagnostic and repair tasks

When an application requests elevation or is run as an administrator, UAC will prompt for confirmation and, if consent is given, it will allow access as an administrator. See Figure 5-3.

Figure 5-3

UAC confirmation with Secure Desktop

UAC can be enabled or disabled for any individual user account. Of course, if you disable UAC for a user account, your computer will be at greater risk. However, if you perform a lot of administrative tasks on a computer, repeated UAC prompts can be annoying and can stop you from doing certain activities, including saving to the root directory of a drive if you have an application that is not compatible with UAC.

ENABLE OR DISABLE UAC

GET READY. To enable or disable UAC, follow these steps:

1. In **Control Panel**, click **User Accounts**.
2. On the **User Accounts** page, click **User Accounts**.
3. Click the **Change User Account Control settings**.
4. Slide the slider to the desired options, as shown in Table 5-1. (See Figure 5-4.)

Figure 5-4

UAC settings

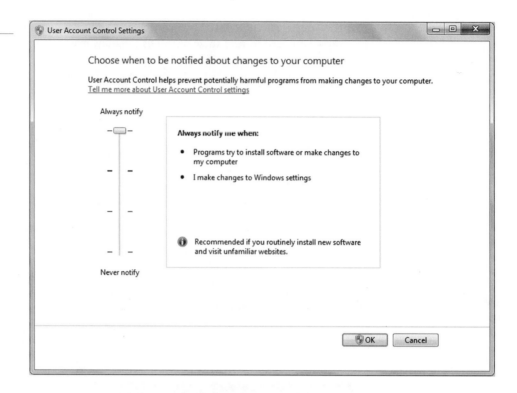

5. When prompted to restart the computer, click **Restart Now** or **Restart Later** as appropriate for the changes to take effect.

Table 5-1

UAC settings

SETTING	DESCRIPTION	SECURITY IMPACT
Always notify	You will be notified before programs make changes to your computer or to Windows settings that require the permissions of an administrator. When you're notified, your desktop will be dimmed, and you must either approve or deny the request in the UAC dialog box before you can do anything else on your computer. The dimmed desktop is referred to as a secure desktop because other programs can't run while it's dimmed.	This is the most secure setting. When you are notified, you should carefully read the contents of each dialog box before allowing changes to be made to your computer.
Notify me only when programs try to make changes to my computer	You will be notified before programs make changes to your computer that require the permissions of an administrator. You will not be notified if you try to make changes to Windows settings that require the permissions of an administrator. You will be notified if a program outside of Windows tries to make changes to a Windows setting.	It's usually safe to allow changes to be made to Windows settings without notification. However, certain programs that come with Windows can have commands or data passed to them, and malicious software can take advantage of this by using these programs to install files or change settings on your computer. You should always be careful about which programs you allow to run on your computer.

Table 5-1 *(continued)*

SETTING	DESCRIPTION	SECURITY IMPACT
Notify me only when programs try to make changes to my computer (do not dim my desktop)	You will be notified before programs make changes to your computer that require the permissions of an administrator. You will not be notified if you try to make changes to Windows settings that require the permissions of an administrator. You will be notified if a program outside of Windows tries to make changes to a Windows setting.	This setting is the same as "Notify only when programs try to make changes to my computer," but you are not notified on the secure desktop. Because the UAC dialog box isn't on the secure desktop with this setting, other programs might be able to interfere with the dialog's visual appearance. This is a small security risk if you already have a malicious program running on your computer.
Never notify	You will not be notified before any changes are made to your computer. If you are logged on as an administrator, programs can make changes to your computer without you knowing about it. If you are logged on as a standard user, any changes that require the permissions of an administrator will automatically be denied. If you select this setting, you will need to restart the computer to complete the process of turning off UAC. Once UAC is off, people who log on as an administrator will always have the permissions of an administrator.	This is the least secure setting. When you set UAC to never notify, you open up your computer to potential security risks. If you set UAC to never notify, you should be careful about which programs you run, because they will have the same access to the computer as you do. This includes reading and making changes to protected system areas, personal data, saved files, and anything else stored on the computer. Programs will also be able to communicate and transfer information to and from anything your computer connects with, including the Internet.

Using Windows Firewall

Another important client tool is a firewall. As discussed in Lesson 4, a firewall is software or hardware that checks information coming from the Internet or a network, and then either blocks it or allows it to pass through to your computer, depending on your firewall settings. A firewall can help prevent hackers or malicious software (such as worms) from gaining access to your computer through a network or the Internet. A firewall can also help stop your computer from sending malicious software to other computers.

Microsoft recommends that you always use *Windows Firewall*. However, because some security packages and antivirus packages include their own firewall, you may choose to run an alternate firewall—but you should use only one firewall.

> **TAKE NOTE** *
>
> Although your network may have a firewall to help protect you from unwanted Internet traffic, it's still a good idea to have a host firewall to give you an extra level of protection. This is especially recommended when the client computer is a mobile computer that may be moved outside your organization's network.

In addition, to the Windows Firewall found in the Control Panel, newer versions of Windows include Windows Firewall with Advanced Security. Windows Firewall with Advanced Security combines a host firewall and Internet Protocol security (IPsec). Although Windows Firewall and Windows Firewall with Advanced Security are tightly coupled, the latter allows greater control of your firewall. In addition, Windows Firewall with Advanced Security also provides computer-to-computer connection security by allowing you to require authentication and data protection for communications via IPsec.

⊖ ENABLE OR DISABLE WINDOWS FIREWALL

GET READY. To enable or disable Windows Firewall, perform the following steps:

1. Open the **Control Panel**.
2. If you are in **Category** view, click **System and Security**, then click **Windows Firewall**. If you are in **Icon** view, double-click **Windows Firewall**.
3. In the left pane, click **Turn Windows Firewall on or off**. If you are prompted for an administrator password or confirmation, type the password or provide confirmation.
4. Click **Turn on Windows Firewall** under the appropriate network location to enable Windows Firewall, or click **Turn off Windows Firewall (not recommended)** under the appropriate network location to disable Windows Firewall. See Figure 5-5. You typically want to block all incoming traffic when you connect to a public network in a hotel or airport or when a computer worm is spreading over the Internet. When you block all incoming connections, you can still view most web pages, send and receive email, and send and receive instant messages.

Figure 5-5

Windows Firewall

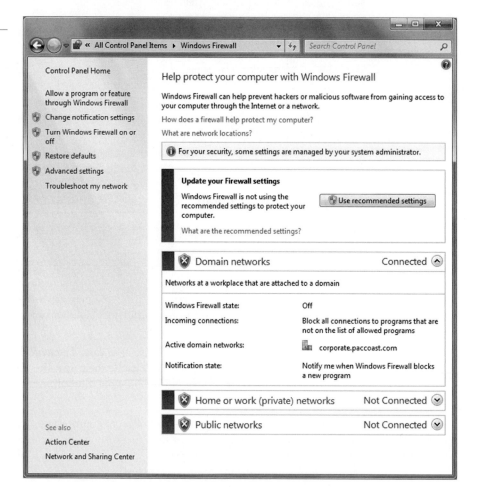

5. If desired, select **Block all incoming connections, including those in the list of allowed programs** and **Notify me when Windows Firewall blocks a new program**.
6. Click **OK**.

By default, most programs are blocked by Windows Firewall to help make your computer more secure. To work properly, some programs might require you to allow them to communicate through the firewall.

ALLOW A PROGRAM THROUGH WINDOWS FIREWALL

GET READY. To allow a program to communicate through Windows Firewall, perform the following steps:

1. Open **Windows Firewall.**
2. In the left pane, click **Allow a program or feature through Windows Firewall.**
3. Click **Change settings.** If you are prompted for an administrator password or confirmation, type the password or provide confirmation.
4. Select the check box next to the program you want to allow, select the network locations you want to allow communication on, and then click **OK.**

 OPEN PORTS ON WINDOWS FIREWALL

GET READY. If the program you want to allow isn't listed, you might need to open a port. To open a port, perform the following steps:

1. Open **Windows Firewall.**
2. In the left pane, click **Advanced settings.** If you are prompted for an administrator password or confirmation, type the password or provide confirmation.
3. In the left pane of the **Windows Firewall with Advanced Security** dialog box, click **Inbound Rules**; then, in the right pane, click **New Rule.**
4. Select **Port** and click the **Next** button. See Figure 5-6.

Figure 5-6

Inbound Rules options

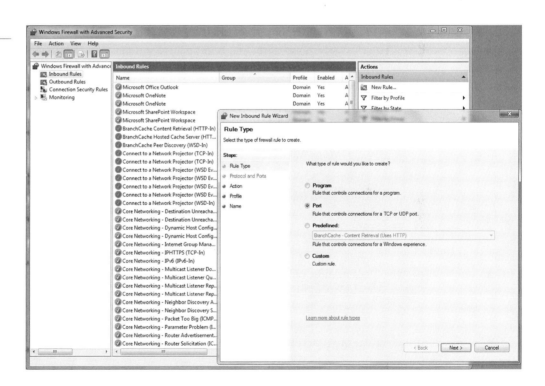

5. Specify **TCP** or **UDP** and specify the port numbers. Click the **Next** button. See Figure 5-7.

Figure 5-7

Opening a port

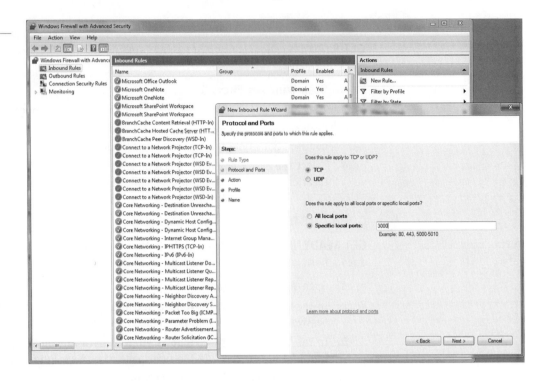

6. Select **Allow the connection**, **Allow the connection if it is secure**, or **Block the connection**. Click the **Next** button.

7. By default, the rule will apply to all domains. If you don't want the rule to apply to a domain, deselect the domain. Click the **Next** button.

8. Specify a name for the rule and a description if desired. Click the **Finish** button.

Using Offline Files

Offline files are copies of network files that are stored on your computer so you can access them when you aren't connected to the network or when the network folder that contains the files is not connected.

Offline files are not encrypted unless you choose for them to be. You might want to encrypt your offline files if they contain sensitive or confidential information and you want to make them more secure by restricting access to them. Encrypting your offline files provides you with an additional level of access protection that works independently of NTFS file system permissions. This can help safeguard your files in case your computer is ever lost or stolen.

 ENABLE OFFLINE FILES

GET READY. To enable offline files, perform these steps:

1. Click the **Start** button and open the **Control Panel**.

2. Search for **offline** in the **Search Control Panel** text box and click **Manage offline files**.

3. Click **Enable offline files**.

4. If prompted, reboot the computer.

→ ENCRYPT OFFLINE FILES

GET READY. To encrypt your offline files, perform these steps:

1. Click the **Start** button and open the **Control Panel.**
2. Search for **offline** in the **Search Control Panel** text box and click **Manage offline files.**
3. Click the **Encryption** tab.
4. Click **Encrypt** to encrypt your offline files, and then click **OK.**

If you choose to encrypt your offline files, you encrypt only the offline files stored on your computer, not the network versions of the files. You do not need to decrypt an encrypted file or folder stored on your computer before using it. This is done for you automatically.

Locking Down a Client Computer

If you work with end users for an extended period of time, you will soon learn that some users are their own worst enemy. Therefore, in some case, you should considering locking down a computer so that a user cannot harm it.

Unless individual users have the need to be administrators on their own computers, they should just be standard users. This will prevent users from installing unauthorized software and making changes to the system that would make the system less secure. In addition, if these users are affected by malware, the malware will only have minimum access to the system. Of course, it would be recommended to use the run as options if needed as discussed in Lesson 2.

When working within an organization, it is often advantageous to standardize each company computer. Therefore, when moving from one computer to another, everything will be similar. To keep computers standardized, an organization may choose to use Group Policies so that users cannot access certain features (including the Control Panel) and make changes to the system that may be detrimental.

Allowing users to install software may:

- Introduce malware to a system.
- Bypass safeguards already put in place to protect against malicious viruses and Trojan horse programs.
- Cause conflicts with software already on a baseline computer within an organization.

If you do not allow your computer users to log on as administrators, you limit what software they can install. You can also use group policies to restrict what software can be executed on a client computer.

Windows 7 supports two mechanisms for restricting applications both of which are based on group policies. They are:

- Software restriction policies
- AppLockerS

■ Protecting Your Email

THE BOTTOM LINE

Email has become an essential service for virtually every corporation. Unfortunately, much of the email received by a company's employees consists of unsolicited messages called *spam* or junk email, some of which can carry malware and may lead to fraud or scams.

CERTIFICATION READY
Do you know how to
prevent viruses from
being sent through email?
4.2

The idea behind spam is to send a lot of unsolicited bulk messages indiscriminately, hoping that a few people will open the email, navigate to a website, purchase a product, or fall for a scam. For the people who create it, spam has minimal operating costs. Over the last few years, spam amounts have increased exponentially, and today, spam accounts for at least 90 percent of all the email in the world.

Besides the risk of malware and fraud associated with spam, there is also a loss of productivity for email recipients as they sort through unsolicited emails. In addition, the IT department will need to install additional storage and provide sufficient bandwidth to accommodate the extra email. Therefore, you should always install a spam blocking device or software that includes antivirus protection. The program will provide a second layer to protect your network from viruses.

Dealing with Spam

To keep your systems running smoothly, you—the network administrator—must put some effort into blocking spam.

The best place to establish a spam filtering system is on a dedicated server or appliance or as part of a firewall device or service. You can direct all email to the spam filter by changing your DNS Mail Exchanger (MX) record to point to the antispam server or device. Any email that is not considered spam will be forwarded to your internal email servers.

When establishing a spam filtering system, keep two things in mind. First, spam filtering systems will not catch every single spam message. Like an antivirus package, a spam filtering solution needs to be kept up to date and constantly tweaked. You may also need to add email addresses, email domains, IP address ranges, or keywords into a black list. Any email with traits on the black list will automatically be blocked. Of course, you need to take care when using a black list to make sure you don't make the criteria so broad as to start blocking legitimate email.

Many antispam solutions also use a real-time blackhole list (RBL) or DNS-based blackhole list (DNSBL) that can be accessed freely. RBLs and DNSBLs are lists of known spammers that are updated frequently. Most mail server software can be configured to reject or flag messages that have been sent from a site listed on one or more such lists. Because spammers look for ways to get around this, it is just one tool that can help reduce the amount of spam that gets through.

As email is identified as spam, it is usually quarantined or stored temporarily in case a legitimate email has been mistakenly placed in this category. While the number of miscategorized messages should be relatively low, you will need to train your help desk personnel and possibly your users to access quarantined email so they can release misplaced messages to their destined email box. In addition, you need to add the sender's email address or domain to a white list so that it will not be identified as spam in the future.

Detecting spam can be a daunting task if you've ever had to do it manually. Besides the obvious advertising phrases and other keywords, spam systems will also look at an email's header to analyze information about the email and its origin. For example, if you have email in Outlook 2003, open one email message, open the View menu, and select Options. Under Internet Headers, you can see the history for an email delivery path. To do this in Outlook 2010, first select the message, then click the File menu and select Properties under Info.

To make a spam message look like a legitimate message, sometimes spammers try to spoof an email address or IP address where a message comes from. For example, if email was sent from a yahoo.com domain, an antispam system could do a reverse lookup using the DNS PTR record to see the IP address of the yahoo.com domain. If that IP address does not match where the email said it came from, the message is considered spam and will be blocked.

Sender Policy Framework (SPF) is an email validation system designed to prevent email spam that uses source address spoofing. SPF allows administrators to specify in DNS SPF records in the public DNS which hosts are allowed to send email from a given domain. If email for a domain is not sent from a host listed in the DNS SPF, it will be considered spam and blocked.

Today, antispam packages use special algorithms, such as *Bayesian filters*, to determine whether email is considered spam. These algorithms usually analyze previously received emails and create a database using a number of attributes. Then, when a computer receives an email, it will compare that email with the attributes it has collected to determine whether the message is spam.

Relaying Email

> Simple Mail Transfer Protocol (SMTP) is one of the primary email protocols. SMTP is used to transfer email from one server to another, and it is responsible for outgoing mail transport. SMTP uses TCP port 25.

Although you may think your email servers function only for users to send and retrieve email, they also may be used to relay email. For example, web and application servers may relay email through their email servers, such as when you order something over the Internet and a confirmation email is sent to you.

Usually, you only want your internal servers to relay email through your mail servers. Unfortunately, spammers frequently look for unprotected SMTP servers to relay their email through. As a result, not only do the spammers use your SMTP servers to send emails, but other organizations may flag your server or domain as a spammer, and you may be placed on one of the RBLs or DNSBLs. To get off this list, you will need to close up your security hole so that other people cannot relay email through your server. Then you can contact the organizations that host the RBLs or DNSBLs to get taken off their list.

■ Securing Internet Explorer

THE BOTTOM LINE

Because browsing a website can expose you to a wide range of hazards, you also need to look carefully at your browser to help protect both you and your system. Today's browsers include pop-up blockers, zones, and other built-in security features.

CERTIFICATION READY
Where do you think most malware comes from?
1.3

Looking at Cookies and Privacy Settings

> When you use a browser to access the Internet, you may be revealing personal information and a great deal about your personality. Therefore, you need to take steps to ensure that this information cannot be read or used without your knowledge.

A *cookie* is a piece of text stored by a user's web browser. This file can be used for a wide range of purposes, including user identification, authentication, and storing site preferences and shopping cart contents. Although cookies can give a website a lot of capability, they can also be used by spyware programs and websites to track people. Unfortunately, some websites will not operate without cookies.

 DELETE COOKIES IN INTERNET EXPLORER 8

GET READY. To delete cookies, perform these steps:

1. Open **Internet Explorer**.
2. Click the **Tools** button, and then click **Internet Options**.

3. On the **General** tab, under **Browsing history**, click **Delete**. See Figure 5-8.

Figure 5-8

Deleting cookies and
temporary files

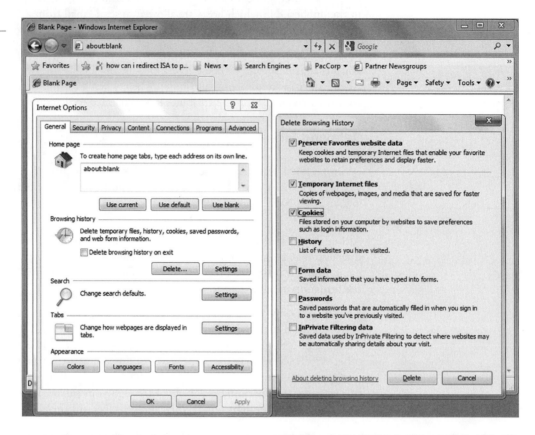

4. Select the **Cookies** check box, and then click **Delete** if it isn't already checked. Clear or select check boxes for any other information you also want to delete. If you want to keep cookies for your saved favorites, select the Preserve Favorites website data check box.

Being aware of how your private information is used when browsing the web is also important to help prevent targeted advertising, fraud, and identity theft. Here, it's important to use the appropriate privacy settings.

 CHANGE PRIVACY SETTINGS

GET READY. To change Internet Explorer's privacy settings, perform these steps:

1. Open **Internet Explorer**.
2. Click the **Tools** button, and then click **Internet Options**.
3. Click the **Privacy tab**. See Figure 5-9.

Figure 5-9

Privacy tab

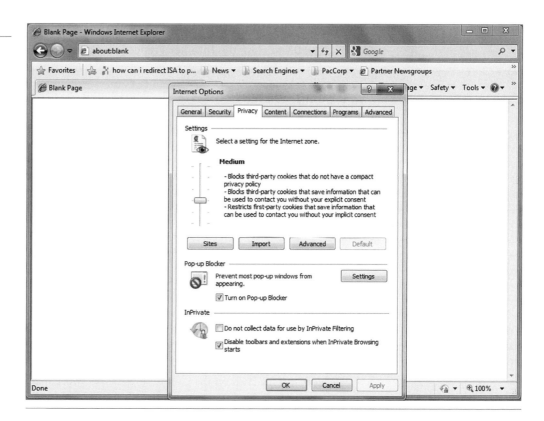

To adjust your privacy settings, adjust the slider to a new position on the privacy scale. The default level is Medium; it is recommended that you configure your settings for Medium or higher. If you click on the Advanced button, you can override certain settings, and if you click the Edit button, you can allow or block cookies from individual websites.

Pop-up windows are very common on the Internet. Although some pop-up windows are useful website controls, most are simply annoying advertisements, and a few may attempt to load spyware or other malicious programs. To protect your computer, Internet Explorer has the capability to suppress some or all pop-ups. To configure the pop-up blocker, use the following procedure:

 CONFIGURE THE POP-UP BLOCKER

GET READY. Log on to Windows 7, then perform these steps:

1. Click **Start**, and click **Control Panel**. The **Control Panel** window appears.
2. Select **Network and Internet > Internet Options**. The Internet Properties sheet appears.
3. Click the **Privacy** tab. Make sure the **Turn on Pop-up Blocker** option is selected.
4. Click **Settings**. The Pop-Up Blocker Settings dialog box appears.
5. To allow pop-ups from a specific website, type the URL of the site in the **Address of website to allow text box**, and then click **Add**. Repeat the process to add additional sites to the Allowed sites list.
6. Adjust the Blocking level drop-down list to one of the following settings:
   - **High:** Block all pop-ups
   - **Medium:** Block most automatic pop-ups
   - **Low:** Allow pop-ups from secure sites

7. Click **Close** to close the Pop-Up Blocker Settings dialog box.

8. Click **OK** to close the **Internet Properties** sheet.

Examining Content Zones

To help manage security when visiting sites, Internet Explorer divides your network connection into four *content zones* or types. For each of these zones, a security level is assigned.

The security for each zone is assigned based on dangers associated with the zone. For example, it is assumed that when you connect to a server in your own corporation, you are safer than when connecting to a server on the Internet.

The four default content zones are as follows:

- **Internet zone:** This zone is used for anything that is not assigned to another zone and anything that is not on your computer or your organization's network (intranet). The default security level of the Internet zone is Medium.

- **Local intranet zone:** This zone is used for sites that are part of an organization's network (intranet) and do not require a proxy server, as defined by the system administrator. These include sites specified on the Connections tab, network, paths such as \\computername\ foldername, and local intranet sites such as http://internal. You can add sites to this zone. The default security level for the Local intranet zone is Medium-Low, which means Internet Explorer will allow all cookies from websites in this zone to be saved on your computer and read by the website that created them. Finally, if the website requires NTLM or integrated authentication, it will automatically use your username and password.

- **Trusted sites zone:** This zone contains sites from which you believe you can download or run files without damaging your system. You can assign sites to this zone. The default security level for the Trusted sites zone is Low, which means Internet Explorer will allow all cookies from websites in this zone to be saved on your computer and read by the website that created them.

- **Restricted sites zone:** This zone contains sites that you do not trust and from which downloading or running files may damage your computer or data. These sites are considered a security risk. You can assign sites to this zone. The default security level for the Restricted sites zone is High, which means Internet Explorer will block all cookies from websites in this zone.

To tell which zone a web page falls into, look at the right side of the Internet Explorer status bar.

 MODIFY SECURITY LEVEL FOR WEB CONTENT ZONE

GET READY. To modify the security level for a web content zone, perform these steps:

1. Click the **Tools** button, and then click **Internet Options**.

2. In the **Internet Options** dialog box, on the **Security** tab, click the zone on which you want to set the security level. See Figure 5-10.

Figure 5-10

Configuring security content zones

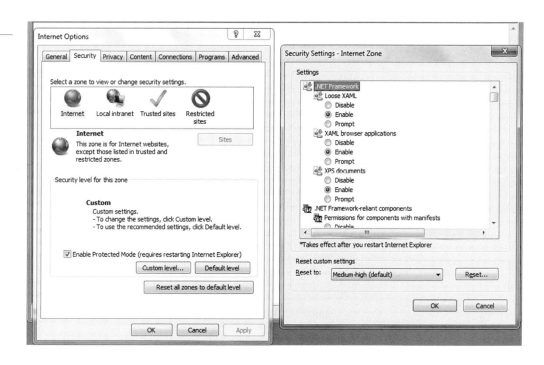

3. Drag the slider to set the security level to **High**, **Medium**, or **Low**. Internet Explorer describes each option to help you decide which level to choose. You will be prompted to confirm any reduction in security level. You can also choose the **Custom Level** button for more detailed control.

4. Click **OK** to close the **Internet Options** dialog box.

For each of the web content zones, there is a default security level. The security levels available in Internet Explorer are as follows:

- **High:** Excludes any content that can damage your computer
- **Medium:** Warns you before running potentially damaging content
- **Low:** Does not warn you before running potentially damaging content
- **Custom:** A security setting of your own design

The easiest way to modify the security setting that Internet Explorer imposes on a specific website is to manually add the site to a security zone. The typical procedure is to add a site to the Trusted sites zone to increase its privileges, or to instead add it to the Restricted sites zone to reduce its privileges. To do this, use the following procedure:

 ADD A SITE TO A SECURITY ZONE

GET READY. Log on to Windows 7, then perform these steps:

1. Click **Start**, and click **Control Panel**. The Control Panel window appears.
2. Select **Network and Internet > Internet Options**. The Internet Properties sheet appears.
3. Click the **Security** tab.
4. Select either the **Trusted sites** or **Restricted sites** zone to which you want to add a site.
5. Click **Sites**. The Trusted sites or Restricted sites dialog box appears.
6. Type the URL of the website you want to add to the zone into the **Add this website to the zone** text box, and then click **Add**. The URL appears in the Websites list.
7. Click **Close** to close the Trusted sites or Restricted sites dialog box.
8. Click **OK** to close the Internet Properties sheet.

To modify the security properties of a zone, use the following procedure:

 MODIFY SECURITY ZONE SETTINGS

GET READY. Log on to Windows 7, then perform these steps:

1. Click **Start**, and click **Control Panel.** The Control Panel window appears.
2. Select **Network and Internet > Internet Options.** The Internet Properties sheet appears.
3. Click the **Security** tab.
4. Select the zone for which you want to modify the security settings.
5. In the **Security level for this zone** box, adjust the slider to increase or decrease the security level for the zone. Moving the slider up increases the protection for the zone, and moving the slider down decreases it.
6. Select or clear the **Enable protected mode** check box, if desired.
7. To exercise more precise control over the zone's security settings, click **Custom level.** The Security Settings dialog box for the zone appears.
8. Select radio buttons for the individual settings in each of the security categories. The radio buttons typically make it possible to enable a setting, disable it, or prompt the user before enabling it.
9. Click **OK** to close the Security Settings dialog box.
10. Click **OK** to close the Internet Properties sheet.

Phishing and Pharming

Phishing and pharming are two forms of attack used to lure individuals to bogus websites in an attempt to spread malware or collect personal information.

Phishing is a technique based on social engineering. With phishing, users are asked (usually through email or websites) to supply personal information in one of two ways:

- By replying to an email asking for their username, password, and other personal information, such as account numbers, PINs, and Social Security number
- By navigating to a convincing-looking website that urges them to supply their personal information, such as passwords and account numbers

For example, say you receive an email stating that your credit card account has just expired or that you need to validate your information. The email offers you a link to click on. When you click on the link, you go to the fake website. However, by "logging in" to the site with your real information, you are actually providing your username and password to the hacker, who can then use this information to access your account.

To help protect against phishing, Internet Explorer 8 includes SmartScreen Filter, which examines traffic for evidence of phishing activity and displays a warning to the user if it finds any. It also sends the address back to the Microsoft SmartScreen service for comparison against lists of known phishing and malware sites. If SmartScreen Filter discovers that a website you're visiting is on the list of known malware or phishing sites, Internet Explorer will display a blocking webpage and the Address bar will appear in red. From the blocking page, you can choose to bypass the blocked website and go to your home page instead, or you can continue to the blocked website, although this is not recommended. If you decide to continue to the blocked website, the Address bar will continue to appear in red.

One of the best ways to avoid such ploys is to know that they exist. Accordingly, when you get an email requesting personal information, look for signs that the email is fake and that links within it go to bogus websites (e.g., instead of going to ebay.com, a link goes to ebay.com.com or ebay_ws-com). Don't trust hyperlinks. Never supply a password or any other confidential information to a website unless you type the URL yourself and you are sure that it is correct.

Pharming is an attack aimed at redirecting a website's traffic to a bogus website. This is usually accomplished by changing the hosts file (a text that provides name resolution for host or domain names to IP address) on a computer or by exploiting a vulnerability on a DNS server. To protect against pharming, you need to make sure your system has the newest security patches and that it is a up-to-date antivirus software package. In addition, UAC will help protect the hosts file since it is located in the System32 folder, which is one of the areas UAC helps protect.

■ Protecting Your Server

THE BOTTOM LINE

When considering security, remember that you need to secure your network, your clients, and your servers. By securing all three, you adopt a layered approach that makes it more difficult for hackers and malware to breach your organization. In previous lessons, we discussed how to keep your network secure. Earlier in this lesson, we discussed how to keep your clients secure. Now, in this portion of the lesson, we'll focus on securing the server.

CERTIFICATION READY
Do you know how to protect your servers so that they are always up and running?
4.3

As you already know, servers are computers that are meant to provide network services and applications for your organization. Unlike a workstation, if a server fails, it will affect multiple users. Therefore, it is more important to keep a server more secure than a workstation.

Placing the Server

The first step in securing a server is determining where to place the server. Of course, the server should be kept in a secure location. In addition, servers should be on their own subnet and VLAN to reduce the traffic reaching them, including broadcasts.

In some instances, you may need to place servers at a branch office. In situations in which you need to install a domain controller in a low physical security environment, you should consider installing a Read-Only Domain Controller (RODC), which holds a nonwriteable copy of Active Directory and redirects all write attempts to a Full Domain Controller. This device replicates all accounts except sensitive ones. Therefore, if the domain controller is compromised, attackers are limited in what they can do when writing information to Active Directory.

Hardening the Server

The next step in securing a server is to harden the server to reduce the attack surface, thereby reducing the server's vulnerabilities. To harden a server, you should look for security guidelines and best practices for Windows servers and for the specific network services you are installing, such as Microsoft Exchange or Microsoft SQL Server.

One of the most important steps in securing a server is to make sure that Windows, Microsoft applications, and other network applications are kept current with the newest security patches. As with clients, you can do this using Windows updates, WSUS, and SCCM. Of course, before applying patches to a production system, make sure that you test the security updates.

To reduce a server's attack surface, you should disable any service that is not necessary so that this service cannot be exploited in the future. In addition, you should consider using host firewalls (such as Windows Firewall) that will block all ports that are not being used.

To reduce the effect of losing a server, you should separate the services. Never install all of your services on one server! You also need to plan for the rest and hope for the best. This means that you need to anticipate that a server will eventually fail. Therefore, you should consider using redundant power supplies, RAID disks, redundant network cards, and clusters.

You should also disable or delete any unnecessary accounts. For example, although you cannot delete the administrator account, you can rename it to something else so that it will be more difficult for a hacker to guess what it is. In addition, you should not use the administrator account for everything. For example, if you have to run a specific service, create a service account for that service and give it the minimum rights and permissions that it needs to run. Of course, the guest account should be disabled.

Besides disabling or deleting any unnecessary accounts and only assigning the minimum rights and permissions necessary for users to do their jobs, you should also minimize who can log on locally to the server.

In addition, you should disable any unsecure authentication protocols. For example, you should not use Password Authentication Protocol (PAP) when using remote access protocols. You should not use FTP with passwords. Instead, use either anonymous that does not require passwords (assuming its content does not need to be secure) or use secure FTP, which will encrypt the password and content when being transmitted over the network. For similar reasons, you should not use telnet. Instead, use SSH.

Finally, you should enable a strong audit and logging policy and review these logs on a regular basis. If someone tries to hack a server or do something that he or she should not be doing, you will have a record of that person's activities. This should include both successful and failed account logins.

Microsoft Baseline Security Analyzer (MBSA) is a software tool released by Microsoft to determine the security state of a system by assessing missing security updates and less-secure security settings within Microsoft Windows components such as Internet Explorer, IIS web server, and products such as Microsoft SQL Server and Microsoft Office macro settings. See Figure 5-11.

Figure 5-11

Microsoft Baseline Security Analyzer

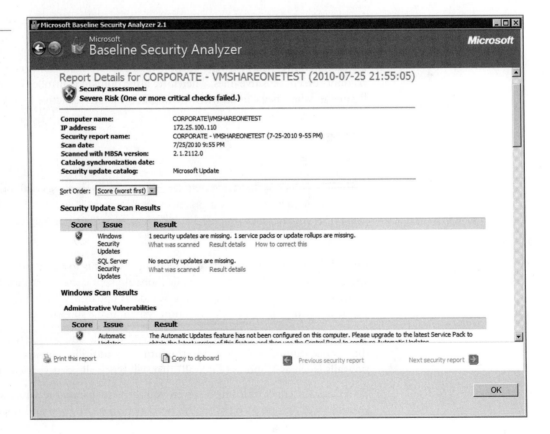

Microsoft often publishes security guides and best practices guides for various products. In addition, Microsoft has published the Threats and Countermeasures—Security Settings in Windows Server 2008 and Windows Vista, which can be found at http://www.microsoft.com/downloads/details.aspx?displaylang=en&FamilyID=037d908d-6a1c-4135-930c-e3a0d6a34239.

Using Secure Dynamic DNS

Since Windows Server 2003, Windows servers have provided support for the DNS dynamic update functionality. Dynamic DNS lets client computers dynamically update their resource records in DNS. When you use this functionality, you improve DNS administration by reducing the time that it takes to manually manage DNS zone records. You can use the DNS update functionality with DHCP to update resource records when a computer's IP address is changed.

With typical unsecured dynamic updates, any computer can create records on your DNS server, which leaves you open to malicious activity. To protect your DNS server, secure it so that only members of an Active Directory domain can create records on the server.

SKILL SUMMARY

IN THIS LESSON, YOU LEARNED:

- Because client computers are connected to an organization's network and may have direct and indirect access to servers and network resources, it is important that these computers are protected.

- A virus is a program that can copy itself and infect a computer without the user's consent or knowledge.

- A backdoor in a program gives remote, unauthorized control of a system or initiates an unauthorized task.

- Some viruses, worms, rootkits, spyware, and adware work by exploiting security holes in Windows, Internet Explorer, or Microsoft Office.

- The first step to protecting yourself against malware is keeping your Windows system (as well as other Microsoft products, such as Internet Explorer and Microsoft Office) up to date with the latest service packs, security patches, and other critical fixes.

- A virus hoax is a message warning the recipient of a nonexistent computer virus threat, usually sent as a chain email that tells the recipient to forward it to everyone he or she knows. This is a form of social engineering that plays on people's ignorance and fear.

- User Account Control (UAC) is a feature that helps prevent malware. UAC was first introduced with Windows Vista and is included with Windows 7.

- Microsoft recommends that you always use Windows Firewall.

- Offline files are not encrypted unless you choose for them to be. You might opt to encrypt your offline files if they contain sensitive or confidential information and you want to make them more secure by restricting access to them.

- If you do not allow users to log on as administrators, you can limit what software these users install and you can better protect the system from malware.

- You can also use Group Policies to restrict what software can be executed on a client computer.

- Most email is unsolicited; such messages are called spam or junk email.

- The best place to establish a spam filtering system is on your email relay on a dedicated server or appliance, or as part of a firewall device or service.

- To make a spam message look like a legitimate message, sometimes spammers try to spoof an email address or IP address where a message comes from.
- Spammers look for unprotected SMTP servers to relay their emails through.
- Although some pop-up windows are useful web site controls, most are simply annoying advertisements, and a few attempt to load spyware or other malicious programs.
- To help manage security when visiting websites, Internet Explorer divides your network connection into four content zones or types. Each of these zones is assigned a security level.
- Phishing and pharming are two forms of attack used to lure individuals to bogus websites in an attempt to spread malware or collect personal information.
- All servers should be kept in a secure location. In addition, servers should be on their own subnet and VLAN to reduce the traffic reaching them, including broadcasts.
- You should also secure a server by hardening it to reduce the attack surface. When hardening a server, look for security guides and best practices for Windows servers, as well as for the specific network services you are installing.
- To secure your DNS server, make it so that only members of an Active Directory domain can create records on the DNS server.

■ Knowledge Assessment

Multiple Choice

Circle the letter that corresponds to the best answer.

1. Which type of malware copies itself onto other computers without the owner's consent and will often delete or corrupt files?
   a. Virus
   b. Worm
   c. Trojan horse
   d. Spyware

2. Which type of malware collects personal information or browsing history, often without the user's knowledge?
   a. Virus
   b. Worm
   c. Trojan horse
   d. Spyware

3. Your computer seems to be slow, and you notice that you have a different default web page than usual. What is most likely the cause of problems?
   a. Your ISP has slowed your network connection.
   b. Your computer has been infected with malware.
   c. You did not update your computer.
   d. You accidentally clicked the turbo button.

4. Besides installing an antivirus software package, you should always _____ to protect your computer against malware.
   a. keep your machine up to date with the latest security patches
   b. reboot your computer on a regular basis
   c. change your password on a regular basis
   d. spoof your IP address

5. A thoroughly tested, cumulative set of hotfixes and other patches is known as a _____.
   a. Recommended update
   b. Hotfix pack
   c. Service pack
   d. Critical update

6. What technology is used by Windows to prevent unauthorized changes to your system?
   a. UAC
   b. Protected mode
   c. Windows Defender
   d. ProtectGuard

7. When using UAC, which of the following requires administrative permissions or rights?
   a. Installing updates from Windows update
   b. Changing the date and time
   c. Resetting the network adapter
   d. Installing drivers from Windows update or attached with the operating system

8. What mechanism is working when you try to change a computer's display settings and you get a pop-up asking whether you wish to continue?
   a. Windows Firewall
   b. Protected Mode
   c. Windows Update
   d. UAC

9. What host-based firewall software comes with current versions of Windows?
   a. Windows Firewall
   b. Windows Protected Mode
   c. UAC
   d. Windows GuardIt

10. What program would you use to configure IPsec on a computer running Windows Server 2008?
    a. Windows Firewall with IPsec Plugin
    b. IPsec Monitor
    c. Windows with Advanced Security
    d. IPsec Configuration console

11. If you have sensitive or confidential information stored in your offline files, it is recommended that you
    a. Clear your cache
    b. Encrypt the offline files
    c. Clear your cookies
    d. Execute ipconfig /renewip

12. You determine that legitimate emails are being blocked by your spam-blocking device. What should you do?
    a. Flush out the quarantined items
    b. Reboot the spam-blocking device
    c. Add the address or domain for these emails to the white list
    d. Add the address or domain for these emails to the black list

13. SMTP uses TCP port _____.
    a. 43
    b. 25
    c. 80
    d. 443

14. How many content zones are there in Internet Explorer?
   a. 1
   b. 2
   c. 4
   d. 8

15. Say that you receive an email stating that your account has just expired and asking you to log in to a legitimate-looking website to fix the problem. This is most likely an instance of _____.
   a. Phishing
   b. Pharming
   c. Phaking
   d. IP address spoofing

Fill in the Blank

Complete the following sentences by writing the correct word or words in the blanks provided.

1. _____ is software that is designed to infiltrate or infect a computer, usually with ill intent.

2. A(n) _____ is a self-replicating program that copies itself to other computers while consuming network resources.

3. Microsoft's antispyware program is called _____.

4. For antivirus software to be effective, it must be kept _____.

5. An example of a(n) _____ is a message saying to delete the win.com file because it is a virus.

6. If you want to control what updates get pushed to clients within your organization, you would use _____ or _____.

7. _____ is when you are asked if you want to continue with an action and your desktop is dimmed and other programs are temporary halted until you approve the change.

8. _____ are copies of network files that are stored on your computer so that you can access them when you are not connected to the network.

9. _____ is another name for junk email.

10. _____ is an email validation system that is designed to verify that an email is coming from the proper email server.

■ Competency Assessment

Scenario 5-1: Checking Physical Security

You were just hired as an IT administrator for the ABC Company. Across from your desk, there is a table with seven physical servers. You go to your boss and ask why the servers are out in the open and not locked up. He says there are located on the table so that they can be easily monitored and watched. How should you respond to your boss?

Scenario 5-2: Programming Backdoors

You have been hired as a security consultant for the Contoso Corporation. One day, you are working with the CIO on a new comprehensive security policy for the company. Although the CIO is not a programmer herself, she wants to understand how she can keep programmers from creating a backdoor on the programs they create for the company. What do you tell her?

■ Proficiency Assessment

Scenario 5-3: Scanning with Microsoft Baseline Security Analyzer

Download and install the newest Microsoft Baseline Security Analyzer on a Windows server, then scan the computer for missing security updates and less-optimal security settings.

Scenario 5-4: Looking at Windows Updates

Go to http://www.microsoft.com/technet/security/bulletin/advance.mspx. Read the most recent advance notification or most recent security bulletin summary and review the executive summary. Determine how many security bulletins there are for the most recent month. Then run Windows Update to bring your system up to date with the newest patches.

 # Workplace Ready

Keeping Up with Security

Maintaining security for an organization is often a full-time job that usually requires multiple people with various skill sets. For example, you may have a person who is responsible for routers and firewalls, another person who is responsible for servers, and another person who is responsible for client computers. You may also have a security manager who oversees all items related to security, including physical security. Of course, a company's CEO, CIO, and other executives are the ones who are ultimately responsible for security.

However, for security to be effective, you need to remember that everyone needs to participate. This includes the executives who support the IT department and help enforce and support security-related decisions, as well as the IT staff members who establish the security measures and monitor them. But don't forget that the weakest link could be the end user. Best practices, awareness training, and constant reminders are key to communicating to all employees why security is so important.

Objective Domain	Skill Number	Lesson Number
Understanding Security Layers		
Understand core security principles.	1.1	1
Understand physical security.	1.2	1
Understand Internet security.	1.3	5
Understand wireless security.	1.4	4
Understanding Operating System Security		
Understand user authentication.	2.1	2
Understand permissions.	2.2	2
Understand password policies.	2.3	3
Understand audit policies.	2.4	2
Understand encryption.	2.5	2
Understand malware.	2.6	5
Understanding Network Security		
Understand dedicated firewalls.	3.1	4
Understand Network Access Protection (NAP).	3.2	4
Understand network isolation.	3.3	4
Understand protocol security.	3.4	4
Understanding Security Software		
Understand client protection.	4.1	5
Understand email protection.	4.2	5
Understand server protection.	4.3	5